HEAVY DATE OVER GERMANY

HEAVY DATE OVER GERMANY

The Life and Times of B-17 Tail Gunner Ray Perry

Edited by Jewellee Jordan Kuenstler
Foreword by former Texas Governor Rick Perry

State House Press

State House Press

State House Press
Abilene, Texas
325-660-1752
www.mcwhiney.org

Copyright 2019, State House Press
All rights reserved

Cataloging-in-Publication Data

Names: Jordan Kuenstler, Jewelee, editor. I Perry, Rick, 1950- , writer of foreword.

Title: Heavy Date Over Germany: the life and times of B-17 tail gunner Ray Perry / Jewelee Jordan Kuenstler.

Description: First edition. I Abilene, TX: State House Press, 2019. I Includes bibliographical references and index.

Identifiers: ISBN 9781933337807 (softcover)

Subjects: LCSH: Perry, Ray, 1925-2017. I World War, 1939-1945 – Aerial operations, American. I World War, 1939-1945 – Personal narratives, American. I B-17 bomber.

Classification: LLC D790.2 (print) I DDC 940.54

No part of this book may be reproduced in any form unless with written permission from State House Press, except for brief passages by reviewers.

First edition 2019

Distributed by Texas A&M University Press Consortium
800-826-8911
www.tamupress.com

With all my love, Tracy, TJ and Daddy

CONTENTS

vii	Foreword by former Texas Governor Rick Perry
ix	Editor's Preface
1	**CHAPTER 1** Haskell County Farm Boy
12	**CHAPTER 2** Basic Training: Fort Sill to Sheppard Field
24	**CHAPTER 3** Gunnery School: Kingman, Arizona
40	**CHAPTER 4** Meeting the Crew: Lincoln, Nebraska
47	**CHAPTER 5** Overseas Training: Dyersburg, Tennessee
63	**CHAPTER 6** Combat Destination: England
79	**CHAPTER 7** Missions 1–5
94	**CHAPTER 8** Mission 6: The Deadly Mission
105	**CHAPTER 9** Finishing out 1944: Aiding the Victory in Europe
127	**CHAPTER 10** A New Year: 1945
152	**CHAPTER 11** Going Home
162	**CHAPTER 12** Life Goes On
171	Epilogue
177	Endnotes
205	Bibliography
208	Index

FOREWORD

"If the situation presents itself . . . give 'em hell!"

—Wayne Perry (Grandfather) to Ray Perry (Grandson), Summer 1943

Char · ac · ter (noun)
1. The mental and moral qualities distinctive to an individual.
2. A person in a novel, play or movie.

From 1943 to 1945, my father was engaged in his personal development of both these definitions. He was an honest, loyal and patriotic son of American and Texan pioneers who defended beliefs in liberty as they saw them, in both the American Revolution and the Civil War.

He considered it an honor, a privilege, and a responsibility to serve his country.

Dad didn't talk much as a general rule . . . he made his points, if asked, and moved on.

I learned about his time with the Ninety-Fifth Bomb Group listening to snippets of conversations between him and his aircrew buddies who came to visit from time to time; poking around his uniforms and memorabilia in Grandmother Perry's chifforobe; and, later in life as Mom compiled his mementoes in a scrapbook. Finally, learning about his life-changing experiences culminated in a well-planned and most anticipated trip in Summer 1999 to his old airbase in East Anglia. In our lifetime of great experiences, it was possibly the most memorable of all. To go back to England, within a short distance from my own Air Force duty station, with my father, my friend, and my hero, was a dream come true.

My serious study of World War II did not begin in earnest until after I had completed my military service to our country.

Reading the following helped me realize just how unique these boys of the greatest generation were: "You had a higher percentage of being killed, wounded or captured while flying in the 8th AF than if you were in the infantry in the front line." Like all statistics, this fact is high when you compare the Eighth Air Force losses against all personnel in the units that were considered "in combat." In actuality, it was even higher if you count the front-line regiment combat personnel and not the whole division. A U.S. division was 16,000 or so personnel with only 3,600 being the front-line infantry combat troops—all the others were support personnel.[1]

According to Dad, the first few missions were not that difficult. "Milk runs" was a common description until fate raised its tragic head October 7, 1944. Then it became very real . . . and deadly.

These letters and this narrative are a glimpse into the anything but routine life of a nineteen-year-old American tail gunner, longing for home, family, and a girl left back in Texas. I will, as well as my family, be eternally grateful to Jewellee Kuenstler for her diligent and loving compilation of this collection. She vividly brought Dad's observations and desires back from seventy-plus years ago in a pleasing and professional way. Well done, Jewellee.

Mother gets the lion's share of the credit for keeping Dad's records and maintaining his scrapbook. As usual, Mother gets the credit for holding everything together. She always did. Dad knew how blessed he was to have met, married, and shared a wonderful life with a magnificent woman.

The last time I saw Dad was April 22, 2017, in Hendrick Hospital after the boys of Collins Creek had come by to sing him Happy Birthday.[2]

We had a bit of alone time as he asked me about my day job in Washington. Dad knew where he was headed as this adventure was coming to a close. With that crooked half smile, he said, "I love you, Rick." And I replied, "I love you too, Dad. I'll see you later."

And I will . . . .

(Mathew 25:23)

Rick Perry
Faithful Son, 1950–Present

EDITOR'S PREFACE

The idea behind this book began with a scrapbook. An old, falling apart, purchased-at-a-Five-and-Dime scrapbook. Not one with photos, but newspaper clippings. You see, my grandfather joined the army right out of high school in June 1941, before America entered World War II. This was my great-grandmother's youngest child and only son. They were from the poor, rural community of Berryhill and made their living farming, mainly with cotton. They did not have the luxury of electricity, phone lines, or even running water. My grandfather was stationed in San Antonio, and although that was still in Texas, it was far enough away that they did not see each other very often. His mother did not want him to miss all the local events that were happening at home, so she kept a scrapbook of newspaper clippings that highlighted events that he might be interested in. The first few pages are clippings of fish caught, local couples getting married, babies being born, etc. But as the year 1942 began, the clippings began to be interspersed with local boys that were joining up for the military and a few that had already lost their lives in the war. By the end of the book, the clippings looked more like an obituary page from the newspaper. Clipping after clipping showed young men, cut down in their prime, in the war. Every one, forty-one in all, were young men from their community or someone they knew personally.

Growing up, I didn't really appreciate this book of memories. To my young mind, it was rather dull. I didn't know the people that were in this book. It was much more fun to see my mom, or my aunts and uncle as young people in the photos that graced the other scrapbooks. But that all changed when I got married and had a son of my own. I rediscovered this scrapbook, and this time it made my mother's heart constrict with the anguish that those mothers from sixty years earlier must have felt. I could see in my mind, my great-grandmother painstakingly clipping out news articles or pictures that she thought my grandfather would enjoy reading or hearing about when he got to come home on leave. But as I continued to read each article, my heart was overwhelmed with sadness. How heart-wrenching it must have been for her to clip out the names of my grandfather's friends, or children of her friends, that had been killed in the war. These were young men—eighteen-, nineteen-, twenty-years-old—dying far from home, and many not able to have their bodies returned to America for burial. World War II took an entirely new meaning for me from that point on. These were people that were from my community. I knew their descendants. These were not just stories in a book, or pictures taken by some journalist in a far-off land, these were sons, husbands, brothers, cousins, and fathers. I felt like these stories needed to be told. Not in a strictly academic sense, but more in the genre of my great-grandmother's purpose, to remember their sacrifice. These were boys that were loved and cared for. These were not just nameless thousands that perished in a war that happened more than seventy years ago, these were boys whose deaths caused great sadness to envelope an entire community when one of their own perished. Their stories and sacrifice needed to be told in a way that everyone could feel the emotions that these young soldiers were experiencing, feel the anguish that their parents were going through, and understand why they were willing to do what they did. The idea to somehow tell this story was always in the back of my mind, but had not taken form quite yet.

To give a little bit of background to my own story, I grew up in the Berryhill community on a farm around twenty miles southeast of Paint Creek. My dad was the person that instilled in me a great love of history. As we would drive through pastures or down county roads, he would tell me stories about the people that used to live there or events that occurred there. He also passed this on to my son, TJ. He is especially interested in World War II, and admires those men and women that were so young, yet did so much to preserve the freedoms we tend to take for granted. So, when I found out that Ray Perry had been in World War II, I thought that this would be a great opportunity for my son to really get to speak to someone that lived through it.

I had heard of Ray Perry growing up, but just knew that he was a farmer and a rancher from the Paint Creek area. I really got to know him and his wife, Amelia, after I married my husband, Tracy Kuenstler. The Kuenstler homestead was one-half mile from the Perry home. They were good family

EDITOR'S PREFACE

friends. My husband, who pursued a career in aviation, told me his first airplane ride was with Ray's son, Rick, when he was just a little boy. I had known Ray personally for almost twenty years before I heard he had been in World War II. I called the Perry family and asked if I could interview Ray about his World War II experiences, and they graciously agreed. TJ. and I met them at their home and Ray told us of his adventures as a tail gunner on a B-17 Bomber named *Heavy Date*. Amelia brought out a scrapbook of photos Ray had taken while he served in the Army Air Force. They also produced a bound copy of an interview completed about ten years previously by Dan K. Utley from the Texas Historical Commission. This was a well laid out interview recalling Ray's life from birth to his return from the war. This wealth of knowledge was used extensively in telling Ray's story. The visit was fascinating. We did a follow up interview about a year later. It was at this time that Amelia brought out an orange Tupperware tub. When she opened it, it was like a treasure chest. Inside were all the letters Ray had written home to his parents, all lovingly preserved by his mother and then given to Amelia. With the interview, personal photos, and war time letters, I knew this was a story that needed to be told. And what a story. Ray was the embodiment of every "good ol' boy" I had known growing up. Tough, hardworking, a little rough around the edges, but moral, and always stuck by his values. Those values included helping others and doing your duty. If you gave your word, you stuck by it, and you never shirked your responsibilities.

I knew Ray had been ill, his sight was almost gone, but I was still rather shocked when he died early the following year. I admired this man. I also admired the job he did in World War II. I knew a hundred other men like this that would never be recognized, beyond their small communities, for their life's work. And I knew there were thousands of veterans that were never properly appreciated for what they endured during World War II. I wanted to honor all those people by telling Ray Perry's story. That idea in the back of my mind was finally taking shape.

Ever since I read my great-grandmother's scrapbook of clippings, I have wanted to tell this story. I found when I was writing and putting the information together, that it became very emotional. Knowing Ray personally, I could imagine him as an eighteen- or nineteen-year-old boy. I could almost envision being in the plane with him, or in the barracks when he was far from home, or concentrating so much on doing your job, that you do not have time to feel fear. Coming from a farming family and living close to the community that Ray did, I could empathize with his interest and concerns about the family harvest, in his brothers and sister's going-ons, on news of people in his community which were more like family than simply neighbors.

Without giving any spoilers, just know that when writing the eighth chapter of the book, I often had to stop early for the day, because I could not see the screen for the tears I was shedding. Maybe I was more sensitive because my upbringing mirrored Ray's just fifty years later. Maybe it was because of the great impact that the scrapbook of newspaper clippings had on me. Maybe it was because my own son was eighteen-years-old and has explored the possibility of a career in the military. His interest was mainly because of the admiration he has for World War II veterans like Ray. TJ. is my only child. When he announced he looking into joining the military, I was devastated. One day I sat him down and told him, "What if I lose you? You are my only child!" His reply could have just as easily come out of Ray Perry's mouth. My son turned to me without any fear or tears, held my hands and said, "But Mom, what if I could die helping others to live." Poignant words coming from a young man, words I was quick to dismiss due to his age and inexperience. But how many thousands of young men his age during World War II felt the same way. Ray did. He was junior in high school (the same grade as my son when I wrote this book) when Pearl Harbor was attacked, and he wanted to go and do his duty. He said he never had any second thoughts about it. It needed to be done and he wanted to play his part. These heroic men have influenced my son to see that he has a duty to America as well. He has a servant's heart, just like Ray, and just like thousands of other "good ol' boys" in America.

I want to thank the Perry family. Their willingness to share such a personal part of their lives with me was extremely generous. Amelia was so gracious in answering my hundred and one questions. Rick was an amazing editor and offered up some more great photos of his dad. Milla was kind enough to let me share her wonderful daddy with the world. Thank you for letting me share this truly amazing story.

I hope that you too can personally enjoy this ride with Ray. I hope it tugs at your heart strings and perhaps even gives you a deeper understanding of the sacrifice these very young men, boys really, made for our country. But above all, my greatest hope is that this does justice to the story of Ray Perry. He was a great man and I'm proud that I got to call him friend.

HEAVY DATE OVER GERMANY

CHAPTER 1
HASKELL COUNTY FARM BOY

"The prospect ahead is indeed flattering. The several industries surrounding us have prospered for the past two years . . . the country is on a big boom, and the farming interests promise to keep the boom going. It is our sincere wish that the New Year will swell the lowing herds, double the fleecy flocks, fill the granaries and larders of the farmer, and add brilliancy to the pen and yellow gold to the purse of the Haskell Free Press."

—*Haskell (TX) Free Press*, January 4, 1890[1]

I can't remember a time that I ever saw Ray Perry without a hat on. Not just any hat, but a perfectly creased, slightly worn cowboy hat. It was part of him. Like his hair or his arms. I'm sure I did see him once or twice without it, but when I picture him in my mind, he always has a hat on. A hat and a grin. One of those lopsided grins that shows your teeth and puts a sparkle in your eye. Words can only describe so much, but a person's look can speak volumes. His look was one of a man who loved life, people, and a good story. He was the epitome of a West Texas good ol' boy—generous, fun loving, liked to visit, loved the land. Amelia, his wife of almost seventy years, put it better than any words I could arrive at. She summed Ray up by saying: "He loved his God, he loved his family, and he loved his country, in that order!"

As I sat across from this ninety-year-old man, his face tanned and leathered from a life spent outside, his back stooped from hard labor, his eyesight gone with age, he still looked every bit a Texas cowboy. A man who enjoyed every moment on this earth, and looked forward to every adventure around the corner. He loved his life. You could tell by the way he spoke about his children. Whether he was telling a story about them growing up, or accomplishments they had made as adults, the pride he felt literally burst out of him. The same was true as he talked about his grandkids and great-grandkids. These were his proudest accomplishments.

But his greatest adventure? His greatest adventure was at the ripe old age of eighteen. You remember, the age where you feel invincible—the age where now you look back and say, "What was I thinking?" Although he was telling me his story at the age of ninety, he became so animated you could see that eighteen-year-old country boy that couldn't wait to sign up to be a part of the war. Hoping that it wouldn't be over before he could experience it. And experience it he did!

It's important to know how Ray came to be the man he was. It seems that the Perry family was always farmers. Some say farming runs in the blood. The great state of Texas was admitted into the Union in 1845, and sometime between 1845 and 1850, Ray's great-great-grandfather, J. W. Perry, arrived in Texas, and began farming. Census records consistently listed his place of birth as Alabama. The 1850 U.S. Federal Census records placed him in Harrison County in East Texas, along with several other Perry families, most of which were also listed as farmers. J. W. was eighteen years old and probably saw this as *his* great adventure, never dreaming that a descendant in his direct line, would one day be governor of this state.[2] Sometime prior to 1856, J. W. Perry married a young lady named Jane, and on April 3, 1856, his first child, a son, John Michael Perry, was born.[3]

As J. W.'s family grew, he sought bigger and better farming opportunities. Texas at this time was still a frontier land, with great opportunities available, but also with great risks as well. Frederick Law Olmsted undertook a saddle trip through Texas during 1856 and 1857. He recorded details about the land and the people to run as feature articles in the *New York Daily Times*. His description of East Texas, very close to the land settled by J. W. Perry, was full of stories of abandoned farms and quick-shod shacks for new settlers, and he found the land to be not quite the rich farmland that had been described, "the pines gradually disappear and a heavy clay soil, stained by an oxide of iron to a uniform brick red, begins. It makes most disagreeable roads, sticking close, and giving an indelible stain to every article that touches it."[4] When describing the homes, he wrote, "We called at a plantation offered for sale. It was described in the hand-bills as having a fine house. We found it a cabin without windows. The proprietor said he had made ten bales [cotton] to the hand, and would sell . . . for $6 per acre."⁵ Although Olmsted's rough description of the land and less-than-civilized area might deter some, to a young man seeking a living to support his family, this was paradise. Lots of land just waiting to be tilled and civilized, and the boasts of "ten bales [cotton] to the hand" was a strong pull. Before 1860, J. W. and Jane moved to Grand Bluff, Texas, in Panola County, just one county south of Harrison County. The census records for 1860 tracked his growing brood to now include not only his eldest, John Michael, but two more sons, James and William.⁶

Shortly after the 1860 census, the first shots of the Civil War at Fort Sumter echoed through every household in the north and south. Even a family man with a wife and three small children was not exempt. J. W. Perry joined the Nineteenth Texas Infantry, serving in Company E. This was part of Capt. F. B. Dixon's Company, which was attached to Col. Richard Waterhouse's Regimental Texas Volunteers.⁷ According to his Confederate military record, J. W. joined up on March 30, 1862, in Panola County for a period of three years or until the end of the war. Gone were the days when both sides thought that war would last only a few months. Each was committed now for the long haul, and every man in the South was needed. Apparently, J. W. was musically inclined, because in June 1862, he was promoted to Fifer. J. W. is listed as "wounded & at hospital Monroe, La." on the Company Muster Roll sheet for May and June 1863. Records indicate that he was wounded in the "engagement of Milliken's Bend in Louisiana, June 7, 1863." He appears to have rejoined his Company by the end of August that same year.⁸ When the war ended in 1865, one can assume J. W. returned home to his family in Panola County, Texas.

The family put down roots in the East Texas area for at least ten years. By 1870, J. W. and Jane had added two more children, Joel and Ida.⁹ But then the Perry family moved again, this time to Hill County, Texas. This was not unusual for farmers to move often, seeking better land and better opportunities as well as following the progression of settlers as Texas became more populated and a little more civilized. In 1880, the family expanded to include three more boys, John C., W. J., and Frank.¹⁰

In 1880, his eldest son, John Michael, was eighteen years old and ready for his own adventure. According to records, shortly after moving to Hill County, he met and married Winneyfred Catherine Berry on December 1, 1881.¹¹ Winneyfred was born in Hillsboro, Texas. According to one source, her parents lost their plantation during the Civil War, and moved to Texas for a fresh start. She was born shortly thereafter.¹² John Michael and Winneyfred Perry lost no time in starting their family. Ten months from their wedding day, they welcomed a son on October 21, 1882, named Wayne Willing Perry.[13]

Texas was slowly losing its frontier status especially in West Texas, in the area that eventually became Haskell County, the place that the Perry family put down deep roots. This part of Texas was still considered wild and unhospitable to settlers following the Civil War, but that would change. Haskell County was formed in 1858, and was named in memory of Charles R. Haskell who died in the Goliad Massacre. Due to hostile Indian tribes, the county would remain unsettled for twenty years. A former Civil War hero named Ranald Slidell Mackenzie battled against these tribes for about five years, finally forcing the last remaining Comanche tribe to a reservation in Oklahoma. (Although sworn enemies, Mackenzie and the Comanche chief, Quanah Parker, both had a grudging respect for each other that actually turned into a friendship in the latter part of their lives.[14])

With the Indian threat neutralized, ranchers moved into Haskell County starting around 1877. In 1880, the U.S. Federal census documented forty-eight people living in the county and two ranches had been established. In 1882, the county's largest community was named Rice Springs, but changed its name to Haskell and became the county seat in 1885 when the county was formally organized.[15]

With the organization of the county, settlers began to move in and farm the land. Among these pioneers, John Michael Perry brought his family, including his seven-year-old son, Wayne. The family began farming in Haskell County in 1889.[16] In 1890, 105 ranches and farms were recorded, a huge jump from just two ranches ten years previously. Creating farms out of a frontier was a long and laborious undertaking, therefore it only makes sense that ranching was the main economic industry. But early farmers to Haskell County, those sons of the South, brought with them the knowledge and skill to raise cotton. Cotton farming in Haskell County included 340 acres in 1890, yet just a decade later, this jumped to 3,674 acres. If one figures that most of these were tenant farmers with just 160 acres to work with, this would be approximately twenty-three farms that had been carved out of the land in a short amount of time. The Perry family worked one of these farms.[17]

The next census in 1900 listed the Perry family still living and farming in Haskell County.[18] Wayne, now eighteen years of age, was listed as a farm laborer. The family had grown considerably. Wayne now had five brothers and sisters, ranging in age from two to fifteen.[19] Just two years later, Wayne Perry married Gertrude Hamilton in Haskell, Texas, on November 4, 1902. Their first child, Hoyt Alfred Perry, was born on December 22, 1903, in Haskell County.[20] By the next U.S. Census in 1910, Wayne and Gertrude's family expanded to include another son, Press, and a daughter, Thelma. The family made their living farming. The census showed them living near Sagerton, still in Haskell County.[21] Wayne's family moved again in the next ten years, presumably to a different farm. According to the 1920 U.S. Federal census, they were still living in Haskell County, but were listed in a different precinct.[22]

The year 1922 was when Hoyt Perry married Thelma Dinsmore and began farming with his in-laws. The farm was located on Paint Creek before it was dammed up to create Stamford Lake. Three years later, Hoyt and Thelma welcomed their first child, a son, Joseph Ray Perry, on April 23, 1925. When Ray was asked where he was born, he replied, with a twinkle in his eye, "Born here in Haskell County, I was born down there in the bottom of that lake!"[23] Just to clarify, Paint Creek was dammed up in 1953 to create what is now Stamford Lake. This was to provide a steady water source for the city of Stamford and surrounding communities.[24] So, the Dinsmore Place, or the farm they worked, is now covered up by water. The 1930 U.S. Federal census indicated that Hoyt and Thelma settled in Haskell County. Ray was joined by sister and brother, Frances and Gene.[25]

When asked where he attended school, Ray grinned and said, "Started right here, where this house sits." After he chuckled at my perplexed look, he put me out of my misery and explained, "Post [the Post school stood on the property that now has the Perry home on it]. Of course, they consolidated all these little schools, '37–'38, formed Paint Creek."[26] He continued to explain that when the little schools consolidated and formed the Paint Creek School District, he was in the seventh grade. This was where he finished his education, graduating from Paint Creek in May 1943.[27]

Paint Creek and Haskell County, were "covered up with people." Tenant farmers usually farmed 160 acres. A section of land was 640 acres or one square mile. Usually four families lived on one section. Ray stated, "It was just covered up with people . . . there was a family that lived on just about ever' quarter section out here, you know, houses with families. There was a lot of people out here."[28] He continued to reminisce and talked about Haskell being the main town they frequented for supplies, "back in those days you might not even find a parking place in Haskell around the square."[29]

Ray described his life on the farm during the 1920s and 1930s. Ray explained that his parents moved from the Dinsmore place (his mother's parents' place) to another farm further west that belonged to his dad's parents. He proudly stated that he still owned that farm.[30] A quick note for those of you that did not grow up on a small farm, farming is in the blood and is often passed down through generations, but to own the farm, especially when you grew up during the Depression years, was, and still is, a source of pride for old farmers. It is a mark of success. Not just to own a piece of land, but land you have poured sweat and blood into, land you have prayed over during times of drought, and land you have rejoiced over when the harvest was good. Land that holds your family's memories and thus their history. This was what this piece of land meant to Ray. "You know, back in those days, tenant farmers, they might rent a place, live on it two years and then rent another one," Ray described. He explained that farmers at that time farmed on the quarters, which meant that whatever money they received for their crop, one-quarter would be paid to the landowner as rent. This was the gross amount made off a crop, not taking into consideration the overhead or bills accrued during the cotton season. The first quarter went straight to the landlord. This practice is still used today in farming in this area.

Perry explained that due to lack of underground water in the Paint Creek area, the type of farming that his family did was called dry land farming.[31] This simply means that one relied totally on the rainfall to water the crops. At the age of nine or ten years old, Perry was in the field picking cotton with his family. Not to confuse this process with other areas of Texas where cotton was picked, Ray's family picked the bolls off the plants that were open with the cotton spilling out. He did not pull out the cotton fibers and leave the bolls. The cotton in this area had shorter fibers, therefore, the time it would have taken to pull the cotton out, would have made the crop too labor intensive. So, they pulled boll and all, and the gins would separate them. The Perry family would haul their cotton to either the Haskell or Stamford Gin to be processed. This was approximately fifteen miles either way. He commented that they mainly used the Haskell Gin.[32] Their farm was pretty typical for the day, no electricity or running water.[33] His father, Hoyt, had an old Farmall tractor and his granddad, Wayne, had a smooth-mouthed John Deere tractor. These were improvements that were appreciated, because Ray commented that he "come along early enough that I got to drive teams. Granddad put me down there running two horses and a plow, to plow the third row out."[34] The third row referred to how cotton was planted in those days. A farmer would plant two rows of cotton and skip the third row. This was due to the size of their planting rigs, cultivators, and later, the size of the headers on their

Cotton Strippers. The cultivators on the tractors would only plow around the two rows, so to keep the weeds and grass out of the third row, Ray's grandfather, Wayne Perry, would hitch up a team to a plow that was on wheels with a sweep. This was referred to as "plow the third row out". Ray recalled the instructions his granddad gave him, "You make so many rounds here, and then stop and let them horses rest a few minutes."[35] Chopping cotton was also a chore that Ray did with his mother in the fields. This technique required using a hoe to clean out the weeds and grass in the cotton row that the cultivator missed.

Cotton was a cash crop, and its success was totally up to that year's weather. So, farmers would raise gardens and animals to supplement their income and for personal consumption. Ray remembered, "they all canned stuff in the summertime, yeah and of course, we always had hogs, and we'd have hog killing in the wintertime and cure that pork, you know, the hams and the bacon . . . sometimes there'd be three or four groups kill hogs at the same time . . . down here on Paint Creek there was a guy lived down there, his name was George Weaver, that in the summertime he would kill a beef and he'd quarter it up, or cut it up to some extent, and he'd put it in the back end of that old car, and he'd drive around over the community, and if we wanted a roast or some steak, or whatever—cause you couldn't keep it—we didn't have any refrigeration at all, and that's the way we got what beef we eat. We'd eat mostly pork and chickens. Now, I ate enough dadgum chickens that I won't hardly eat a chicken anymore! Oh yeah, I hunted a lot. I'd shoot rabbits and I'd shoot coyotes and skunks . . . there wasn't any deer here at that time. Not up here. They was on down there on the river a good long ways down there."[36] The river Ray referred to was the Clear Fork of the Brazos River which was approximately ten miles east from the Paint Creek community.

Ray, immersed in memories and having a great time telling them, continued, "I know my junior and senior year in high school—we moved [to another farm] in 1940, I believe it was, and Paint Creek run here, and California Creek run here, and they both run together down yonder at Scott's Crossing. We lived about halfway between them. Well, in the wintertime, I'd set me a trap line in them pastures along that California Creek, and there was just a lot of days that I'd go to school smelling like a skunk! I'd run them when I come home after school. I had an old horse, and I'd ride him down there running the trap line. And I've been trying to think what those skunk hides brought. They were pretty valuable, I mean, maybe a dollar, you know, or something like that, and a dollar's as big as a bedsheet back in them days. I sold them at the produce house in Haskell. I say produce house—it was a feed store. They bought them." When asked what his weapon of choice was Ray replied with pride, "Little old single shot .22. I've still got it, yep! . . . I was a good shot . . . well, you know, we always raised chickens to eat, you know fryers. And back before I got that .22, well Mother'd get ready for a chicken to kill and cook, she'd send us boys out there in the yard to catch a rooster, a little fryer-size rooster. We'd have to run him down (laughs). But after I got that .22 that eliminated that (laughter). That rooster didn't have a chance then; I'd shoot him in the head."[37]

Sadly, the conversation moved from fond childhood memories, to the reality of war, a war that affected every household in America, even a small rural area in Haskell County, Texas. When asked where he was when he heard the news about the Pearl Harbor attack on Sunday, December 7, 1941, Ray recalled, "We didn't have electricity, we didn't have radios, and I didn't know about December 7th until I got back to school Monday morning— next morning. That's when I first knew about Pearl Harbor . . . They just announced at our school that Pearl Harbor had been bombed, and course, you know, I didn't even know where Pearl Harbor was. But we knew the Japanese had jumped on us, you know. That's the main thing we knew. And of course, we were all, I don't know if you'd say bitter or what, but we had a bad taste in our mouth about the Japanese all the time after that, you know, because we had got attacked." When asked if he considered quitting school to join up, he said he did not consider quitting, but wanted to hurry up and finish, so he could join.[38]

While still in school, Perry commented on what the community was doing to help the war effort. These were rural, poor farmers, still feeling the effects of the Depression. But Ray proudly remembered how they did their part, "they were gathering a lot of metal. And things were rationed. Gasoline was rationed, sugar was rationed, tires were rationed. You couldn't hardly buy a tire for the old car. And people just didn't go very much. They pretty well stayed at home." He recalled that a few families left to pursue defense jobs that were opening up due to the war. "I know one family went to California. Their name was Earles, and there's still a bunch of them here, but there was a good many families that went into defense work. You know, you had to go to California or Fort Worth. Seemed to me like they had an airplane manu-facturing [plant] in Fort Worth. Yeah, there was some of these farmers that just wasn't getting along too good, went and took defense jobs . . . Agriculture

Ray Perry as a junior at Paint Creek High School in 1941-1942.

didn't start coming back until after World War II and these farmers went to making a little money. No, it was pretty tough out here back in the thirties and forties."[39]

For a lot of young men, like Ray Perry, living through the depression relegated their life to the farm, barely surviving above the poverty level, and never really leaving or seeing any place farther than a twenty-mile radius from home. The war not only touched the pride of these young men, but was an opportunity to get out of this rural community and be part of something much bigger than themselves. Patriotic fervor was high. Ray explained that his whole family anticipated his going to war when he graduated high school. Out of his immediate family, he was the only one old enough to enlist. His father had not been in the military, being too young to join in World War I and considered too old for World War II.[40]

As graduation approached, Ray recalled how "all the boys that was in my class, they were ready to go to service. They were all ready . . . fact, there was one I know of that quit high school maybe a year earlier and went into service. They were all ready to go help. I can't think of a one that wasn't prepared to go to service."[41] A common thread in these small communities was pride. They may not have much money, but pride was a trait that was consistently instilled in the rural West Texas areas. Pride to defend yourself, or others; pride in your family; pride in your work; and pride for your school team. With farming, the work was feast or famine. Times of constant labor was interspersed with down time, waiting for the next rain, or the crop to ripen. Because of this, many rural communities had their own baseball teams, or other social events that were separate from their local school. They may not have had much materially, but pride was something they all carried like a badge. Therefore, it was not odd to hear Ray discuss how all the boys in his class were ready to do their part. Even though they may have been hesitant or even afraid, their pride would not allow them to show that side. This was considered a weakness. Earlier, when Ray's wife, Amelia, summed him up by saying, "He loved his God, he loved his family, and he loved his country, in that order!," these were traits that were taught to the children of this era. As Ray talked, you can tell there was never any doubt about him signing up to do his part in the war effort. It was expected, not just by others, but for himself.

Picture taken when Ray was inducted into the Army Air Force.

With a grin, he remarked, "I was scared to death that it was going to be over before I got out of school!"[42]

Ray graduated from Paint Creek High School in May 1943. Since the bombing of Pearl Harbor, Ray had mulled over his plans for enlisting following his graduation. He dreamed of being a pilot. Someone had told him that his best bet was to go to Dallas to the Army Air Force office there, instead of signing up locally. So, with the confidence only an eighteen-year-old can project, Ray went to Haskell and boarded a bus for Dallas, not really knowing where he was going, just that he needed to find the federal building. He later laughed at his younger self as he'd never been farther than Fort Worth! Describing his experience, Ray remembered with mirth, "I got down there and found that building that they was talking about, and I went in and found the Air Force recruiting place where they recruit you. Went in and told them what I wanted to do and they give me a physical, and all this and you know, I believe they swore me in and inducted me, you know, and they said, 'Now you go on back home and we'll send you your orders.' Well, I come on back home and it wasn't—I don't know how long it was, it wasn't very long until I got my orders and it said, 'Fort Sill, Oklahoma.' I said, my gosh, I thought I joined the Air Force!"[43]

CHAPTER 2
BASIC TRAINING: FORT SILL TO SHEPPARD FIELD

"The War Chest is a worthy drive; We all know what it's for, So beat them to the dash, turn in your extra cash, And help to bring our boys home alive. This is our war, our men are in it—at the front or on their way . . . we can give our fighters, our allies and their families, the greatest weapon of all—'The will to win.' Contributing to the War Fund Chest can help to bring this about."

—Haskell (TX) Free Press, October 29, 1943[1]

Ray Perry, all of eighteen-years old, and with the confidence that only a young man of that age can have toward an uncertain future, prepared to follow his orders and report to Fort Sill. In 2006, Dan K. Utley, with the Texas Historical Commission, interviewed Ray about his service. Utley asked him if he had any second thoughts about going into the military. In true Texas fashion, Ray replied, "No, no, I was scared to death I wasn't going to get here in time. I wanted to finish high school, and I'm glad I did, but I got there just in time. In fact, I was only in service two years, training and overseas duty."[2] This optimistic view about serving his country continued throughout the war. Although at times there were undercurrents of missing home, overall Ray loved being in the Army Air Force, meeting new people, and exploring new places.

When it was time to report to Fort Sill, Ray's dad, Hoyt, gave him a two-dollar bill with the corners torn off. One can only imagine the range of emotions this tough West Texas farmer battled within himself—pride, worry,

BASIC TRAINING: FORT SILL TO SHEPPARD FIELD

overwhelming love, and a desire to protect his son—knowing Ray would most likely be sent far away. Watching his oldest child report for war duty must have been gut-wrenching. When Hoyt handed the two-dollar bill to Ray, he said, "That's for good luck." Ray would carry that bill in his pocket for sixty years.[3]

Ray's first stop was the Wolverton Hotel in Lawton, Oklahoma, the location of Fort Sill, where new recruits were inducted. Ray wrote a letter home upon his arrival:

Dear Folks,   *Dec. 22, 1943*

I got here at 5:30 this morning and slept until 10:00. We had to lay over an hour & half at Wichita Falls.

I am staying with the two boys I left Haskell with and a boy from Lamessa [sic] we met him at the bus station in Lawton.

I really did enjoy the Christmas dinner and am still full. I have really been having a lot of fun with these boys. I have to close and mail this.

Lots of Love, Ray[4]

Ray remembered that at Fort Sill about forty young men came from the West Texas area. In describing his time at this base, he explained, "it's just where they inducted us, give us our shots and put us on KP [kitchen police duty] one day. And then they put us on a bus and sent us to Sheppard Field, and that's where we took our basic training."[5] While at Fort Sill, Ray wrote two letters home. The mood of the letters was very optimistic. They were also very telling for a young man from a rural community, whose family was still feeling the effects and depredations of the Great Depression:

Dear Folks,   *Dec. 24, 1943*

I got out to Ft. Sill on time yesterday morning and everything is going fine.

We have nice barracks with cots. On our cots we have two sheets two wool blankets one mattress and pillow. Our chow is fine.

I have to get up at 4:00 Xmas morning and be on K.P. by 5:00. Every one in our barracks except two is on K.P. I got my clothes yesterday and I got more clothes . . . [than I] ever saw. We got 6 pairs of pants [missing piece] . . . 1 blouse, 1 overcoat, 1 raincoat and a bunch of other stuff . . . You can write me to the outside address.

Love, Ray[6]

From his letter to his parents, Ray seemed excited about the accommodations and the amount of clothes he received. For this poor Haskell County farm boy, this was definitely a very abundant Christmas. And as with any teenage boy, he had to mention the "chow," a common topic in many of his letters home. In his second letter, Ray included a copy of the bulletin for the church service he attended the day after Christmas.

Dear Folks, Dec. 26, 1943

I went to church this morning and got back just in time for chow. I sure hope I get a letter at mail call today. We took 3 tests Thursday and you had to pass them or get out of the Air Corps, I passed. One was on Math, one on mechanics, and another on radio. We haven't got our shipping orders yet, but may get them this evening at mail call. . . .

Lots of Love, Ray[7]

Although optimistic, as almost all his letters would be, the undercurrents of missing home were starting to show. Ray never traveled much farther than twenty miles from his home. Now in this new, unfamiliar military world, surrounded by lots of different people, he relied on the mail as his link to home.

Ray's forthcoming orders took him to Sheppard Field, in Wichita Falls, Texas. Just 118 miles from his family home, Sheppard Field would be the closest station to his family during his time in the Army Air Force. Ray's first letter home, after reaching Sheppard Field, provided a view into this new world:

Dear Folks, Dec 29, 1943

I thought I would write you a line and give you my address. We got to Sheppard Field this morning and got our barracks.

BASIC TRAINING: FORT SILL TO SHEPPARD FIELD

> I like the army OK so far, I really like it at Fort Sill, but we got up here with a bunch of Yankees, and I don't like them at all . . . We start our training about next Monday (Jan. 3) and it will last about 48 days. We get one 4 mile hike, one 14 and one 30 mile hike. On our 30 mile hike we carry a 60 lb pack.
>
> I haven't got a letter from you. I got one from Pearleta yesterday and was really glad to get it. I must close as I am tired.
>
> Love, Ray[8]

Ray's next letter home showed a young man, away from home for the first time, missing his family, but trying to reassure them as well.

> Dear Folks, Jan. 2, 1944
>
> I got two letters from you today that were sent to Fort Sill. I got a letter from Pearleta and the Sunday School paper. I got a letter and the box of candy from you yesterday, the candy was really good. You asked if I wanted candy and cake, sure I want it for the grub is not very good here at Sheppard Field.
>
> I don't think you had better come up here Sunday for we are confined to the post for 14 days after we get here. I could see you in the guest house, but I had rather get out and go somewhere. I hope you can come up here Sunday after next. Weldon's folks are up here today, but they can't go anywhere and have to stay in the guest house.
>
> I have a slight cold but it isn't very bad so don't worry. On Sunday we can stay in bed all day if we want to. I didn't get up until about 10:00 this morning. I sure enjoy getting those long letters from home, but I can't think of anything to write. I really was glad to hear about that new heifer calf . . .[9]

When Ray wrote inviting his parents to come see him, there was an undercurrent of thoughtfulness on his part. His family was poor, not any poorer than most in his community, but with the new rationing that was implemented on gas and tires, he knew a long trip would be a sacrifice for his family, no matter how much they all wanted to see each other. Before Ray was shipped overseas, he would try to make these visits as easy as possible for his family. As much as Ray missed his family and wanted to see them, he did not want to be the cause of further hardship.

Dear Folks,   *Jan. 5, 1944*

I was going to write you last night but I took a shot yesterday and didn't feel very good last night. My smallpox is taking and has already made a scab.

If you want to you can come to see me Sunday and we will drive over the camp. I am planning on going home weekend after next . . .

                                                                                     Love, Ray[10]

Ray's parents visited him on Sunday, January 9, 1944. His next letter, dated January 10, expressed his appreciation for the visit.

Dear Folks,   *Jan. 10, 1944*

I sure was glad to see you yesterday but I wish you could have stayed longer. I may not get to come home this weekend as we have moved to new barracks and are under different men, but I will try.

We took the tests on coordination today, it wasn't hard. It was fun, we just played games but you had to watch your business. We flew a dummy plane and it was really fun. We take the physical tomorrow and the next day we get an interview . . .[11]

Ray at Sheppard Field, Wichita Falls, Texas

BASIC TRAINING: FORT SILL TO SHEPPARD FIELD

An envelope addressed to Thelma Perry and dated the same day as Ray's letter home arrived not long after. The mail contained a life insurance policy for Ray in the amount of $10,000 "payable in case of death." Ray had made the beneficiary his mother, Thelma.[12] They recently spent the day with Ray, assuring themselves that he was safe and in good health. But this letter showed the uncertainty of war, and reminded them of the danger in which their son would soon find himself.

Ray's thoughts were never far from home.

Dear Folks, *Jan. 13, 1944*

I have just got up and thought I would drop you a line. I finished the tests yesterday and believe I made it. We took our . . . physical yesterday and I qualified for it. The [physica] is harder than the one I took at Dallas . . . I got my pass to go to town and I went last night . . . I am going to try to get me a pass to go home today I hope I get it.

[written later in the day]

I am planning on going home Sat. night. I will leave Wichita Falls about nine and that will make me get to Haskell about twelve.[13]

Ray wanted to become a pilot. But in 1944, the Army Air Force was not as desperate for pilots as they were at the beginning of the war. Passing the tests and physicals that Ray described proved essential to achieving pilot status. He remarked about the uncertainty of this course in his letters.

Dear Folks, *Jan. 17, 1944*

There has been seven boys to find out about washing out or not. Four of them washed out and three made it. There was only one of the three that made a pilot the other two made bombardier. They are washing out a lot more than they did a little while back. They said they don't expect the war to last long enough to train pilots.

I won't be home this weekend so you can come up here. I would like for you to bring all four of the boys but if you don't have room just suit your self. I guess Frances will have something to say about that . . . I sure hope I get to see you Sunday. Come a little earlier if you can.

Love, Ray[14]

Ray does not identify the four boys, but one can imagine him grinning as he wrote the passage about his sister Frances having a say in who traveled with the family. Frances was around sixteen years old at the time. For any teenage girl, the thought of riding for a couple of hours with four older boys meant she would most certainly want a say in her traveling companions. Ray continued to have concerns about the likelihood of making a pilot.

Dear Folks,   *Jan. 23, 1944*

I have just got back to the barracks and there was a "washout" list there but my name was not on it. There is seventeen men from our flight on it, that is really going to thin us down. Bill is on it, but he hasn't got back yet so he don't know it. They are going to move tomorrow morning at seven o'clock.

I sure did enjoy the day and the dinner was fine . . .[15]

Ray at Sheppard Field with his dad Hoyt, and his mom, Thelma.

BASIC TRAINING: FORT SILL TO SHEPPARD FIELD

Dear Folks,   *Jan 25, 1944*

We went on that hike today . . . it was not as bad as I thought it would be, and it was not as long as I thought it would be. My feet are a little sore, but I think they will be better by tomorrow.

I haven't been classified yet, but I believe I made it for not being on that washout list. Bill didn't even make a combat crew. That is on account of his eyes.

I am going to try to go home this weekend for I might ship next week. I don't believe we will ship, but some of the boys seem to think we will. I am not going to have my coat pressed for it will take all of my money to go home on. We are supposed to get payed [sic] but we might get payed [sic] Saturday. I don't know what time I will get to Haskell, but I guess I will go with the travel [bureau].

Love, Ray[16]

Ray wanted to spend as much time with his family as he could before he transferred to a base farther away. He managed to come home that weekend, arriving on January 29, spending the night, and returning late on Sunday, January 30. He also still held out hope of becoming a pilot. With the possibility of transfer and possible combat looming, the family visits became bittersweet, as evident in Ray's next letter.

Dear Folks,   *Feb. 1, 1944*

I got here Sunday night all right [letter torn] . . . I slept all of the way and didn't wake up except at Munday and Seymour. The boys from Abilene & Stamford were on the bus . . . We didn't do anything Monday morning, but stand in line for our pay. I stood in line from 8 until about 11 and got $21.38. They said they were taking out two months insurance . . . I sure did hate to leave the other night but after I got on my way I was ready to get back to camp.

Love, Ray[17]

One of the boys Ray referenced in the letter, from Abilene, was Raymond Reddell. These two would train together but separated when they joined their respective bomb groups. Interestingly enough, these two found themselves stationed together at the very end of the war.[18] Ray wrote a letter home on February 3, but it did not survive, just the envelope. Ray went home again the following weekend as evident in his next letter.

> Dear Folks, 2-9-44
>
> I got back up here OK but was a little later than the other time. We had a little bus trouble and had to wait for another bus. I don't think I will go home this weekend, but will try to the next. We haven't done much of nothing this week. We went on that hike Monday and it was the same distance as the other one.
>
> I got the package from Miss Warden and it was some talc & shaving lotion . . .
>
> Ray
>
> P.S. I got the letter today with Tommie's address in it, and Bill & I went over to see him at dinner. He washed out and Phillip Colinhead washed out also.[19]

Miss Warden had been one of Ray's high school teachers and his Senior sponsor. In his 2006 interview, he described her "as good as gold. She was a fine lady."[20] Throughout the war, people back home called him, and sent him packages and letters. These reminders of home must have been a great morale booster. Tommie referred to Tommie Davis, a boy Ray knew from Haskell. He would be stationed with Ray several times in the states and overseas. But Tommie's story would take a very different direction.

On February 14, 1944, Ray wrote home to let his family know his plans for the coming week. Ray was a consistent letter writer, and kept his parents informed, but always downplayed any news that might worry them.

> Dear Folks, 2-14-44
>
> I just have time to write a few lines. We are going on bivouac tomorrow and will come back Thursday. I think we are going to have good weather. I

went on sick call today and they gave me some capusles [sic] and painted my throat. I feel as good now as I ever did . . . I sure did enjoy the weekend . . .

Love, Ray[21]

Ray wrote again on February 22, but the letter was lost, leaving just the envelope to show how consistent Ray was in writing home. Sometime between February 22 and February 27, Ray must have made it home for a visit.

Dear Folks,   *Feb. 27, 1944*

I will drop you a line to let you know that I made it in time and everything is OK. We got moved over to the shipping area this morning. There are four other boys besides myself out of our old flight that are shipping together. The orders say we are going to Kingman, Arizona. We have to be there by 2nd of March. I will write more in a day or two . . . I don't think there is any use for you to try to write me for I can't get it before I ship. I[t] will be tomorrow or the next day.[22]

Ray soon found out that his dreams of becoming a pilot were dashed. Although not officially washed out of the pilot program until arriving at Kingman, Arizona, scuttlebutt around camp already predicted the outcome of the men with which he trained. In his 2006 interview, Ray explained that about forty young men from the West Texas area were inducted at Fort Sill and later transferred to Sheppard Field for potential pilot training. These men comprised the "wash out" list. At Sheppard Field, these men worked through basic training and qualifying tests for pilot training. Ray recalled, "that whole bunch—that 40 boys—they washed us all out, and the reason for it was, it didn't make any difference whether you passed them tests or not, they was needing gunners worse than they were needing pilots."[23] His letter home revealed an undercurrent of disappointment.

Dear Folks,   *Feb. 29, 1944*

We are still here and won't leave until Thursday. I don't know what time we will leave but they said it would be sometime Thursday. All we do is lay around on our bunks and sleep. We didn't get up this morning until 7:00.

We are going to get paid this morning and it is a good thing for if we didn't get paid here we wouldn't get paid until next month . . . We won't stay there but for about 8 weeks. It is a gunnery school and they don't last but about 8 to 10 weeks.

I went to town last night to get my money back on this bus ticket and they couldn't give it to me at the bus station I would have to go over to the office in the day time. I wouldn't get but about $35 back for they take out the price of a one way ticket . . . The shipping orders was not the main thing they wanted me back up here for Sunday. They had a few different fires Saturday evening and night and they were guarding the place with live ammunition. All the fires were up in the airplane engine department. Just as I got in the barracks Sunday morning they come in after some guards, but I didn't have to go for I was on shipping orders.

They seem to think it was sabotage and I guess it was or there wouldn't have been so many fires so close together . . . when we get to Kingman we will be only about 250 miles from Los Angleas [sic], California and if we get a 3 day pass I am going over there. I guess I had better close,

Love, Ray[24]

This letter proved particularly revealing about many aspects of a soldier's life. First, it appeared that paychecks were not on a consistent schedule and depended upon which camp a soldier was stationed. Next, Ray seemed to spend a good deal of his pay on his travel expenses home, which explained his frustration at losing half of his ticket fare. An interesting aspect of this letter was his mention of sabotage. Since the sneak attack at Pearl Harbor, Americans became wary of saboteurs, especially on military installations. Finally, Ray's natural optimism reemerged despite his disappointment at not becoming a pilot, as evidenced by his excitement at the prospect of getting to see the big city of Los Angeles, California.

Ray tried to keep his family informed of his whereabouts. Although his group was scheduled to leave on Thursday, March 2, he wrote another letter the day before to remind his family he and his comrades would soon ship out.

BASIC TRAINING: FORT SILL TO SHEPPARD FIELD

Dear Folks,   *March 1, 1944*

We are shipping sometime tonight. I don't know what time we are leaving, but they told us we would leave before sun up in the morning. I don't guess I have wrote you since pay day but I got $29.50 a little more than I got the other time. I will send you my address as soon as I get one. I have to close now.

Love, Ray[25]

Sheppard Field was the closest that Ray would be stationed to his family during the war. But through letters, he remained close to them in spirit.

CHAPTER 3
GUNNERY SCHOOL: KINGMAN, ARIZONA

"Mr. Hunt expressed his sincere thanks on behalf of the Red Cross, 'Haskell County people, as always, have again shown that they are doing every possible [thing] on the home front to back our fighting men."

—Haskell (TX) Free Press, March 24, 1944[1]

Upon his arrival at Kingman, Arizona, Ray soon realized that his dreams of becoming a pilot would not see fruition. In his 2006 interview, Dan Utley asked Ray if they told him that he would not become a pilot. Ray laughingly replied, "Well, no, but I finally figured it out."[2]

Dear Folks, March 4, 1944

We got here yesterday at 2:00. The country around us is pretty, there is big mountains all around us. The mountains have snow all over the top of them. We left Sheppard Field at 8:00 Thursday morning and didn't cross the Texas line until 7:00 that evening.

I think I am going to like it here, it is a real small field. The food is really good. Some boys said they had steak and fried chicken . . . We will not be able to go to town as long as we are here. I don't think we will get paid until we leave, then we get paid for the two months.

The first week we go up in a Flying Fortress up to 18,000 ft. When we leave here we will get our mechanics course or get a gunnery instructor course.

GUNNERY SCHOOL: KINGMAN, ARIZONA

We had a good passenger car to ride up here in. Some of the boys had an old troop car. When we finish here we are supposed to get a private first class rating and a ten-day furlough.

One of the boys got a letter from a boy that is with Bill and he said they really got a poor deal. They said it is really cold up there. The next time you write tell me where Ray Jr. is, I have forgot. Before we are through here we will get 24 hours in the air. I think we will get flying pay . . .

Love, Ray[3]

Kingman, Arizona, was home to Kingman Army Airfield which was built in 1942 specifically to house the Kingman Aerial Gunnery Training School. Sitting on 4,145 acres in Mohave County, Arizona, outside the town of Kingman, this was the perfect location to train and practice aerial gunnery. This was where Ray would spend the next six weeks.[4]

The popular cartoon character Bugs Bunny was used as the mascot for the Kingman Army Air Field.

Ray's optimism radiated from his first letter at Kingman Army Airfield. Being a country boy, Ray first commented on the countryside. These may have been the first mountains that he had seen, and to a West Texas boy, where snowfall only came occasionally, snow was a novelty. His next two thoughts turned to food and socializing. In fact, Ray's overall first impression of Kingman Army Airfield was positive. The two boys he mentioned in his letters were two school mates from Paint Creek. Both were a year ahead of Ray in school, but in a small town, everyone knew everyone. In fact, Ray's junior year in high school saw only a total of seventy-three students between freshman and senior grades, with Ray's junior class having only eighteen students. He developed close friendships with many of his classmates and frequently asked in his letters home about any news concerning those in military service.[5]

Ray's excitement about flying in the B-17 was evident. His love of flying continued to be foremost in his mind in his next letter home.

> Dear Folks,   March 5, 1944
>
> I haven't done anything since I got here. We are going to start to school tomorrow. I don't know how much school we will have but I don't think it is very much. I think we will take a ride in a B17 some time next week just to see how we like it.
>
> I have just come back from the air port, they have a lot of B17s out here. When I come home on my furlough I am going to get a ride on one of the planes to Sheppard Field or some place close like that. It would not cost me a thing, all I would have to do is pay a dollar on a parachute and I would get that back.
>
> Daddy, if you want me to I can get you a carton or two of cigarettes for $1.30 a carton. Everything is cheaper in the PX up here, candy & gum is 3¢ a bar, but you can't get but 3 bars. Tell Aunt Thelma and if she wants me to get her some I will.
>
> When we go on our first flight we will fly over the Grand Canyon and Boulder Dam. We are not very far from the Grand Canyon, I was going to go see it some time but we can't get off, so I don't guess I will . . .
>
> Love, Ray[6]

GUNNERY SCHOOL: KINGMAN, ARIZONA

Growing up in rural Texas and living your entire life feeling the effects of the Depression, money became a common topic in Ray's letters home and he was very conscious of the price of items. Ray's generosity shone through his letters, and his offer to purchase cigarettes for his dad and chocolate for his aunt was an example of this character trait. Ray's generous spirit drew people to him.

Dear Folks, *March 7, 1944*

I have been to school two days and haven't done a thing. All we have been doing is a little drill and lectures. Mother, if you can find me a small suit case I wish you would get it for me. There has been a lot of steeling [sic] going on around here, and I want to lock my stuff up. Tomorrow at dinner I am going over to the Post Office and get a money order for $20.00 dollars and send it home. I don't want to carry it around for someone might steel [sic] it, and I won't need it here for we can't go to town. I got moved to another barracks today and there is just one of my buddies still in the same one with me . . . his name is Reddell . . . While we are here we will get paid for two weeks of flying time . . . We changed to a new mess hall and I never saw such good eats since I left home. They just sit the butter out on the table and let us serve ourselves on the chow line.

[A second letter was enclosed in the same envelope for the same date, presumably written later that day.]

Well I found out for sure about our delay enroutes we are not going to get one. When we leave here we are going to Lincoln, Nebraska and will stay about 3 or 7 days and then we will go to another gunnery school . . . We will get 25 dollars extra a month for flying. There is two of these schools in Texas one is at El Paso and the other is at Delheart [sic]. I sure hope I get sent to one of these fields. We may get a furlough when we finish this field. I sure hope so I would really like to be home. I got the [Haskell] Free Press a day or two ago and was really glad to get it. I really do enjoy reading it . . . J.B. will be badly surprised if he joins the army thinking he can save for in the first place they don't give you much. They are taking all the men who are not in gunnery school in the Air Corps and putting them in the infantry. He had better be glad he didn't get in the Air Corps.

Love, Ray[7]

J. B. from the letter was J. B. Kuenstler, a young man a year behind Ray at Paint Creek High School.[8] The *Haskell Free Press*, the local newspaper, contained news about home and information about his friends. The newspaper began in January 1886 and continued for 131 years, producing its last edition in August 2017.[9]

Gunnery school proved busy for Ray, but for a young man that grew up hunting and shooting, this experience was fun and he excelled. In his letter home on March 8, 1944, Ray sent money home with an added note, "you can use it if you want to."[10] Ever mindful of the hardships back home, he generously offered to let his parents use the money if needed.

> *Dear Folks,*   *March 10, 1944*
>
> *Well, here I am out here in the mountains. This is just a small army camp . . . We went up on our first mission this morning and stayed up about two hours. We fired at a sleeve that was towed by another plan[e]. We only went up to about 10,000 feet but I really did like it. We are going on another mission in the morning at 6:30.*
>
> *I was going to write you last night but I was so tired I just went to bed. We had to ride out here in an old truck and the road was rough and dusty. I got a letter from you today and I thought I wrote you telling you I got the candy and cookies . . .*
>
> *There is still a rumor going around that we might get to go home, but I doubt it. They say we might get one when we leave Lincoln, Nebraska . . .*
>
> *You can send me anything for my birthday you want to it don't make a bit of difference. My watch is still doing ok. No, I don't wear my glasses much for I can't wear them when I am flying and I will be flying most of the time for long time now. There was about five other guys went up in the same plane and two of them urped [threw up] all over the plane. It didn't bother me at all . . .*
>
>   *Love, Ray*[11]

Even with his aspirations of becoming a pilot dashed, Ray was still ecstatic about flying, even if he was not the pilot. His pride in weathering his first plane ride shown through during his story of his comrades getting sick. In his 2006 interview, Ray described what he saw that day, "we flew up pretty high, I don't know how high . . . and I looked out—you know, we might have been at 20,000 feet—Gosh, I can see the world change. Course, that wasn't right, but I could imagine that I could see the curvature of the earth. That's the highest I'd ever been."[12] He laughed as he remembered himself as an awed eighteen-year-old in a plane for the first time. "I loved to fly. Always have. You bet. Never got sick, never got airsick . . . "[13]

From time to time, Ray ran across someone from home during his time of service.

> Dear Folks, March 11, 1944
>
> There was another bunch of boys from Sheppard Field come in here this evening and Tommy Davis was with them. I was at the PX this evening and run on to him. He was really glad to see me, he didn't know a one of the boys he came with. I found two more boys I knew and lived in the same barracks with.
>
> I haven't done much of nothing the last day or two, I went in the pressure chamber again today. We went up to 38,000 feet and stayed about twelve minutes. We stayed at 30,000 for about an hour and took a test.
>
> We had a big parade yesterday and photographers from LIFE magazine were here and made pictures. They made pictures of the firing range last night while they were firing all tracer bullets. I think they made pictures of some of the planes here. It was really hot here yesterday and we had to wear our blouses. We had to stand at attention for about 2 hours and there were a lot of men fainted. You be sure and watch for the pictures. They will come out in about a month. I will get it and cut out the pictures and show you where I was, for you couldn't find me in all that group . . . I really like it here, the officers are a lot better here than they were at Sheppard Field.
>
> We are going to move tomorrow at eight, we will move over to the school squadron, our school starts Monday.
>
> Love, Ray[14]

Tommie Davis was from Haskell and was at Sheppard Field with Ray.[15] Having someone from "home" must have been comforting, not just for Ray, but for his parents as well. Davis became a tail gunner; however, his plane was shot down over Germany during his second mission. He became a German prisoner of war until his release after the surrender of Germany. Ray's mother clipped Tommie's picture and the article describing his homecoming out of the paper and kept it.[16] One can only imagine her prayers for this young man and his family, and her thankfulness that it was not Ray.

Ray loved receiving letters from home, and treats were extra special. With a child so far from home, and the war an uncertain reality, packages of baked goods showed a mother's love and support.

Dear Folks,   *Sunday Afternoon [March 12, 1944]*

I got your cookies and the hand bag . . . and [it was] just what I need. It looks like now I won't get to use the bag for if things don't change we won't get to go home when we leave here. There is a notice on the bulletin board saying there will be no more delays enroute. I am not sure it means us as it says it starts with class 44–20 and we are in class 44–17. Don't look for me to[o] much until you see me walking up.

We have been going out on the range everyday last week and have finished firing the machine guns until we start shooting from a plane. Each day we fire 200 rounds from the hand held and 400 rounds from the turrets.

When we fire the hand helds if we hit 20 times out of 200 shots it is expert shooting. My average is about 18. We shot up 200 rounds in about fifteen or twenty minutes and each shot costs 17 cents, you can figure out where all your tax money goes.

Yesterday when I went over to the post office to get the packages a Lt. handed the big one to me and he saw what it was and he said are you planning on going somewhere and I told him I was and he said I wasn't. He handed me the box of cookies and ask[ed] which barracks I lived in and I told him he said he would be over to see me.

We have already had two final tests and I made 92–90 on them. We will shoot at targets from a pickup with shotguns this week. Next week, we go out to Yucca that is where we start firing from a plane. I don't know if I can write from out there or not, it is about 65 miles from here back in the mountains. The next to last week we will come back here for camera missions.

We got paid Friday night I got $30.00. I didn't sleep a[s] late today as I did last Sunday. I got up and went church. I guess I had better close and write Pearleta.

                                                           Love, Ray[17]

GUNNERY SCHOOL: KINGMAN, ARIZONA

Ray grew up with guns, so his pride at his average on the range was apparent. His joy at shooting for an extended time, up to 600 rounds, was fun and exciting. Although his letter was upbeat, the undertone of missing home was present. Not only did Ray miss home, but he knew his parents and family wanted to see him. Keeping them abreast with the latest furlough developments showed both his and his family's sense of longing.

Ever the dedicated letter writer, Ray wrote home every two or three days. Soldiers throughout history have bemoaned the down time that comes with being in the military. Letter writing helped ease the boredom.

Dear Folks,   *March 13, 1944*

Well I started to school today and I don't think it is going to be very easy. By the last of this week we have to take a machine gun apart and put it together blindfolded. It has about 120 parts.

We are quartined [sic] to our block, some boys have scarlet fever. A day or two ago I had a head ache and sore throat but I have got rid of it now . . . We have had two sand storms since we have been here, we had one today and it was really bad. After each one it has come a shower.

They told us we could volunteer for instructor when we finished. I think I will for after we get our months instructor school we will be sent to one of the five gunnery schools in the U.S. We will have to stay at that field 15 months and I think that will be better than going over seas. Most of the boys don't want that. The boy from Plainview and I have decided we would do that.

Love, Ray[18]

For the first time since joining up, Ray seemed to have a choice about his future assignment. With his outstanding score on the firing range, he had the option of staying in the states and becoming an instructor. His writing indicated that he saw this as the best of both worlds. He loved hunting and shooting and was understandably a little uncertain about overseas service. In his 2006 interview, Ray explained why he felt that most of the boys asked to stay as instructors were country boys: "You take boys that's raised up in the country like I was that shot guns all of his life, didn't nobody had to tell me how to shoot a gun. They had to show me how to assemble and disassemble a .50 caliber machine gun, you know, I had to learn that. But as far as leading a target, I already knew how to do that."[19]

Ray wrote letters on March 15, 16 and 19. His letters indicate that he was still unsure about his path choice, whether it lay as an instructor in the states or in combat overseas. And Ray had still not done much flying during his time at this air field.

Dear Folks,   *March 16, 1944*

I have been going to school all this week and have had to study a lot. I have took three tests and have passed all of them. We have two or three more tests this week . . . If I get instructor, it will be a month later before I get my furlough because I will have to go to an instructors school . . .

The weather out here is very queer. The other day the sand was blowing so you couldn't see a thing and the next morning the ground was covered with snow and by that evening the ground was dry.

We wear our dress clothes all the time and never do anything except go to school. I would not mind being stationed here as an instructor. I could save some money and the people are real nice. We really have a good C.O.

                                                                                                                    Love, Ray[20]

Dear Folks,   *March 19, 1944*

I haven't had time to write you in the last day or two as I have been taking a lot of tests. I took the machine gun apart and put it back together blindfolded yesterday in 28 minutes. I have been getting your mail regular, there is no use to send it air mail for it comes as fast by train.

We will graduate the morning of April 24 at 10:00 if nothing happens. We will get our wings and P.F.C. rating. It will be three or four days before we get to start home. I sure hope those chickens are big enough to eat by then. When D.W. gets to where he is going try to get his address for me. I guess Truett will have it . . . This week we will start to going out on the range and do some firing, we will do a lot of skeet shooting, I think that is going to be a lot of fun. We never did get to go up in an airplane but the last two weeks we are here we will get to fly a lot.

                                                                                                                    Love, Ray[21]

GUNNERY SCHOOL: KINGMAN, ARIZONA

The D. W. he refers to in his letter was D. W. Gipson, a classmate of Ray's at Paint Creek.[22] Truett was Truett Kuenstler who was one year younger than Ray at Paint Creek.[23] Ray always wanted news concerning his friends. His letter from March 21 showed how much he appreciated news from home.

> *Dear Folks,*   *March 21, 1944*
>
> I got your letter and the [Haskell] Free Press you sent today. I haven't got [to] read the paper much yet for I have been busy today.
>
> We signed the payroll tonight and they told us we would get paid by the third of April. I may have to send for the money before I go home for it will cost me about $30.00 to go.
>
> I wrote Aunt Thelma last night. I guess she will be surprised to get it. She sent me a picture and it is really good. She said she finally got her money on her house and Uncle Bill was going to join the Marines.
>
> I read a piece in the paper that Henry Ford said that the war would be over in two months, but I believe it will be a little longer than that. I read about another man said it would be about eight months, I think he is about right.
>
> It has really been cold here the last day or two and we have been out on the range both days. We have been firing the fifties and they are really good guns. They have a lot of power, and will fire 7200 yards . . .
>
>   Love, Ray[24]

His Aunt Thelma was his father's younger sister. The letter described another immediate family member, his Uncle Bill (Thelma's husband), joining the service. Many families across the United States had multiple family members in military service during the war. When discussing the prospect of the end of the war, rumors and speculation abounded, but Ray was right to think that it would be longer than a couple of months.

Ray admired the "fifties," or the .50 caliber machine guns. He recalled his experience with the gun, "It was a fine machine gun. [Manufactured by] Browning . . . I never did have one jam. I think it has happened, but I never did have one to jam on me."[25] He used a Browning .50 caliber machine gun throughout the war.

Following his graduation where he earned his wings and his P.F.C. stripe, he wrote his family.

Dear Folks,   *March 24, 1944*

I was going to write you last night but the Captain wanted all our shoulder patches sewed on so I had to do a little sewing . . . We went out on the range this morning and shot skeet, I have really been having some fun. We go out there and shoot up three or four boxes of shells and don't cost a thing . . . Don't ever ask me if I want you to send me something to eat for something from home is always good. I was glad to get Bill's address and will write him tomorrow night. I would like to know what he is training [for] . . . I guess I had better close.

                                                                                                                       Love, Ray[26]

Most likely, before joining the Army Air Force, Ray had limited ammunition for fun or practice. Skeet shooting with unlimited shot proved a welcome boon compared to all the tests and school he sat through. The war thrust many young men into adulthood, but at the end of the day, these were still boys. Green, wet behind the ears, boys. Reading Ray's open and honest letters one can catch a glimpse of that teenage boy, wanting to have fun, a rule follower, a little homesick, but loving this adventure.

Dear Folks,   *March 26, 1944*

I didn't get a letter from you yesterday or today either. I sure hope I get one tomorrow . . . There is no use to send me anything for my birthday for I will be home about that time. We may finish here a week quicker than we are supposed to I don't know for sure yet.

I slept until about ten this morning and really did enjoy it. I haven't done anything this evening but just sit around with the boys and talk. We have been shooting skeet for the last two days.

I sure thought I was going to get K.P. today. A few mornings ago the sergeant came in during reverlle [sic] and found about twenty of us in bed. He took our names but we didn't get any detail. I never did wake up until about thirty minutes after he had left. . . .

It was really pretty here today, the sun was shining bright and the wind wasn't blowing. It was just like a good old Texas spring day . . .

                                                                                                                     Love, Ray[27]

GUNNERY SCHOOL: KINGMAN, ARIZONA

Dear Folks,   *March 28, 1944*

I got your letter today the one telling about all the boys being home. The reason I am not going home on a plane is that they have stopped all cross country flights from this field. When I go home I will get ten days at home. They will give me enough extra time for traveling.

We went out on the range again today and fired for record. The rest of this week will be for record. Next week we will shoot skeet from a pickup. Then the next week we will go to a place about 65 miles from here and fire from a B17 at a target towed by another plane. Then the last week we come back here and fly camera and high altitude missions. Those last two weeks are the ones we get flying pay for.

We are going to get paid Friday and it is just about time for I am almost broke. I am really glad I sent that money home for it is really going to come in handy when I get home.

We go out on the range next Thursday night for night firing. We have been firing from turrets mounted on trucks. My place on a plane is in the top turret. I guess you know where that is. It is right on top of the plane just behind where the pilot sits. I have a good turret and two fifty caliber machines . . .

Love, Ray[28]

Although Ray thought it would be two weeks from his March 28 letter that they would go to Yucca for their B-17 gun training, the Army must have thought otherwise. Ray next letter was dated April 12, 1944. It was after this flight training, when he was shooting out of a B-17, that all thoughts of staying "safely" in the states as an instructor were put aside. His skill with a gun and his love of flying made his choice for him.

Dear Folks,   *April 12, 1944*

I will write you a few lines to tell you what I have been doing and to let you know I am still alright. I didn't get to fly today. I went to school this morning and worked this evening. The work was not very hard, we had to clean guns. We will fly tomorrow for four hours, it will be ground strafing about two hundred feet off the ground going about 150 miles per hour.

We have been flying over in California both times we went up. One of the boys flew over Needles [California], the Bolder [sic] Dam and Los Vages

[sic], Nev. Today. I sure hope I get to fly over some those places tomorrow. I believe I could have made a pilot if they had give me a chance. It looks easy, to watch the pilots fly the planes. We have really been flying with a good pilot.

I have "TEXAS" wrote on the bill of my work cap, and I have really been running on to a lot of guys from Texas. A week or two ago I run onto a sergeant from Georgetown and he knew Mr. Hughes and old man Tom Hughes . . .

Love, Ray[29]

Ray described the training in the B-17s: "an AT-6 is a single seat trainer and they put a rope on the tail end of it, with a . . . well it was a big round thing, that air would catch in and it was made out of ducking. The B17 would be flying along here and the AT-6 would be flying out there and they would be making all different kinds of maneuvers, and you'd shoot at that target, which was on the end of that rope. And . . . I don't [know] how they done that, but there would be a certain color of paint on the end of my bullets . . . and the other gunners. They'd get that thing back to the base, and they'd tell how many I hit or how many he hit. And that was the way we done our training . . ."[30]

Dear Folks,　　　　　　　　　　　　　　　　　　　　　　　April 16, 1944

. . . I liked it out at Yucca but they worked us pretty hard out there. When we wasen't [sic] flying or in class we had to unload ammo. The boxes weighed 98 lbs. each and we unloaded several box cars of it. We flew ten hours while we were up there. I like it fine, but it don't take it long to get old. On our last mission the weather was pretty rough and the guys kept the bomb bay full, three got sick and urped all over the place. I never did get sick some guys can take it and some can't. I fired 1500 rounds while I was out there. The best thrill was when we were ground strafing about 150 feet off the ground.

This week we are going to fly three, four hour missions. They are going to be camera and high altitude missions. I don't think we will go any higher than 25,000 feet. They issued us flying helmets and oxygen mask. When we start flying they will issue us fleece lined flying suits. We will have on those [with] fur lined shoes.

I never did apply for instructor but they have picked me to go up to interview me. I am really going to try to get out of it. Out of the four guys I run

GUNNERY SCHOOL: KINGMAN, ARIZONA

with they have picked two of us. The other one is the boy from Rotan. I really would hate to see the other boys leave here Monday morning without us. I really am going to do some high powered talking . . .

Love, Ray[31]

Dear Folks,   April 19, 1944

I was going to write you last night but we had to take a test. I don't know if I passed it or not, it was pretty hard. We took an aircraft recognition test today and I passed it . . . there was 175 out of our squadron that failed it.

If they don't make [me] an instructor we will leave here about 7 o clock Monday morning. I sure do hope I can talk my way out of the instructor deal. I would be stuck out here for about fifteen months and I sure don't want to be here.

Preston Underhill from Rotan, and Clarence "Max" Sturdivant from Blackwell, were two of the four friends Ray referenced. They were together at Sheppard Field and Kingman Airfield.

> *I have flew two high altitude missions this week. We went up to about 20,000. We went up high enough we could see the curvature of the earth. We flew over Phoenix, Arizona today. I guess you remember the show "Thunder Bird Field" it is at Phoenix and we flew pretty low over it. They really have some pretty country around Phoenix it is all irrigated and the fields are really pretty . . .*
>
> *. . . I don't know how long it will be before I will have an address after I leave here. We won't have one at Lincoln and won't get one until I get my next field. I thought I would get a furlough when I left Lincoln but don't think I will. I guess I will get one when I finish at my next field. It will take about three months to finish. We will get $25 extra a month for flying time. We will travel around all over the United States when we get with our crew . . .*
>
> Love, Ray[32]

Ray was able to talk his way out of staying and becoming an instructor. When asked how he managed it, his reply was, "It wasn't hard to do. I told them, 'I want to go to combat.' That was my ambition, and I didn't know [at that time] whether I was going to fight the Germans or the Japs, but I'm glad I fought the Germans, because they were more like we were. I mean, the Japs were mean and vicious, and the Germans, they valued their life the same as I valued mine. 'Course, those durn Japanese, those kamikaze airplanes, that sort of thing. I thought I was pretty fortunate to get to fight the Germans."[33]

Ray's next stop was Lincoln, Nebraska, where he met the crew that he flew with for the duration of the war. Ray seemed excited about his position; yet, a sobering letter from Head Quarters may have dampened his spirits some:

> 30 April 1944
> SUBJECT: *Prevention of Desertion.*
> TO: All Heavy Bombardment Groups, Crews, and
>   Components Thereof.
>
> 1. *This letter is written in the sincere belief that no American Soldier whether he be Officer or Enlisted Man will deliberately shirk important service to his Country or seek to avoid hazardous duty if he is in possession of the proper information and realize the importance of his job.*

2. Those who in the past have deserted the Service of the United States have probably for the most part been of the irresponsible type. Not realizing the seriousness of the offense, those men have absented themselves and taken a last fling, intending at all times to return to the Service. The conduct on the part of those men may or may not have been viewed only in a serious manner due to the fact that you are being trained for combat duty.

3. Upon departure from this station you are on the ALERT and the provisions of ARTICLES OF WAR 28 are applicable. These provisions are as follows:

"Any person subject to military law who quits his organization or place of duty with the intent to avoid hazardous duty or to shirk important service shall be deemed to be a deserter."

4. The movement of units from this station is considered important service within the meaning of Article of War 28 and any actual duty from this point on is considered hazardous duty. Failure to appear at the proper time and place is considered sufficient to establish the intent required. The extreme penalty for desertion is DEATH and all of the lesser penalties are severe, involving dishonorable discharge from the service and lots of the rights of citizenship.

5. The irresponsibility and misconduct of a few men can bring discredit upon an entire organization. It is the responsibility of crew members, individually and collectively to prevent unauthorized absences and to insure that the importance of the work being carried on here is fully understood by all.

By order of Colonel Gurney[34]

Although this was a form letter received by all combat personnel, this was a reality check for these young men. It clearly stated that from this point on, any duty was considered "hazardous duty," and that any misconduct, especially desertion, whether coming back to base late, or going out with friends without permission, would not just result in K.P. duty or a reprimand, but could have you prosecuted under military law. From this point on, these young men were considered combat personnel. Ray's "adventure" had taken a sobering turn.

CHAPTER 4
MEETING THE CREW: LINCOLN, NEBRASKA

"Haskell . . . calls [all citizens] to an hour of prayer . . . as the invasion of the continent is announced . . . Each business is asked to close for one hour to go to their churches for prayer . . . all will be at stake and the fate of the world hangs in the balance, when our boys begin to set foot on European soil. Surely everything can stop for one hour . . . and allow each of us to go to his own church for sincere prayer to God . . ."

—Haskell (TX) Free Press, May 12, 1944[1]

When war was declared in 1941, air fields were needed to train air and ground personnel. Lincoln Airfield in Nebraska was chosen as the location of an Army Airfield training facility on February 27, 1942, and was re-christened Lincoln Army Airfield. The airfield provided "flying training instruction to aircrews of B-17 Flying Fortresses," which was the group Ray was assigned to during his stay in Nebraska.[2] At Lincoln Army Airfield, Ray met his crew that he flew with for the duration of the war.[3] The train ride to get to Lincoln, Nebraska, took more than two days, and there was no opportunity to send letters during this trip. His first letter from Nebraska was dated May 1, 1944.

Dear Folks, May 1, 1944

I will really be glad when I leave here. I don't like the camp or the country. I haven't seen the sun since I have been here. All of us boys got split up when we got here. Three of us signed up to be on the same crew I don't know if we will get it or not. I signed up with the boy from Rotan and the one from Blackwell.

Last night I was over at the Soldiers Club and ran on to a boy from Haskell. I didn't know him but he said he knew me. His name is Carrol Sheets, his dad is Will Sheets a truck driver. He finished school in Haskell the same year Pearleta did. When I saw him he shook my hand like he knew me always and I didn't have the least idea who he was.

I got the kids pictures just before I left Kingman. I think they are really good. I will be glad to get a big picture of Frances. I haven't got any mail since I got here maybe I will get some tomorrow.

I got paid today and got $30.45 the next payday I should get about fifty dollars. I have a good bit of money now since I got the twenty and I haven't been spending much.

We saw some pretty country on our way up here especially in Colorado. We saw Pikes Peak which is 14,110 feet high. We went through five states on our way. Arizona, New Mexico, Colorado, Kansas and Nebraska.

You can write to the address on the envelope. I don't know how long I will be here. I must close and write Pearleta.

Love, Ray[4]

For someone that hardly traveled beyond Haskell and Stamford in his entire life, Ray had now been stationed in four camps, in four different states, and had traveled through much more country. The Pearleta that Ray consistently referenced was Pearleta Ivy from Haskell, Texas. The daughter of Judge and Mrs. John F. Ivy, Pearleta attended and graduated from Haskell High School. In one letter, Ray referred to her as "my girl." In another couple of letters, he talked to his mother about a ring that her and Pearleta bought together and gave as a gift to Ray. While Ray and Pearleta were friends and corresponded during the war, Ray and Pearleta did not wed. She married a man named Richard Carothers.[5] Ray married Miss Amelia June Holt after he returned to the family farm following the end of the war.[6]

Ray's next letter was bittersweet, sweet because he received mail from home, bitter because of an Army rumor going around camp.

Dear Folks,   May 2, 1944

    I got the package yesterday and the watch band was really pretty . . . I heard today that the class after us from Kingman are getting delays [furloughs] I guess if they are Tommy is about home by now. If they do it is really going to make me mad.

    I guess you wondered why I didn't write while I was on the train. They would not let us write for they were afreighed [sic] somebody would get hold of the letter. We were on the train about 56 hours and got off twice once somewhere in New Mexico and in Denver, Colorado. It was very comfortable we had regular troop sleepers.

    I sure would like to be home and see all my cows and horses. Can you ride Stormy yet?

Love, Ray[7]

The "Tommy" that Ray referenced was Tommie Davis, the young man from Haskell. Stationed at Sheppard Field together, Tommie arrived at Kingman Airfield just after Ray. The "Stormy" Ray asked after was his horse, given to him by his grandmother. Although Ray was overall optimistic and enjoying his new life, he was also homesick. Ray was not impressed with Nebraska, as his letters reveal, and his thoughts never strayed far from home.

Dear Folks,   May 4, 1944

    I will write you a few lines to let you know I am alright and still here. It is pretty cold here and the wind is blowing hard, the sun has shined one day since we got here. I am all through here and ought to be gone by this time next week. I will probably get some detail like K.P. a time or two before I leave.

    Mother, I can't find a thing to get you for "Mother's Day" so I am just sending you a money order for twenty dollars. Get you a dress or something whatever you need most. I can't even find a good card to send. They had some pretty stuff at Kingman but I thought I could get some better things here. I don't know if I will go to town or not. I don't care too much about it. If some of the boys want to go I guess I will go.

    I found Tommy and Kalenhead today, they come in yesterday. I guess that rumor about the delays was not right. I run onto some of the boys that I knew at Sheppard Field too they had been at Las Vegas, Nev.

I don't know when I will get to make my pictures, the sun never shines here. I'll be glad when we leave this Yankee land and get back down in the good South.

I haven't got a letter since I wrote you last. I will probably get one tomorrow I sure hope so . . .

Love, Ray[8]

While in Lincoln, Ray became a crew member for a B-17. The B-17 crew included a pilot, copilot, navigator, bombardier, top turret gunner/flight engineer, radio operator, ball turret gunner, waist gunner, and tail gunner.[9] At one time, the crew comprised ten and included two waist gunners, but one of the waist gunner positions was eliminated, so this left nine in Ray's crew. Ray recalled how he got assigned the position of tail gunner, "I was strictly a gunner. And Barney Glovick, the pilot, he assigned me to the tail position. The reason he did was because of my score at Kingman, Arizona."[10] Barney and Ray became fast friends. As evident in Ray's interviews and letters, he looked up to Barney. "Barney was a fine feller and a topnotch pilot. He was a little older than most of those pilots; he was 25 or 27. Most of those pilots were 21, 22, and I was always glad to fly with a pilot I thought had a little more maturity than most of those pilots. He was single. I followed him around just like he was my daddy. Course, I was just 18 years old when I got with him," explained Ray.[11] When asked what he admired about him so much, Ray replied, "His ability to fly that durn airplane, 'cause he was sure enough a good pilot."[12]

Even with all his talk about Yankees, his best companion during the war turned out to be from the North. Barney hailed from Grand Rapids, Michigan. The crew consisted of young men from all over the United States. "My radio operator was from Aurora, Nebraska, and he and I buddied up. We were both country boys. He lived in this little old town in Nebraska, and his daddy was a policeman. He and I kind of talked the same language. [His name was] Sandy Herron—W. C. Herron. My co-pilot was from some town in Kansas; I don't recall what town it was. His name was Charlie Clark—C. O. Clark. And the navigator was Norman Sacks, and he was from Stamford, Connecticut. I think he was connected with all them Sacks, them wealthy Sacks up there in the northeast. I never did know for sure, but he was a Jew, and he was a good feller. Good feller. I thought the world of him. And bombardier was from Michigan," stated Ray, recounting his crew. The bombardier's name was William Monkevich and he was from Rosewood, Michigan, outside of Detroit. The waist gunner, Chuck Buda, came from Ohio. The flight engineer was Eugene "Pop" Bowman from Saxton, Missouri. The last crew member, a gunner, was Bert Railton from Glendale, California.[13]

To explain these positions in a little more in detail, Ray described a waist gunner's duties: "Well, he was the gunner, you know. Down the side of the fuselage; in that airplane there's a window, and it's open. About this big a square [demonstrating an area approximately 3' by 3'], and a machine gun mounted right there. He shot out either side." The interviewer, Dan Utley, clarified that the waist gunner was "essentially in the waist of the plane." Ray continued to describe the different gunner positions: nose, waist, tail, ball turret, and top turret, with a total of thirteen, fifty-caliber machine guns, some of which required one man to fire using two different guns. "'course I had two back there, you know, mounted side by side. That's the way the ball turret was. There was two in it, and there was two in the top turret, and the chin gun, it had two fifties, and then on the nose of that airplane there was a gun that come out either side of it on the nose, just a single gun that

(l to r) Eugene "Pop" Bowman, Sandy Herron, Ray Perry, Barney Glovick, Norman Sacks, William Monkevich, Bert Railton, and Charles "Chuck" Buda. Not pictured was Charlie Clark.

the navigator or bombardier either one could use."[14] According to the book *The Mighty Eighth* by Gerald Astor, "The B-17B, standard in 1941, packed just five flexible .30 caliber machine guns, lacked a belly turret and tail gunner, and possessed little protective armor . . . but by the end of World War II the addition of twelve or even thirteen .50 caliber machine guns plus steel padding in vulnerable areas, power-driven turrets, gunners to the rear and below and bulletproof windshields lent some credence to the name [the flying fortress]."[15]

> Dear Folks, May 7, 1944
>
> I will write you a few lines before I go to bed. We flew six hours this evening and I am really tired, flying makes me more tired than driving a tractor all day. We went down into Mississippi today on a high altitude mission although we didn't go but to 16,000 feet.
>
> We got the news yesterday that they started the invasion and it seems they are doing pretty good. They said there was 11,000 planes and 4,000 ships in on it. I would like to have seen all that from the air.
>
> We have been getting reports that the bombers have been going over with[out] any opposition at all, that really sounds good to me. I think by the time we get there they will be going over Europe without gunners . . . Well, I guess I had better close and write Pearleta.
>
> Love, Ray[16]

Ray's news about the invasion prompted the hour of prayer published in the *Haskell Free Press* on May 12, 1944, quoted at the beginning of this chapter. The missions Ray spoke to were preliminary missions before the big D-Day invasion on June 6, 1944. The public and the military personnel knew the invasion was forthcoming, but the actual date was kept top secret. Increased bombing runs and large movements of troops and supplies lead up to the big invasion. Ray's comment that "by the time we get there they will be going over Europe without gunners" may have helped ease his parents' anxiety, as he most likely intended. With his overseas departure imminent, his time training quickly approached its end.

Dear Folks,   *May 8, 1944 3 P.M.*

I had night detail last night and I got to sleep all day today and have just woken up. I had to fire a boiler to keep warm water for the showers. I didn't get off until 5:30 this morning.

I was put on the alert for shipping today. I will ship Thursday. I don't know where I will go and won't until I get there. Some say we are going to Tenn. I would like to go to Tennessee but I would rather go closer to home. The boys I signed up with are shipping with me. I am really glad we are going together. Seems like you ask me what their names are. The one from Rotan is Preston Underhill we were at Kingman I give him [illegible] address and he has been writing to her ever since. He used to go to school with Mr. Underwood, some time when you see him ask him about Preston . . . The other one is Clarence Sturdivant the boy that phone me the night I was shipped from Sheppard. He is from Blackwell. I must close and write Pearleta.

Love, Ray[17]

Clarence Sturdivant was known by his friends as "Max." Ray left Lincoln, Nebraska, on Thursday, May 11, 1944, heading to Dyersburg, Tennessee. They rode on a train for two nights and one day, arriving on Saturday, May 13, 1944. This was the camp where Ray stated he got his "overseas" training—the last stop before heading to war.

CHAPTER 5
OVERSEAS TRAINING: DYERSBURG, TENNESSEE

"**Promoted to Corporal:** *Colonel Merlin I. Carter, Station Commander of Army Air Field Dyersburg, Tennessee, announces the promotion of Joseph R. Perry from private first class to corporal. Cpl. Perry is the son of Mr. and Mrs. Hoyt Perry who reside at Haskell. Prior to his entry into the armed services he was a student at Paint Creek. Cpl. Perry is completing his final phase combat training at this field as a tail gunner aboard a Flying Fortress.*"

—Haskell (TX) Free Press, July 21, 1944[1]

Dyersburg Army Airfield in Dyersburg, Tennessee operated from 1942 to 1945. The Tennessee historic marker for the airfield stated, "Thousands of airmen took their last statewide training here before going into combat overseas. Training received here in B-17 Flying Fortresses played a key role in preparing U.S. bomber crews for combat in World War II."[2] In Ray's 2016 interview, he explained that he was sent to Tennessee for his "overseas trainin'." That's not what they called it. Officially it was called "ETO Indoctrination Course." ETO was military shorthand for the European Theater of Operations. The men he trained with at Dyersburg stayed with Ray until they returned to the states in 1945.[3]

> *Dear Folks,*   *May 14, 1944*
>
> *We got here yesterday morning about nine and have been on the go ever since we got here. We rode the train two nights and a day. We didn't leave*

Lincoln until about nine Thursday night [letter damaged]. There was a big bridge beside the tracks, I guess it was the bridge Frances went over. I thought about her when we crossed it. There was a lot of those great big river boats along the dock.

It is really hot here we had to wear our O.D. clothes [olive drab, heavier material] all day yesterday and I almost burned up. We changed to our sun tans today and they really do fill [sic] good. Mine are a little too big but they will have to do until I can get to a tailor shop and have them cut down. I have gained 3 pounds since I weighed in at Sheppard Field. We took another physical at Lincoln.

At this place we are going to take ten weeks of overseas Training and then will be ready to go across. If things don't change we [letter damaged] . . . a month plus fifty percent of that for flying pay. That is a lot of money for a guy in the army [with] no where to spend it. I guess I had better close and write my gal.

Love, Ray

[P.S.] What has happened to J.B. I haven't heard of him in a long time. Has he ever joined anything.[4]

Ray's general optimism showed in this letter. He loved seeing new places and relating them to his family back home. Enlisted men sometimes received a promotion and substantial pay raise before they went overseas, and Ray looked forward to this promotion. He had just turned nineteen one month before, and was still a very young man. When inducted into the service, Ray could be described as tall and lanky, weighing in at 141 pounds and standing 5'10".[5] Proving yourself as one of the youngest crewmen must have been somewhere in his mind, and he seemed so proud to relate this change in his physical appearance to his parents.

Dear Folks, May 18, 1944

I am sorry I didn't write you before, but they have been keeping us pretty busy since we got here. We have took another complete physical, the toughest I have had yet. We got four more shots and a blood test. The shots were Typhus, Tetanus, Yellow Fever and another one but I can't think what it was. I really like it here we don't have to do anything but about every half day and the rest of the time we can do just what we want to. I can go to town

OVERSEAS TRAINING: DYERSBURG, TENNESSEE

anytime we are off duty. Dyersburg is about fourteen miles from here and a little larger than Haskell. Underhill and I caught a ride to town with three girls last night. The girls were really nice and friendly, other places we have been the girls were unfriendly and didn't seem to care about a soldier.

I really like these Tennessee Belles, but don't tell Pearleta. All these girls want to know all about you and what you have been doing. They are having a big dance here tonight and everyone seems to be having a big time. They have a dance here twice a week.

Well, it looks like I will go overseas without a furlough, there is a little talk of one, but I don't believe we will get one. We will ship out of here on the 25th of July and go to a field in Nebraska and pick up our [letter damaged; plane]. We will spend about two weeks there drawing our equipment and breaking in our plane. When we are through there we will be ready to go.

Frances, I will get you a graduation present the first time I am in town in the day time. You might give me some hints. I must close and write Pearleta and D. W.

Love, Ray[6]

Dear Folks, May 20, 1944

I haven't got time to write you much as it is almost time to go to bed. I haven't done much of anything yet and it don't look like we will. We will start flying in a few days. We will go on cross country flights and they all go out over the Gulf of Mexico. I don't know if any of them will go close to home or not.

If I should happen to get to go home I sure wish you could get a new car. Maybe I can do it with [you] when you can tell if you are going to make a good crop or not.

I get a twenty-four [hour] pass starting tomorrow at dinner, I guess I will go to town and see what it is like to be in town again.

We got a letter from the boy from Wellington that we left back in Lincoln. He is really mad, they are putting him on a B24.

They gave a bunch of boys a fifteen day furlough on Saturday after we left Lincoln on Thursday. There was about 500 of them. We may get one before we go over. It don't look like they would give part of them a furlough without giving us one. I must close it is getting late.[7]

Dear Folks,   *May 23, 1944*

I have just took two more shots. I don't know how many more we will get but I am getting tired of taking them. I haven't did a thing today but get shot.

I think we will start flying in a few days. I sure hope we get our flying time in this month so we can get our flying pay.

I got the papers yesterday and was really glad to get them. I have had plenty of reading to do this morning. I haven't got a letter from you in three or four days. I sure hope I get one today.

[second half of letter written in the afternoon of May 23]

I sent my suntans to the tailor a few days ago and got them back Monday. I had the pants cut down and the shirts cut down in the waist.

I think we are going to fly tonight. If we do we will probably go on a bombing mission. We have to go brief at 7:00.

I got a letter from you and two from Pearleta today, I sure was glad to get them. I guess I had better close as it is almost time to go brief. We will be up until about one o'clock.

                                                                                Love, Ray[8]

Just like most young men, girls were always a welcome distraction. As boredom set in, Ray's optimism waned a bit. Ray also showed how anxious he was to see his family before making the trip overseas. The last time he saw them was in February when he was stationed at Sheppard Field. As always, his thoughts were not far from home and family. His frustration showed as he heard about other soldiers getting furloughs to go home, but no mention yet of his crew getting a furlough. Ray was proud of the money he was making and wanted to help the family with a purchase of a new, or newer, car. The last letter definitely took a more upbeat tone once he began flying again, not to mention the letters he received at mail call.

Dear Folks,   *May 26, 1944*

I could have got a twenty-four [hour] *pass today, but I didn't want to go to town so I stayed here and put out a washing. Laundry is so high here I do most of mine myself. I took two pair of sun tans to the tailor shop to have them cleaned, pressed and cut down in the waist and it cost $3.75. They* didn't get them good and clean then. I am going to try washing a pair of them in a few days, a boy in my barracks has an iron. Most of the boys here does their laundry we have so much time off. I don't know how they will look but I am going to try it.

About the furlough, I haven't heard anything else except that the boys [that] *left here just before we got here got 15 days when they got to their field in Nebraska. If I do get to go home it will be the last of July or the first of August.* There is nothing I can do to get one, if one gets one the whole bunch will get one. When we first got here they had us all to fill out a slip of paper telling if we had had a furlough or not.

Underhill is staying here too, but I think next week we are going to Memphis to see his cousin he is in the Navy Air Corps.

Well guess I had better close and write Pearleta.

Love, Ray

[P.S.] *I have just got back from the meeting and they told us we would fly across!*[9]

When reading an historical account, especially when money was referenced, it helped to have something of that time period to compare it to. Ray complained that two sets of sun tans, to be tailored, cleaned, and pressed was $3.75. One can assume that the sun tans he referenced include two shirts and two pairs of pants. During 1944, in the *Haskell Free Press*, the clothing store, Perkins & Timberlake Co., in Haskell, Texas, advertised "Men's Gabardine Khakis," shirt and pants for $5.73. His tailoring and cleaning cost more than half of the price of buying an entirely new khaki outfit![10]

Ray's next letter, dated June 1, 1944, suffered significant damage, but the gist of the letter seemed pretty clear. He wrote that he received letters from his mother, Pearleta, and his Aunt Thelma. He expressed his satisfaction in the length of the letters, because they held more news from home. Apparently in the letter, his mother asked about a time when she could call Ray. He explained that they had a very irregular schedule and were on call for flying missions all day, so he was not sure if he could set aside a time to receive her call. He then relayed to her the steps they practiced when they went for a mission brief, stopping by a building to check the weather before being briefed on their mission. Keep in mind, these were just training exercises to prepare them for overseas mission trips. He asked his mother to send him some cookies and particularly asked for a cake that his grandmother made. He described it as "that cake with the hole in the middle."[11] He ended the letter by expressing his desire to see the wheat crop, and again conveyed his wish for a furlough.

Ray's wife Amelia remarked that Ray going off to war took a particular toll on his grandmother. According to family stories, Ray's grandmother fretted and worried about Ray's safety until he was home again in 1945. Not to downplay the worry experienced by his other family members, especially his parents, but apparently, she had the hardest time dealing with his time in the service.[12]

> Dear Folks, June 2, 1944
>
> I went to ground school this evening but didn't do a thing this morning. We never have to do anything until 1:30 unless we fly in the morning. We only fly about once a week in the morning and we fly tomorrow morning we have to go brief at 6:00.
>
> I guess I will send you some of my khakis in a few days and let you wash them. I can do the underclothes and hankercheifs [sic] alright. I have about 10 pair of underclothes and about 20 hankercheifs [sic]. I have been buying some all along. I have some bleech [sic] and they are really white when I wash them.
>
> I got a letter from you yesterday and you said the weather was pretty. It rains here almost every day about four and it is cleared off by time for us to fly at night. It is really hot here. I don't notice the heat so much but I sweat a lot, we can't wear a suit of drawers over a day or so. We take a shower every day and sometimes more. Here we wear a pair of shorts (sport) when we are off and we can go anywhere in them even in the PX. We can do anything in this field we want to unless we are on duty. They don't care what we do but we really have to be to classes on time.
>
> I don't know if we are going to get sergeant's stripes or not we may just get corporal stripes. I don't think I will fly overseas with that. I must close and write Pearleta.
>
> Love, Ray[13]

Being from Texas where summer temperatures range from the mid-nineties to 105 degrees, Ray seemed unbothered by the heat, but the humidity, something that West Texas does not often experience, appeared to bother

OVERSEAS TRAINING: DYERSBURG, TENNESSEE

him. However, his optimism shown through. He was young, seeing new places, flying, and for the first time in his military experience, given lots of freedoms.

> *Dear Folks,*   *June 5, 1944*
>
> *I didn't go to Memphis on my pass, we went to Union City it is a town about the size of Haskell. We are going to Memphis Thursday and have some pictures made . . .*
>
> *We flew a high altitude mission Sunday morning and went all over Tennessee. We went over Nashville. Our mission before that we went to a town in Mississippi, I think it was Meridian. I have to go to school tomorrow at 11:30. And we fly tomorrow evening. I got back out to camp this morning about four and didn't wake up until 10:30. We didn't have to go to school until 1:30.*
>
> *I got your cookies a day or two ago and they were really good. They didn't last very long. Pop got some today and I got some of them. He is one of my crew members we call him Pop he is 27 years old.*
>
> *I got your letter today you said you were planting cotton I wish I was home to help. I really would like to see LaVern and Jack.*
>
> *I have just talked to a boy from Fort Worth he has a car and if we get a 52 hour pass I think he is going. If he does I will go and you can meet me there. If we do and get a pass I may not know it very long before and I will phone Pearleta. I phoned her the other night I like to never got her. I would have never got her but another soldier put an emergency call through to Dallas and they got it through with it someway. She told me LaVern & Jack was home. I guess I had better close and write her.*
>
>   *Love, Ray*
>
> *[P.S.] Mother my shoes are about wore out and I wish you would get me a pair. Get plain toes and about 9 ½. Frances I can't think of or find a thing to get you for graduation so if you want a calf you can have Faye's next one. I know before I come in the army you was wanting one. I would give you one of my heifers but I am going to need them when I get out of the army.*[14]

Later, in his 2006 interview, Ray explained the "bombing missions" or training they participated in while at Dyersburg, Tennessee, "we were flying as a crew and we were doing a lot of bombing—not real bombing, but you know, training the bombardier and training the gunners to work as a crew, and we weren't there but about six or eight weeks, something like that."[15]

The "Pop" in his letter was his flight engineer, Eugene Bowman from Saxton, Missouri. Considering most of these young men were late teens and early twenties, at the age of twenty-seven, Pop must have seemed old and in an entirely different league. Pop was married and had children back home. He and Ray had a life-long friendship.

Ray still sought to get home. Rumors of furloughs given or not given ran rampant, and these young men grasped at any opportunity to get home to see their families before being shipped overseas. He mentioned a young man that may try to head to Fort Worth on a two and one-half day pass. A drive to Fort Worth would still be a good distance for his family, but it would get him closer than he was at that time.

Ray's next letter, written around June 7, was lost to time, and only the envelope remains.[16] The following letter, dated June 10, suffered heavy damage. From what was legible, Ray went to Memphis and had his picture taken. He complained about the price, which he considered very high, and asked his mother to send him some money from his savings. He talked about how expensive it was to go places or do things, which he did infrequently. He explained that it took about ten days before the pictures were ready, and that he had some of the pictures tinted. Ray then listed some of the people that he wanted his mother to give the pictures to, including his grandmother and Ruby. He ended the letter by asking after his herd of cows and whether any had calved yet.[17]

Although Ray was young, he was very prudent about money. Maybe because he had so little of it growing up, or he was frugal enough to want to set aside for the future, but he sent home money when he could and began an allotment of pay during this time. A portion of his paycheck would automatically be taken out and sent to his mother.[18] In many of his letters, Ray's generosity shown through, when he told his parents to use the money if they need to, or when he offered to go in with his dad on a car. His mother even kept the copies of the bank deposit receipts, where she would deposit this money into an account for Ray. He also had a monthly amount taken out for life insurance.[19] Right before Ray left to begin his trip to the European Theater, he raised the amount of his allotment.[20]

OVERSEAS TRAINING: DYERSBURG, TENNESSEE

Dear Folks,   *June 13, 1944*

We get another pass today . . . there is no place to go . . . [some] of the crew were going to Union City and celebrate his birthday, but they went on a Gulf mission and haven't got back yet. They probably won't get back until about five. He will be 19 tomorrow, he looks older than that he weighs about 175. He has gained a lot since he got in the army. We were supposed to go on a Gulf mission this morning but our engineer was sick so we couldn't go. We were called up yesterday and they told us we would not get any rating here. This is really a mad bunch of boys. I think most of them are [going to go] A.W.O.L. if they don't give us a furlough.

If they keep fooling with us I am going home before I go overseas. I got your letter yesterday saying you were planning [to come see] me. I sure hope you can . . . I haven't heard from that [boy from] Fort Worth say anything more about going. I could be there for more than 5 or 6 hours anyway. I think you would enjoy the trip, there is a lot of pretty country up here. It really is pretty from the air. All the people up here farm with teams and it is a lot of fun to watch them scratch around with their walking plows.

I guess I had better close and write Pearleta.

                                                                                                Love, Ray[21]

Commanders throughout history have lamented about how low morale becomes when soldiers sit for too long. Even though Ray and his crew ran practice missions, the end of their training never left their mind, and their number one priority was to get home to say a final goodbye to family and friends. Their future seemed uncertain, and the thought of leaving without that farewell bothered these young men, most away from home for the first time. To add to their low spirits, news arrived that they would not receive the promised promotions and pay raises. News about the war, about victories and defeats, were most likely discussed and dissected in their many hours of down time as well. Ray rarely wrote about the war's progress in his letters, which remained pretty upbeat, but the added anxiety over the casualties relayed from friends and family surely increased the airman's anxiety.

Ray Perry, c. 1944

Dear Folks,   June 16, 1944

    I got the shoes yesterday and the letter with the money today. I really like the shoes and they fit alright. I also got the proofs for the pictures and they are not very good, but I will have one of them made.

    We have flew all evening and I am so tired I can hardly write. We went on a air to [illegible] mission and the old guns . . . work very well. I am getting so [tired] of this army I don't know what to do. First they cut our furloughs and then they cut out our ratings. Maybe it won't be long till it is over. News came over the radio today that we bombed Japan with the big B29 that is the big Super Fortress.

    Frances wrote that Uncle Welsh wants us to go see him. If you come to see me maybe we can go see him, if it is not very far from here to where he lives. We have another pass tomorrow. I don't know what I will do. I may stay here and try to get some rest. [letter damaged]. I must close and write Pearleta a few lines.

                                                      Love, Ray[22]

    This letter was the lowest point in all of Ray's letters home, before and after. He was missing home terribly, he felt unfairly treated, and down time had lost its allure. Since Ray was not naturally a pessimist, his next letter home was more upbeat.

OVERSEAS TRAINING: DYERSBURG, TENNESSEE

Dear Folks,   *June 18, 1944*

I have decided not to send my clothes home to have them washed. There is a lady here about a quarter of a mile from the field. She does our laundry real good and don't charge very much. She lives by herself, her husband is in the army. She has a washing machine and we get it in about four days. There is about six of us boys that take our laundry to her.

Well, I went on a cross-country hop to Texas last night. We flew over Fort Worth and Dallas and went on to Sherman. Dallas is really a big town, the lights are really pretty from the air. It was a low altitude mission and we could see the lights good. It took us about two hours to get there.

I have to go to ground school for three hours today and then fly again tonight. I don't know what kind of a mission it will be.

While we were over Ft. Worth and Dallas I was really hoping about two engines would go out so we would have to land there, but of course they didn't.

I think I will write Uncle Press and Aunt Clarie and tell them about flying over Ft. Worth. I must close as I have two more letters to write.

Love, Ray[23]

Ray's Uncle Press and Aunt Clarie Perry lived in Fort Worth. Press was Hoyt Perry's brother. Before joining the military, visiting his Uncle Press in Fort Worth had been the extent of Ray's traveling. Whether it was just being over Texas soil again, or Ray's natural optimism returning, his next letters seemed more hopeful.

Dear Folks,   *June 21, 1944*

I will write you a few lines although I don't have a thing to write. We had to get up this morning and fly at four and landed about four. We went on a mission down to the gulf and back. We went from here to Gulfport, Miss. and out over the gulf a little ways and back.

I got the pictures yesterday and was really glad to get them. Some of them were good and I really enjoyed looking at them. I guess all the kids had a good time on their trip. I wish we could have gone on a senior trip.

They didn't give us any reason for not giving any ratings except that it was a second Air Force order and that don't have anything to do with going overseas. They have to give us at least sergeants stripes before we go into combat. I may get corporal stripes here, I think all the Pfc.(private first class) are. That still isn't all they said we would get.

We get another pass tomorrow, but I doubt if I go anywhere. I will probably stay here and go to the show. I must close as it is getting late.

Love, Ray[24]

Dear Folks,   June 22, 1944

I got two letters from you today and was really glad to get them. I don't know what to tell you about coming to see me. I have heard we may get a furlough, but I have not heard any of the big shots say anything about it. I'll go see the captain in the morning and see what he says about it. If you come you will go through Memphis and you will get to the field before you get to Dyersburg. I think you can get on the post and when you do go to the service club and you can ask there where barracks 2263 is, that is where I live. Daddy can go over to the barracks and find me. My barracks is just a little ways west from the service [entrance]. You can ask someone on the field where [it] is.

If you let me know what day you are going to get here and about what time I will try to meet you at the gate if I am off. Let me know when and who all is coming and I will try to get a place to stay.

I didn't know anything was on my letter but I got to asking and one of my crew members had mailed the letter and put that on it. S.M.R.L.H. means Soldiers Mail Rush Like Hell. I must close and go take a shower. I will let you know more in a few days if I find anything out.

Love, Ray[25]

Dear Folks,   June 24, 1944

I got the pictures yesterday and will send you some of them . . . I got your cake today and it was really good. Underhill and I have just finished eating it. Two boys on my crew and Underhill and I ate it. They really did like it and so did I.

I don't know what to tell you about coming to see me. I can't find out anything for sure. The boys that are leaving here in a day or two are going to get about five days I think. I expect to get a few days, but five is not very much and again they may not give us any at all. Let me know what you are going to do and just do what you think is best for I don't know what to tell you they won't tell us a thing. I would hate for you to drive all the way up here and then I get a furlough in a few days.

I must close and write Pearleta. I really did enjoy the cake.

Love, Ray[26]

Dear Folks,   June 25, 1944

I got a letter from you today and was very glad to get it. I didn't get one from Pearleta, but I got one yesterday.

You had better come to see me I guess for I don't know if I will get a furlough or not. I have just found out the boys that just left here just got three days instead of five. If I just get three days I am going home anyway. I don't care if I get back late or not. The boys that got the three days are the ones that haven't had a furlough in 6 months. I haven't had one, but three days is not much.

I think I can be with you most of the time you are here. They have been letting boys off ground school when their folks are here. Be sure and let me know if all of you are coming or how many and I will try to get a place to stay.

The cake was just the kind I like and it was really good. I must close and get to bed as I am tired. I flew about six hours this evening.[27]

Since these "bombing missions" were for training purposes only, in later years Ray explained what they practiced and prepared for on these flights. He recounted that although everyone had their job, such as flight navigator, radio operator, etc., if they came under attack, several men would shift to a gun and begin to protect the plane. "Anytime we were under attack by fighters, German fighter planes," the navigator and bombardier gave up their duties to become temporary gunners. "The bombardier, the only time he ever did anything was when we was going over target, and they would switch that airplane from the pilot to the Norden bombsight. See, actually that bombardier he flew that airplane, because you had to fly it straight and level . . . But anyway, I don't know how he done it, but that Norden bombsight was quite an instrument, because somehow or another they'd switch it, I guess, from automatic pilot, if there was an automatic pilot, and he'd fly that airplane with that bombsight."[28]

The B-17s Norden Bombsight was kept top secret in the beginning of the war. Although the plane was on autopilot, the bombardier would have limited control of the aircraft but could only alter the course a few degrees one way or the other. After the bomb was dropped, the bombardier relinquished control of the aircraft back to the pilot. According to an article in *Aviation History*, "Bombs fall in a curved path; from 20,000 feet, for example, they must be released approximately 2½ miles from the target. Many factors contribute to accurate bombing, including optical and mechanical principles; direction, movement and speed of the airplane; aerodynamics of the bombs; weather conditions; and enemy action."[29] These were the maneuvers that the crew practiced over and over to prepare for combat bombing missions overseas.

Dear Folks,   *June 29, 1944*

I got your letter today, the first in about four or five days. I haven't heard from Pearleta in about the same time, I don't know what is wrong. I am sorry I have gone so long with writing but have been pretty busy lately.

I guess you had better plan on coming to see me if you want to see me for I can't find out a thing. The last group got three days and a lot of them aren't back yet. If you come, try to get here about the twelfth [sic] of July for they are going to try to finish us up by the fifteenth.

After that we are going to just make up what we have missed. Our crew hasen't [sic] missed anything so I guess we will just lay around and do nothing.

On those long missions I usually just stay in the radio room and sleep if I can. We can't land on those missions unless it is an emergency. I try to carry a sandwich or two with me.

There was no use in sending me the three dollars for the five was enough. If you need some money cash my bonds. I get another one this month. After that I am having them cut out or they are stopping. I am just going to send the money home. After I get overseas and get some more stripes and go to drawing flying an overseas pay.[30]

OVERSEAS TRAINING: DYERSBURG, TENNESSEE

Dear Folks,   July 2, 1944

    I got a letter from you today and was very glad to get it. I am glad you are coming on to see me for I want to see you. If you come between the twelfth [sic] and fifteenth I might get to go back with you. I think we will get a few days. They told us a few days ago if we finished up early we might get a few days off. We are having our final processing the 9-10 and 11. After that we will do flying we have skipped. Our crew is ahead of most of the others, but probably won't get anymore off.

    I went to Memphis yesterday and got the pictures. They are not a bit good but I will send them to you anyway. We stayed in Memphis all night and had a good time. One of our crew members had a good friend down here and he payed [sic] all our expenses. He is about fifty I guess.

    Be sure and write me all your plans pretty soon and I will see about a place to stay. If I should find out a day or two before you come that I am going to get a furlough I will phone Pearleta and she can get you word some way.

    I must close and get to bed.

                                                                                            Love, Ray

    [P.S.] I got promoted today I am now a Cpl. My base pay is $66 with 33 flying pay.[31]

Ray was not only a faithful letter writer, but he was also a faithful picture taker. His pictures showed what life for the everyday G.I. consisted of and told a story all their own. The excitement and relief was palpable in Ray's letters when he knew his parents were coming to see him. Ray's family did indeed make the trip from Texas to Tennessee. Ray related the story with a smile, "My mother and daddy and my sister and two brothers come to see me one time. They got in an old car Daddy had, I think a '37 Ford, and drove from here to Dyersburg, Tennessee. I think they slept in the car. Course, Mother was the kind that always carried plenty to eat. They didn't have to stop at a restaurant, or didn't have the money I don't imagine. But anyway, they come to see me."[32] Don Perry, Ray's youngest brother, added more details about the trip. In a 2017 interview Don recalled, "the whole family went to Tennessee in our '37 Ford to see him off before he went overseas. I remember we slept in the car [while traveling]. It took us two days to get there and two days to get back. I remember we broke down coming back home about 1/2 mile from our house."[33]

The Perry family visited Ray in Dyersburg, Tennessee, before he went overseas. (Clockwise): Frances, Ray, his mom Thelma, Don, and Gene.

Several items found in Ray's service records proved very telling about this time before being shipped overseas. A notation dated July 11, 1944, stated that Ray was "offered opportunity to make will and power of attorney."[34] If Ray managed to keep the dangers of war at bay in his mind, the opportunity to draw up a will would have brought them uncomfortably close to home. The next notation of interest, dated July 15, 1944, reported that Ray was "favorably recomended [sic] for good conduct medal."[35] This was not surprising given Ray's character. He was at last given a furlough. According to his service record, he received a six-day furlough from July 21 to July 27, 1944.[36] The final notation for this period, dated August 15, 1944, stated "ETO Indoctrination Course Completed." Ray's "overseas trainin'" was over, and the war in Europe still raged on.

CHAPTER 6
COMBAT DESTINATION: ENGLAND

"*Is Gunner* – Sgt. Ray Perry has arrived in England. The son of Mr. and Mrs. Hoyt Perry of Paint Creek, he is a gunner on a Flying Fortress."

—Haskell (TX) *Free Press*, September 15, 1944[1]

Ray received a short leave after all and returned home, "As soon as we finished our training, well they did send us home for a little short furlough, and we went back to — our orders read 'Kearney, Nebraska.' And we picked up a brand new airplane, [and] the crew . . . got back together at Kearney . . ."[2] Kearney Army Air Field was actually the second of that name. As the war gained momentum in Europe, and the military began to increase production of everything from planes to pilots, the city invested time and money to entice the government to build an airfield near their city. The first airport opened in August 1942, but it quickly became evident that the military needed an air field for heavy bombers and the new airport was not meeting those needs. So, the city tore down the first airport and built another in its place to the military's specifications. Construction ended on February 1, 1943, and the first B-17s arrived on February 4, 1943. The air field became a "processing unit for B-17 crews and planes."[3] According to Ray's service record, he was given a furlough from July 21 to July 27. He reported for duty at Kearny, Nebraska, on July 29, 1944.[4]

Dear Folks, July 30, 1944

I got to camp about seven yesterday and got settled. We don't have to do anything until about two this afternoon, then we just go to a lecture. I don't think we will be here very long. Some say we are going to leave the last part of the week.

I wish you would send me some pictures as soon as you can. I was going to get some before I left, but just forgot it. Be sure and send me one of you and Daddy. Just send me some that you think I would like.

I never saw so many planes in my life. There is four lines just as far as you can see. I saw a boy from Houston that I went through gunnery school with . . . I guess I had better close. I will write you again tomorrow.

Love, Ray

[P.S.] I have just got back from the meeting and they told us we would fly across![5]

Ray's service record held a wealth of information. On July 31, 1944, 1st Lt. Raymond D. Holmes, a Personnel Officer for the Air Corps, wrote that Ray's character was excellent and his efficiency rating as a solider was also excellent.[6] Anyone who knew Ray would not be surprised. Ray was a hard worker and felt this was his duty to serve. These traits had been instilled in him by his family, traits that governed his adult life, and traits which he would pass on to his children.

Dear Folks, August 2, 1944

I got paid yesterday and drew $92.50 and will draw the traveling pay today which will be about $30.00. I don't know if I will send any of it home or not. I have bought a lot more stuff to take across with me.

Part of the crew is flying today, but the gunners are not. They are on an instrument check. I have not done a thing today, but lay around. We are going to start processing tomorrow. I will get a physical and a lot of new equipment.

I looked at one of the new planes yesterday and they are really the thing. The tail has more armor plating than I had expected. The whole tail is redesigned and the guns will cover a lot more territory.

Mother, I tried to find you something for your birthday, but couldn't find a thing. I am going to send you twenty dollars, just spend it like you want to.

> By [sic] you something that you need most, it don't make any difference with me, though.
>
> It is about time to go get that thirty dollars so I guess I had better close.
>
> Love, Ray
>
> [P.S.] I had my hair cut off today and really am a sight. It is about a quarter of an inch long. Most all of the boys are having theirs cut off.[7]

The tail gunner's position was unique and the plane had been redesigned to accommodate and aid the tail gunner in being more efficient. In his 2006 interview with Dan Utley, Ray laid out the steps he took to get into position, "Well, I had to crawl from the waist on my hands and knees back to the tail position. Nobody else [was back there] and it was a good ways . . . I had to crawl around the tail wheel; I had enough room . . . and, there was more room back there than you would think. Couse, I wasn't near as big then as I am now. When I went into service I only weighed 142 pounds and was five feet ten. I grew up after I went into service . . . Course, I had to carry my chute, my parachute. You know, we used those chest chutes. I think I already had my flak jacket back there, and they had a big old helmet that you'd put on if you was in antiaircraft fire, you know. And I think I already had them laying back there before we took off, and probably had my parachute back there. I don't know for sure. I didn't get too far from that parachute (laughs). Course, we always had our harness on, our chute harness. And there were two snaps right here in front and you'd just snap that parachute if you were fixing to jump — snap that parachute on, that was all there was to it. It just laid behind me, you know, when we was flying."[8]

When asked about what it was like to operate out of the tail gunner position, Ray clarified that although the area looked very small he "could move around. I wasn't all that crowded. I flew backwards, you know, all the time, but I had plenty of room to turn my guns, you know, and things like that. You know, some people have got the idea that the tail gunner just couldn't move at all. Fact, I've had people ask me if I laid on my belly. Originally, when those B-17s were first built back in the thirties, they did lay down, but they figured out they didn't have any mobility. See, I sat on a little old — well, it looked kind of like a bicycle seat; little bigger than a bicycle seat, and it was about, oh, that high off of the floor — eight or ten inches off of the floor, and you sat with your knees folded back like this, see, and you just sat down with your feet behind you . . . it wasn't all that uncomfortable. Course, you sat there eight or ten hours and you'd get sort of tired of it."[9]

Parachutes were of vital importance to the crew. Their training had included learning when to exit the plane, how to exit the plane, and how to work the parachute. The main exit for the tail gunner was to maneuver his way back up the tunnel in the waist of the plane. But Ray detailed a second escape hatch for the tail gunner. "right to my left and behind me a ways there was a little old door. It was big enough that . . . if you had to bail out . . . you just roll out with your chute. You just barely could get out." Up until this point, all Ray had experienced had just been preparation for what he could expect in combat. The reality was something quite humbling, "What would happen a lot of times, those old B-17s become disabled from antiaircraft fire or whatever and they'd start down. Well, they'd always go into a spin . . . you see one of them going down like that it looks like that spin is real slow, you know, but the centrifugal force in there would pin those people against the wall and they couldn't get out. That happened time and time again. You know, just watching it you wouldn't think it was spinning that fast . . . We'd watch them go down and we'd sit there and count the boys that got out, and maybe one or two would manage to get out."[10]

Being the tail gunner was a rather lonely position in the plane, isolated from the other crew members. "See, the waist gunner was the closest neighbor I had, and course the only way I could talk to any of them—see, only communication I had was intercom. I could talk to the crew, but I couldn't even hear the communication between airplane and airplane. I wasn't even hooked up to that. The radio operator was and of course both pilots were. But all the communication I had was intercom."[11]

Dear Folks,   *Kearney, Nebraska, August 3, 1944*

I am sorry I told you in my last letter I was sending the money, but I just forgot to put it in the letter. I will send it in this letter if I don't forget it.

We drew all our equipment today and we really got a lot of stuff. We are loading in the morning and will probably leave [letter damage] sometime.

I don't think I am going to the same place as Underhill and Sturdivan. They drew a lot different equipment from me. I believe they are going to the Pacific.

Just keep on writing me to the same address and I will get some letters when I get over there. I don't know if I can write you any more or not. If I have a chance I will write you tomorrow . . . It is really hot here tonight. Almost as hot as it gets in Tennessee. I guess I had better [letter damage] *to take shower before I go to bed.*

Love, Ray[12]

The crew still did not know their final destination. They assumed Europe, but there were a lot of options in that vast arena and the Pacific theater was opening up as well. By the equipment they were given, crews could speculate as to their destination, as Ray did when he predicted his two buddies would be stationed somewhere warm. His thought was the Pacific, but Underhill would actually be stationed in Italy. He, of course, did not know this at the time. Ray told his parents about all the equipment he drew. Later in his 2006 interview, he described some of that equipment and the reason for it: "We had our longhandles and then our heated suit over that, and then we had a . . . set of coveralls, flight suit. And then on top of that we had those old fleece-lined britches and top. And of course our gloves and socks, they were heated. [And we] had great big old boots . . . and like those gloves, you know, they'd snap together. They hooked up to your other suit . . . I know one day we started out and we'd already got up pretty high, and it was cold, and my heated suit didn't

Ray and Sandy Herron in the Radio Room of a B-17.

work. It wasn't heating. Course, we always carried some extras in the airplane, and I had to strip down to my longhandles and put on another heated suit (laughs)." When asked how cold it could get in that unpressurized plane, Ray recounts, "Well, one day my right ear stuck to my headset. It was 56 below—56 below! And see, those airplanes are open, you know, wind coming through there."[13]

Flying a new B-17, Ray's crew left Kearney, Nebraska. The crew consisted of the pilot, Barney Glovick; co-pilot, C. O. "Charlie" Clark; bombardier, William "Monk" Monkevich; navigator, Norman Sacks; flight engineer, Eugene "Pop" Bowman; radio operator, W. C. "Sandy" Herron; ball turret gunner, Bert Railton; waist gunner, Chuck Buda; and, last but not least, tail gunner, Joseph Ray Perry.

The first stop for this crew was at Grenier Field in New Hampshire. Grenier Field, originally Manchester Airport, was renamed when it became a military base.[14] This air field was listed as a "primary staging base for heavy bombers en route to war in Germany."[15] Ray's service record noted that the crew left Grenier Field on August 8, 1944.[16] The crew did not fly straight across to England, but made several stops along the way. Ray must have been so excited to see the ocean and lands he had only read about in books. This rural, country boy had come a long way! In his later years, Ray recounted the trip, "from there we went to Presque Isle, Maine. Landed there, and from there we went to Goose Bay, Labrador, landed there. And from Goose Bay we went to Rekjavik, Iceland, and from there we landed in I guess it was Northern Ireland at that time . . . we landed . . . and they left that airplane there . . . see, this new airplane it wasn't ready for combat. It wasn't equipped, and I'm sure what they done there at that air base in Ireland, they equipped that airplane ready for combat and then sent it to whatever base in England that needed a new airplane. And they paddled us across that little old stretch of water over to England and put us on a train and sent us to our base which was Horham."[17]

While Ray was making his way to the European theater in England, life continued at home. Yet, war was never far from the minds of everyone. Ray's father, Hoyt, received a letter from one of his farm's landlords, Dimmitt Hughes. Hughes lived in Georgetown, Texas. The letter told about the farming concerns during 1944, but more importantly, it showed that the concern about the war was foremost in everyone's thoughts:

COMBAT DESTINATION: ENGLAND

Dear Mr. Perry, *August 14, 1944*

    I got the deposit slip for $90.80 from the Stamford bank. I see you was able to get a truck to take the rest of the maize to Fort Worth. Maize here is making about 800 lbs and bringing $1.90 delivered. Cotton will not make more than ½ as much as last year and perhaps not that much. It is very dry and hot here and a rain will not help the early cotton much. The country will do well to make 30,000 bales.

    I guess land sales there is about like it is here, that is very slow. I had planned to try and sell out every thing I owned in that country [Haskell County] this year for I do not own very much there now. When I was out there about a month ago [I] wanted to talk with you about it. As I remember last year you said something about you might try and buy ½ of the place. I am very well pleased with the way you worked the place this year, in fact you did an excellent job. I would like to sell the place, but I certainly want you to work it again if I can't. When I was out there I told Jim Free if he could get $35 per acre to sell it. I doubt if the place will bring that much this year unless that country makes a larger crop than I now think it will. I am sure you would like to know about renting again so as to make your plans but let me suggest that you go ahead and do your plowing and I will guarantee payment for all that you do in case the place sells. I am trying to make every effort to get out there sometime this month . . . the first week [or] next. Go ahead with the plowing and I will get out as soon as possible, but would like for you to let me know before you try to rent another place. If you can get a tractor to build the other tank go ahead but would let [me] know about it if you do.

    This war looks better every day now. I don't [know] but what the Germans are hard pressed. Surely hope it will end in Europe by Christmas.

    Yours very truly, Dimmitt Hughes

    P.S. I should have answered your letter sooner but have been very busy. This ration board work along with my own at times keeps me on the jump. Have been trying to get off the board but they will not release me now. One of the other members is in the hospital and the other about to die from heart trouble.[18]

Although optimistic, Hughes' hope that the war would end by Christmas was unfulfilled. In fact, history teaches us that it would be another nine months of constant fighting to achieve this goal, not to mention another three months of brutal island hopping in the Pacific before World War II was completely over and the world could begin to pick up the pieces.

Around the same time that Hughes wrote this letter, Ray and his crew were stepping on to British soil. The first letter that was saved since leaving Kearny, Nebraska, was dated August 27, 1944:

> Dear Folks, August 27, 1944
>
> I haven't received any mail since I got here and we landed in England on the 14th of August. I should get some this week I sure hope so anyway. I guess you are getting my mail O.K. Let me know which gets there the quicker, Vmail or air mail. I can get all the air mail envelopes I want they have them in the P.X.
>
> I was going to send a hundred dollars home, but I bought me a bycicle [sic] so I guess I won't send quite so much. I don't have any idea how long it will be before we make a mission. We don't even have all our equipment yet. The boys fly every day the weather permits and seem to be doing O.K.[19]

Ray and his crew had been assigned to the Ninety-Fifth Bomb Group which was based at Horham, England, about one hundred miles northeast of London. It seemed an odd thing for Ray, in his first letter home since arriving in England, to tell his family about purchasing a bicycle. When asked about this later, Ray explained, "when we got to England everybody bought a bicycle. That was the way we got around on the base. You know, go from our huts over to the mess hall, which was about a mile over there—maybe less than a mile, but pretty good little ride over there. And we'd all get on our bicycles at night if we weren't flying the next day, and we'd go down to the Green Dragon Pub." At this memory, he laughed.[20] There definitely were not any "pubs" in Paint Creek.

According to the American Air Museum in Britain, "Horham Airfield was planned and built for RAF use, but . . . instead . . . became the final UK base of the 95th Bomb Group, who flew B-17 missions from the airfield until the end of the war in Europe."[21] The Ninety-Fifth Bomb Group was part of the Eighth Air Force under the command of Lt. Gen. James E. Doolittle, who became a household name for his bombing raid on Japan following the surprise attack at Pearl Harbor. The Ninety-Fifth Bomb Group was comprised of four

COMBAT DESTINATION: ENGLAND

Norman Sacks, Clarence Miller, and Charles O. Clark on a bicycle in England.

bomb squadrons, the 334th, 335th, 336th, and the 412th. Ray was part of the 336th Bomb Squadron.

Ray discussed those first few weeks in England, "Well, we did a few training missions around over England . . . 'course these pilots, they hadn't flown a whole lot of formation, you know, in their training, and we done a little of that for a few days. I don't remember how many, but just getting us ready for combat mission."[22] He also discussed the differences in this base's hierarchy compared to other military set ups, "You know combat crews were different from the Old Army. The officers and enlisted men on a combat crew associated—unless we were dressed up in our formal uniform, you couldn't tell an officer from an enlisted man. We associated together, we ate together at combat mess, they called it. There was a mess hall that was just for the combat crews, and we ate together. See, I was in the 336th Squadron, and the enlisted men's hut was just across a hedgerow from the officers' huts. The officers' huts were just like ours and they were just real close together."[23] There was a hierarchy in the military and normally enlisted men and officers did not associate outside of their units, but this crew did everything together, on and off the airfield. They became each other's family. Ray remarked that the pilot, Barney, was "like a daddy to me."[24]

Barney Glovick

The layout of the base was rather spread out, but Ray explained that there was a good reason:

> There were four squadrons on that base [in] the 95th and they were scattered out. There'd be one here and maybe, oh, maybe not hardly half a mile over there there'd be another one. The reason they had them scattered out like that is on account of bombings. The main headquarters and everything was about three-quarters or a mile from our huts . . . You had the main runway. There was a cross runway, but it wasn't very long. It was kind of like an emergency type of thing. But the main runway run north and south, generally, and those hard stands were scattered around that perimeter. Now, a hard stand is where you drive an airplane off the main runway out here and then there's a pretty good size paved area out there that you'd turn that airplane around. And there would be a tent, pretty good sized tent, behind it that the ground crew, which was mechanics and armament people that stayed in there—they didn't stay all

Norman Sacks, William Monkevich, Clarence Miller, and Charles O. Clark in Horham, England.

the time. They had Quonset huts in a different area also. They were out there to work on the airplane and prepare it for the next mission, and they had cots in there and a stove, you know, in this tent. This tent was probably, I don't know, twelve by twelve. It was just a regular old GI tent, pretty good sized tent, you know, that they stayed in. They were assigned to a certain airplane, and this airplane after every mission come back to this same hard stand and they would repair it, do whatever needed to be done to get it ready to go on the next mission.[25]

Militaries throughout time have fought against the greatest enemy to their armies, boredom. Being far away from home, in a combat area, was stressful, but add to that the down time where the men had nothing to do but worry and think, and that was a recipe for chaos. The book, *Contrails II*, about the Ninety-Fifth Bomb Group, shows a base that was more like a mini city. The men could enjoy sports, spending time in the English countryside or with locals, and entertainments such as dances and shows.[26] Through Ray's letters, it appeared Ray enjoyed all these diversions, but his favorite distraction was with an elderly English couple that seemed to have adopted Ray and Barney. "[Barney] got acquainted with a farm family not very far from our base . . . we'd ride the bicycles over there. And this old man and old lady, English people, we'd go over there and carry our shotguns and some ammunition, and they would let us hunt partridge on their farm. You know, a partridge is kind of like a quail, only maybe more like a pheasant, only not that big. They didn't run in coveys, but we'd walk around over those fields and shoot us a partridge or two and then we'd carry them back to the base. We had an old stove there that we burned coke in, and we'd have partridge for supper."[27] One cannot help but speculate that this rural couple, that so generously took these two young men in, reminded Ray of his own family and neighbors back home.

Dear Folks *Sept. 1, 1944*

I still haven't received any mail from you or anyone else as far as that goes. Some of the boys got some today. I am hoping to get some in a day or two. I hope you are getting my mail. I am going to send my mail Air Mail. It is supposed to go faster that way. I can get all the Air Mail stamps I want.

All our stuff around here is rationed. We get a weeks ration every time. In a weeks ration we get four candy bars, two bars of soap, three packages of cookies, one package of gum, and seven packs of cigarettes. I already have two cartons of cigarettes saved up. If I keep on getting my ration of cigarettes I guess I will have more than I can carry home when I get ready to go.

I am O.K., and like it pretty well over here. They really treat us good over here. I haven't done a thing in the last two or three days. I hope you can send me something to eat in a few days. I guess I had better close. I sure hope to get some letter from you in a day or two.

Love, Ray[28]

Ray appeared in good spirits. It was touching to see this nineteen-year-old trying to reassure his parents by saying he was "O.K.," followed by his homesickness in the next sentence with his wish for letters and news from home. Uncharacteristically, since Ray was such a consistent letter writer, his next letter was dated September 16th. Reading the letter, it appears that other letters dated in between must have been lost to time.

Dear Folks,   *Sept. 16, 1944*

The last letter I wrote was a false alarm. We didn't go on the little spin we were planning on. I haven't flew a real mission yet and don't know when we will start.

You asked if I could send any cigarettes. I can't send any for they are sold to us very cheap and if they caught me at it they would be pretty rough on me. I get more cigarettes than I use. We get seven packs a week and I don't smoke that many.

I didn't get a letter from you today, but I got one from Pearleta. My mail has been getting here in about eight days.

Pearleta said they were expecting John M. home real soon. I bet they will be glad to see him. Sandy's brother is home now after three years in Italy. He has been wounded twice since he has been overseas.

I guess I had better close and write Pearleta.

                                                                                 Love, Ray[29]

The "Sandy" mentioned in his letter was presumably Sandy Herron, the crew's radio operator. Ray described the relationship he had with Sandy, "He was raised up . . . in Nebraska. I buddied with him more than I did any of the rest of the crew. Course, we were all together all the time, but he was raised in Aurora, Nebraska, and he was from a poor family like I was. His daddy was a policeman there in Aurora . . . a rural town, and he knew about farming. You know, it was different from West Texas farming, but we had that connection."[30]

Sandy Herron

Dear Folks,   *Sept. 21, 1944*

I got a letter from you yesterday mailed to Kearney. That is the first one that has been delayed. All your mail has been coming in about eight or ten days. We still haven't flew a mission yet, but expect to fly before long.

I got a letter [from] Aunt Thelma a few days ago. I guess I will write her tonight. She said Bill was going to ship out. Our ratings came through today. I was really glad to get it. I am a staff sergeant now. Sandy and Pop will get another stripe at the end of the month, but the rest of us won't get anymore.

We made lead crew and that took five missions off ours. Lead position is a good place in the formation. There is nothing to write about so I will close and write again soon.

Love, Ray[31]

The lead crew was the first airplane in the squadron. The navigator in the lead plane set the course for the squadron, although the other planes' navigator kept up with their own coordinates in case the lead plane dropped out of formation. From the lead position, one B-17 flew off the left wing and another off the right wing. At times, more planes flew directly behind the lead

Picture taken by Ray's crew during a mission showing the lead crew in the middle of a squadron. If you look closely, you can see the planes dropping their bombs. The Heavy Date often held the middle position during bombing runs.

plane, depending on how many planes flew during any given mission.³² Crews oftentimes saw this position as a catch-22: on one hand, your plane was more vulnerable to attack as the leader; on the other hand, flying in the lead position knocked five missions off the total number of missions the crew had to finish to round out their tour of duty. For those who flew, it boiled down to: do you take a slightly higher risk position for thirty missions, or risk completing the full thirty-five missions, never knowing which might be your last? Gerald Astor, in his book *The Mighty Eighth*, explained the military's reason for bumping up the total number of missions, "Bomber crews who had hardly adjusted to the increase from twenty-five to thirty missions before relief now learned they would have to complete thirty-five missions before going home. (Some extra credit accrued to those who served as lead pilots, navigators or bombardiers and their gunners.) The explanation given to the unhappy fliers was that the advent of more fighter groups capable of ushering the bombers to and from the target had so increased the chances of survival it was reasonable to tack on the additional number."³³

Dear LaVern, *Sept. 23, 1944*

I am sorry I waited so long to write you, but it is hard to write from over here. We can't tell everything we want to. I was going to write a long time ago.

We haven't been on a real mission yet, but expect to go on one in a few days. We don't do a thing around here. We have been very rudely interrupted from sleep several nights by the buzz bombs. Some have got pretty close but no damage done. All they do is scare the devil out of us.

If you want to and have time you can make me some candy and good things to eat. I haven't got a package from home yet, but hope to get one real soon. Mother said she had started one. I will really be glad to get some good eats from home. I think I will write Aunt Ruth and ask her to send me one of her good Angle [sic] food cakes. She really can make good ones.

I am a sergeant now and will get staff sergeant when I make six or seven missions. I must close and write another letter or two.

*Lots of Love, Ray*³⁴

Ray was writing to an old classmate and cousin, LaVern Livengood. According to the Museum of Flight in Seattle, Washington, the Buzz Bomb mentioned by Ray in this letter was in fact a "Fieseler Fi 103 'flying bomb' a small, pilotless, medium-range cruise missile . . . which German propaganda called . . . the Vengeance Weapon 1 (V-1) . . . the entire V-1 was a disposable vehicle powered by a primitive yet powerful 'pulsejet' engine which gave the V-1 a loud, raucous noise that could be heard from more than 10 miles away . . . [earning] the nickname 'Buzz Bomb'. Over 20,000 of these bombs were targeted at Belgium, England, and France."[35]

These bombs carried out a lot of damage to the city of London. Besides the potential for airplanes and hangars to be hit, the base was storing their own bombs and ammunitions. Ray explained, "there was a big ammunition and bomb storage area . . . two or three hundred yards away from any tents or anything like that. They had them in bunkers, you know, these bunkers that were covered with dirt."[36]

Ray itched to get busy with the work he trained to do. Although his crew flew training missions, he was ready for the real thing. This first mission would come soon enough. In fact, just three days from this last letter to LaVern, Ray got his first glimpse of Germany.

CHAPTER 7
MISSIONS 1–5

"**In Just 10 Minutes They'll Need Your Help** — Back home the headlines read — 60 U.S. Planes Lost. Actually about 60 percent of all airman shot down over enemy territory survive — as prisoners of war . . . in all, the men behind the barbed wire live the same empty life. There is nothing to do but wait — wait — and try to hold on to your sanity while you wait. That's why War Prisoner's Aid was formed. It provides the wherewithal to buy for prisoners of war the things that will help them hold on to their sanity during those empty days of waiting. Give Generously to Your Community War Fund."

—Haskell (TX) Free Press, October 6, 1944[1]

MISSION 1: BREMEN, GERMANY – SEPTEMBER 26, 1944

Ray's first briefing. The Quonset hut where the briefing took place held the crews from more than thirty B-17 bombers. In the front of the room hung a large wall map with a red string showing the mission route. A chalkboard showed the crews a good view of the lead plane along with the formation to be flown that day. Reconnaissance photos of the intended targets lay scattered around the room. The target for Ray's first mission on September 26, 1944, was Bremen, Germany, and the B-17s of the 336th Bomb Squadron would carry six 1000-pound bombs. This was Ray's first real bombing mission. More experienced crews in the room may have felt like old hands at these briefings, but all aviators, regardless of the number of completed missions, probably experienced the same range of emotions at every briefing: anxiety, adrenaline, fear (whether of failure, capture, or death), pride, and that overwhelming need to throw up! For Ray, the wait was over, the mission was here.[2]

Mission No. 1
9-26-44
Breman, Germany
6 – 1000 lbs. [bombs]
6 hours 50 minute flying time
Medium Flak

When Ray came home from the war, he brought with him a tag from every bombing mission in which he participated. Each bomb had a corresponding identification tag which was removed before the bomb was dropped from the plane. After each mission, Ray took time to write about that particular mission on the tag. Later, his wife, Amelia, put these bomb tags in chronological order in a scrapbook.[3] The "Mission 1" bomb tag says: "Bremen, Germany, 6–1000 lbs. [bombs], 6 hours 50 minutes flying, medium flak."[4] The recorded time was from takeoff to landing. Ray explained that the flight engineer activated the bombs about an hour out from their target. Each bomb tag had a pin attached to it, which once removed, armed the bomb. The flight engineer collected the bomb tags as he armed each bomb, and when the crew returned to base, he passed the tags out among the crew.[5]

Escort of fighter planes.

When Ray's plane, the *Heavy Date*, left on a bombing mission, they flew in formation with approximately thirty-six other bombers. Ideally, twelve planes flew on each wing of the formation, though this number changed depending upon the number of flight-worthy planes. An escort of fighter planes rendezvoused with the B-17s over Germany and escorted them close to their intended target. Ray explained, "After we crossed the English Channel and got over in Germany a ways, they'd show up out there off our wing . . . we could see them . . . nearly always P-51s. Once in a while we'd have a group of P-47s, but the P-47 wasn't near the fighter plane that the P-51 was. And after they got the wing tanks on them P-51s, they could go plumb to the target with us. Course they didn't go over the target with us; they'd hold up. They knew where we was going to come out over there and they'd meet us on the other side."[6]

Ray described his job while the crew flew to their destination:

> By the time we'd get over the English Channel, I was already back there in my tail position, and we always had to test fire our guns. We'd do that over the English Channel . . . [and] make sure we didn't hit one of the airplanes in formation! I didn't do a dadgum thing except just sit there and watch for fighter planes, and if one of them got close enough I'd take a shot at him! (laughs) I'm just along for the ride . . . after we'd get over Germany, I'd spend most of my time looking, you know, watching for aircraft, fighters. And we were trying to identify our aircraft and German aircraft, all kinds of German aircraft. We spent a lot of time even after we got to our base at Horham . . . viewing pictures of fighter airplanes. So, we had to be real good at identifying them way out yonder. That's what I spent most of my time doing was looking for aircraft.[7]

Each mission had a different objective. Some were strategic, such as railroad centers or ammunition factories, but some operations were to simply put fear into the hearts of the Germans and break their morale. The Allied Chiefs of Staff signed a document stating their aim for the bombers in Europe, "Progressive disruption and destruction of the military, industrial, and economic structure of Germany, and undermining the morale of the population to a point where the ability for armed resistance is decisively weakened."[8] The Allied strategy was apparent to the military leaders of Germany as well. Adolf Galland, a General in the German Luftwaffe as well as a flying ace during World War II, wrote in his autobiography, *The First and the Last*, "Psychologically the war at that moment had perhaps reached its most critical point . . . Hamburg . . . was right in the heart of Germany."⁹ Although Galland spoke of a particular raid that occurred in 1943, Hamburg was the destination of Ray's seventeenth and twenty-ninth missions in 1945. By flying right to the center of Germany, the Allies were making a pretty clear statement—you can't stop us!¹⁰

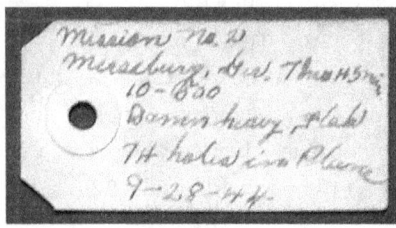

Mission No. 2
Merseburg, Ger. 7 hrs 45 min.
10 – 500 [lbs. bombs]
Damn heavy Flak
74 holes in plane
9-28-44

MISSION 2: MERSEBURG, GERMANY – SEPTEMBER 28, 1944

Two days after his first successful mission, Ray's crew embarked for Merseburg, Germany. Recorded on the bomb tag, "7 hrs 45 min, 10–500 [lbs. bombs], damn heavy flak."¹¹ Ray recalled after landing, their ground crew counted seventy-four holes in their plane.¹² According to Ray, he felt flak was more destructive than the bullets they faced from the fighters.¹³ "German fighters – they wouldn't come into attack us when we was going over a target, because we were receiving an awful lot of antiaircraft fire [flak] and they didn't want to get into that, see. So, when we're going over target, none of us would be shooting, cause the Germans wasn't going to come in there. But when we left that target and got off out yonder somewhere, well they'd come get us."¹⁴ Ray praised the Norden bombsight with autopilot, explaining that the plane flew in a straight line over the bomb target. Right before getting to the bomb target, the pilot released control of the plane to the bombardier. The autopilot feature turned on, and the bombardier had a small degree of variance to ensure the plane flew straight and level over the target. As a pilot "that's pretty hard to do, sit there and just fly straight and level in antiaircraft fire," Ray added.¹⁵

Author Edward Jablonski in his book, *America In the Air War*, emphasized just how destructive flak was to the bombers, "From August 1942 to May 1945, almost 20,000 American fliers were killed over Europe. Among the deadliest perils the bomber crews faced were exploding antiaircraft shells that caused the loss of 2,439 heavy bombers in Europe, and the crippling of countless more."¹⁶

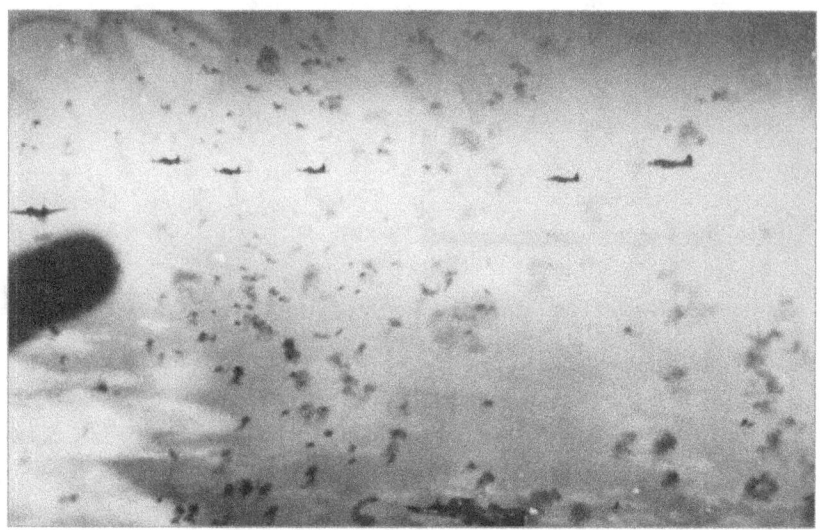

Ray took a picture of the flak they experienced during bombing missions. He felt flak was more destructive than the bullets from the German fighters.

Aviators utilized many tactics to combat antiaircraft fire. Ray described one method called chaff:

> Well, it's shredded tinfoil is what it is, and it's rolled up in a package . . . maybe a foot long and three inches in diameter, something like that, and rolled up in brown paper . . . those two windows on either side of the waist part of the airplane were open. There wasn't no glass over them or anything . . . [the waist gunner would] throw that out. You know, if we was going over an area where we knew there was antiaircraft fire, antiaircraft guns and radar places . . . it would drift down below us, behind us. When you throwed [sic] that out it just come apart. It was just a whole bunch and the sky was full of those little old shreds of tinfoil. And their radar a lot of times would pick that up instead of hitting us, see, and it worked a lot of times because I'd be sitting back there, and of course that stuff going down behind me and below me, there's where the antiaircraft fire was exploding instead of hitting us. It didn't work every time.[17]

Mission No. 3
Bielefeld, Ger
12 – 500 [lbs. bombs]
5 hrs 35 min
Light Flak

MISSION 3: BIELEFELD, GERMANY – SEPTEMBER 30, 1944

Written on the tag for Mission 3 was, "12–500 [lbs. bombs], 5 hrs 35 mins, light flak."[18] Ray was getting into the swing of things. What was once new, was becoming old hand. During his hours of sitting in the tail gunner position, he took photographs of what he saw, although personal photos during combat was strictly forbidden.[19] It was these photographs, however, that truly illustrated his experience. Some pictures contained images of flak exploding all around the B-17s flying nearby. In another photograph, an American escort of fighter planes flew by fast, leaving contrails behind them. Some pictures showed bombs falling out of the belly of other planes, while a particularly poignant image showed another tail gunner in a neighboring bomber. One photo gave a view of what Ray saw through the sights of his gun. He took pictures of the targets after the bombing runs, showing the smoke as it rose up to the sky.[20]

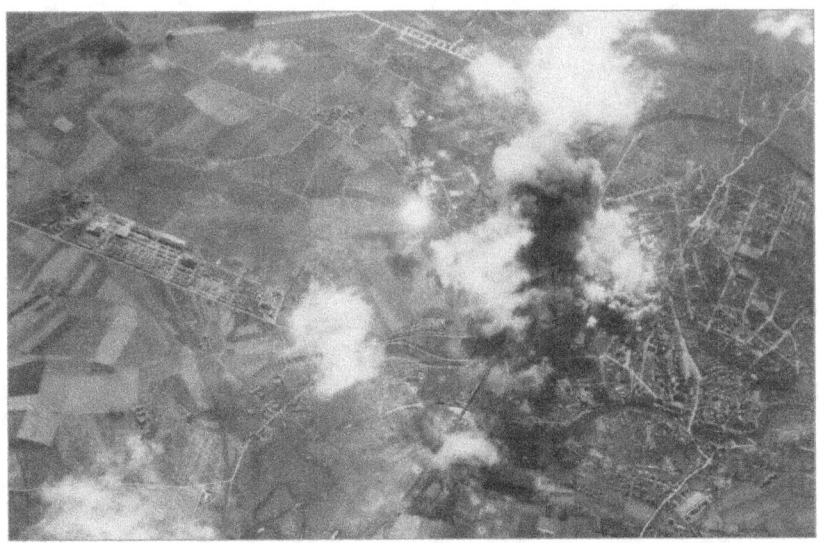

After the crew released their bombs over the intended target, they would "make a turn, depending on where we were supposed to go . . . and then kind of start heading back to the English Channel."[21] The military would then send in P-38s "for reconnaissance to take pictures" of damage inflicted and possible vulnerable targets for future attacks. Ray described the P-38s: "See, the P-38

was real fast. They were unarmed. They didn't have any armament on them because [of] . . . reconnaissance. Now, if they were assigned for combat duty or anything, they did have the armament, but those recons, all they had was a camera mounted under there somewhere and they flew over that target and made pictures and they'd hightail it back to 8th Air Force Headquarters, and they would look at those pictures. Lot of times they would have those pictures

developed and look at them before we got back, because that P-38'd fly 500 miles an hour unarmed."[22] In reality, the top speed of a P-38 averaged about 400 miles per hour, much faster than the bulky B-17s.[23]

When the crew returned from a bombing mission, they were sent to debrief. A truck waited for the men at the airfield to take them to headquarters. During the debrief, Ray and his crew explained what they saw during the mission that might be of a benefit for future operations, specifically, the number of fighters and antiaircraft fire they encountered.[24] This debriefing included an RAF tradition of drinking a shot of liquor to calm the nerves, "Every time we went to a [de]briefing . . . we had good whiskey . . . they'd give us a little shot of that just to kind of relax us, you know. And they finally run out of good American whiskey, they went to filling their glass with cognac, French. I didn't like that at all."[25]

Ray's parents back home received a surprise in the mail. Where they normally looked for letters from their son, they instead received a letter from Ray's buddy, Preston Underhill. Preston was one of the Texas boys that trained with Ray, and the two were stationed together at Kingman, Arizona; Lincoln, Nebraska; and Dyersburg, Tennessee. They hoped to get on the same crew overseas, but ended up in different locations. Preston met Ray's parents during their visit to Dyersburg to see Ray off before going overseas, and they had heard a lot about him in Ray's letters.

Somewhere in Italy   *October 1, 1944*
Dear Folks,

I suppose you will be pretty muchly surprised to hear from me. I've been intending to write every since I've been here but somehow I just haven't.

Ray and I got separated when we left the States. He went to England and I came here. I sure hated to leave him after we had been together so long. We have had some mighty good times. I've written him a couple of times but haven't gotten an answer yet. Haven't had time, I guess.

I got a letter from my little sister today. She had just gotten home from Haskell. She wrote about two pages about going over to see you and what a good time she had. How is Frances and the boys? I guess the boys are busy going to school now. My little brother has been coming out for football and Mother writes about how tired he is every night. I know just how he feels because I used to play.

I have in twelve missions now. Part of them are pretty easy and some are really rough. We have to complete [censored] here before we go back to the States. We haven't flown in over a week so it will take a long time to complete them. It has been raining here for several days now and will probably be this way most of the winter.

How did the crops turn out this year? I remember Mr. Perry said that the rain that came while Ray and I was home was just about two weeks too late. Maybe it helped some anyway.

How long does it take to get Ray's letters and he to get yours? It takes mine about one week to get home and takes theirs about three weeks to get here. I hope he hears sooner than that. Today was the first mail I had gotten in over a week.

Well, I'd better stop now and get into bed before I freeze to death. Take it easy and I'll be expecting to hear from you in about a month.

Love, Preston Underhill[26]

Letters from home were treasured when these young men were overseas. Although the families did not know each other before the war, they felt close enough to visit each other and write to each other's sons. Preston's hometown

Picture of Preston Underhill from the local newspaper.

of Rotan, Texas, was also a small town, about the size of Haskell, and was approximately fifty-five miles southwest from Haskell. A newspaper article that Ray saved told about a lucky break that Preston had while in Italy. According to the article titled, "Rotan Gunner Missed Raid in Which His Crew Went Down," Preston was visiting some friends at a neighboring base and was late reporting back to his base. Another tail gunner, anxious to get his missions completed, offered to take his place as a sub. The plane did not return from the mission, and only three of the crew were known to have survived, all three prisoners of war with the Germans. To make up for missing this flight, and because he did not have a regular crew, Preston became a "tail gunner-at-large," subbing on crews as needed. By the war's end, Preston had completed thirty-four sorties and a total of fifty-seven missions. He finally returned home to Rotan without a scratch.[27]

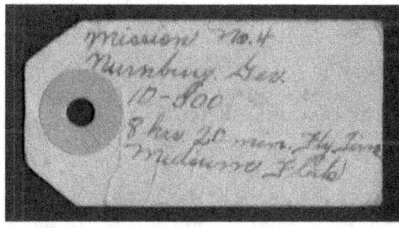

Mission No. 4
Nurnburg [sic], Ger
10 – 500 [lbs. bombs]
8 hrs 20 min. Fly Time
Medium Flak

MISSION 4: NUREMBURG, GERMANY – OCTOBER 3, 1944

On the morning of October 3, 1944, before reporting to their mission briefing, Ray enjoyed a hearty breakfast. The most consistent themes in Ray's letters were his critique of the food and his longing for home. "They fed the combat people a little better than they fed the ground crews. And over there at headquarters, where the mess hall was, they had what they called Combat Mess. That's where the combat crews eat their meals. It was a good ways over there [to the mess hall] . . . we didn't have to ride them [bicycles] in the mornings when we was going on a mission. They would send GI trucks around to pick us up and haul us over there to the mess hall. And we'd eat our meal there and get ready. Put our flying garbage on and then they'd pick us up there and haul us out to the airplane. We didn't have to walk."[28] Home cooked breakfasts must have been on his mind the morning of October 3, 1944, as his next letter home that day reflected his culinary longing instead of the mission planned for later that day.

> Dear Folks,	England Oct. 3, 1944
>
> *I got a letter and paper from you today. I was really glad to get your letter. A few days ago I had a bright idea that I wanted some sausage. When you kill hogs I wish you would fry about a half gallon and try to send it to me some way. Every time we go on a mission we get fried eggs and I will have the cook to warm a piece each for us boys and then we will have a good breakfast . . .*

On the outside of the envelope, Ray had written, "Request for Sausage," underlining 'sausage' several times.[29] October in Texas meant hog slaughtering season, when meat was cured into hams, bacon, pork chops, and sausage. Home proved never far from Ray's mind.

The fourth mission was over Nuremburg, sometimes called the "most German of cities" during World War II. The mission bomb tag read: "10–500 [lbs. bombs], 8 hrs. 20 min. flying time, medium flak."[30] When asked about the accuracy of the bombing missions, Ray pointed out that "it was carpet bombing . . . you take 36 airplanes in formation, that's a pretty good area, and they all drop them bombs at the same time, every one of them. And every airplane did not have the Norden bombsight. We would drop off of the lead airplane."[31]

Ray tried to explain the sheer size of the formation that flew on bombing missions:

Those bases were probably five miles apart, you know, the 95th here and the 100th over there, and the 390th over yonder. I would guess it would be five miles. I'm not sure about that. You'd take off and you'd fly so many minutes, and then they'd start circling, every airplane, they'd start circling just over that base. And this is what was always kind of a mystery to me. You know, a lot of times the fog would be pretty high, but they done it by timing, those pilots and navigators. Those airplanes was taking off, you know, 10-15 seconds apart, maybe a little more, I don't recall. But they would do the same thing and we'd just start circling over that base and gaining altitude until we got up there where we could see. Course, on a clear day you could see, but anyway, still, just the whole world was full of airplanes doing that circle to gain altitude and get in formation. When you got up there a ways, well, course number one airplane and then here'd come his wing man and they'd just go to falling into position and they'd do that until they got all those formations together . . . they already had it figured out who was going to be where. And it was just a whole string of B-17s and sometimes B-24s . . .[32]

Ray brought home a copy of the October 4, 1944, edition of *The Stars and Stripes* magazine. One of the headlines on the front page read, "Nearly 2,000 U.S. Planes Raid Reich War Plants." This article appeared in direct relation to the bombing missions that Ray and his crews participated in the weeks before. Another article that Ray cut from an edition of *The Stars and Stripes* and kept with his war memorabilia was titled, "Heavies Strike Nazi Ordinance."[33] He indicated that this article referenced the damage done following their fourth mission.

According to German Gen. Adolf Galland, in 1944, "the Eighth AAF from England was to raid works and installations at Politz, Zeitz, Maddeburg, Leuna, and Ruhland in Lower Silesia as well as refineries at Hamburg, Harburg, Bremen, and Hanover."[34] Many of these cities appeared on the bomb tags throughout the *Heavy Date's* combat missions.

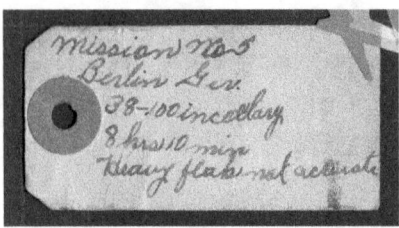

Mission No. 5
Berlin Ger.
38 – 100 [lbs.] incendary [sic]
8 hrs 10 min.
Heavy flak not accurate

MISSION 5: BERLIN, GERMANY – OCTOBER 6, 1944

Ray wrote a letter home the day before his fifth mission, but only the envelope remained in the collection. This mission was the first for Ray's crew to drop a different type of payload—incendiary bombs. It was also the first time Ray participated in a bombing run over the German capital. According to the bomb tag, the plane carried "38-100 [lbs.] incendiary [sic]" bombs, and the mission took "8 hrs. 10 min."[35] Ray recorded on the bomb tag that the plane experienced heavy flak and their bombs were not "accurate," which Ray explained as they did not hit their intended target. Ray recalled, "When we left the target, when we got back [over] . . . the English Channel, I could still see the smoke of Berlin."[36]

Ray's tail gunner position enabled him to protect the plane using two .50 caliber machine guns from German fighter planes coming up from behind. Ray thought the range of his guns was about 600 yards. He elaborated that "our ammunition had five different bullets in it. You had the regular .50 caliber . . . incendiary . . . armor piercing . . . tracer . . . and [another] one . . . that burn real hot . . . they were that way in the ammunition belt. And what I'd do a lot of times just to let them durn fighters know that I knew he was out there, you know, and it would stop them a lot of times from coming in. I'd just give a few bursts cause he could see those tracers."[37] Ray estimated that his .50 caliber could fire something like 600 rounds a minute.[38] The machine gun was air-cooled, so gunners shot in short spurts, allowing time for the barrels to cool in between firing.

Even with five missions under his belt, Ray found himself with a lot of down time. He recalled one day, when he and his fellow crewman, Sandy Herron, were standing on the flight line, a little bored, when all of a sudden this P-47 blew down the runway right in front of them. "I imagined he completed his mission . . . and he was coming back home and he buzzed our air base. He had that ol' thing wound up just as tight . . . I mean he was hooking 'em . . . he was right down on the ground, and then when he got to the end of the runway . . . he pitched her up, and that tail went down, and that tail wheel drug the runway. It didn't hurt anything. There's no telling how fast he was going. He was celebrating!"[39]

Many years after the war, Ray explained his feelings after his fifth mission, "The first five missions I flew, I thought, well dang, if there ain't no more to this war than this it's going to be easy, you know, but they made a believer out of me on that sixth one."[40] With only five missions behind him, Ray still had thirty missions left to complete before he could return home, and the very next mission would prove to be the worst of all.

CHAPTER 8
MISSION 6: THE DEADLY MISSION

"Haskell County was soaked with 3.19 inches of rain that fell Monday . . . cotton picking will be at a standstill for several days in the county."

—Haskell (TX) Free Press, October 6, 1944[1]

While cotton harvest was delayed back home, Ray prepared for another mission. Today's target was Bohlen, Germany, close to the city of Leipzig. According to Ray, Bohlen proved a tough target due to fuel and trains on the ground that the Germans were trying to protect.[2] Unlike the first five missions, this operation became Ray's most memorable, in a very tragic sense. Ideally, thirty-six aircraft flew on a mission, but on this inauspicious day, only twenty-five planes were airworthy enough to launch. Every bombing mission resulted in damage to the bombers, and several were grounded for repairs. According to the Ninety-Fifth Bomb Group mission report for October 7, 1944, the planes forming the 95A and 95B squadron began to take off to join formation at 7:15 a.m. Twelve aircraft comprised the 95A group and thirteen aircraft the 95B group.[3] Ray recounted the formation, "We were flying . . . what they call 'tail-end Charlie' in the formation that day. After you have flown a few missions — course, they always used the green crews or the crews with the least experience in those most vulnerable positions . . . back end and lowest [positions]. And there were three airplanes in that wing . . . we were flying the lead plane and there was one on each wing flying with us."[4]

Shortly after takeoff, four planes returned before reaching their target due to engine troubles. The first returned at 10:45 a.m. with a #2 engine failure,

MISSION 6: THE DEADLY MISSION

the next about fifteen minutes later with #3 and #4 engine failures. The third had an engine system out, and the last made it about forty minutes east of the English Coast when it was forced to turn around due to failure in the #1 engine.[5] This left the formation with twenty-one bombers to complete the mission. Normally, when the heavy bombers reached the German border an escort of American fighter planes waited to see them through enemy territory, but on October 7, 1944, no escort arrived. The official "Mission Report" for October 7, 1944, stated, "Beginning at 1201 hours with both Groups subject to a mass fighter attack by 30 to 40 FW 190s and ME 109's the attack lasted till 1216 hours."[6] Ray shared his memories of that fateful day, "the whole sky was full of fighter planes, and we didn't have any escorts . . . [later] they told [us] we had a security leak . . . that the Germans knew when we were to meet this group of fighter escorts, and they sent up a group to pick a fight with them before we got there . . . and then they sent this other group up and jumped on us."[7] In a 2016 interview, Ray said, "I didn't get a count [of the German planes], I was busy."[8] Although the first main battle lasted only fifteen minutes, its effects lasted a lifetime.

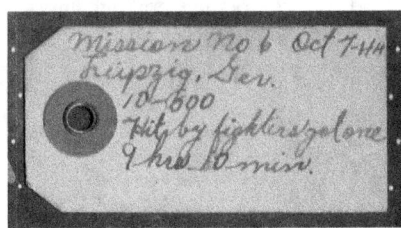

Mission No 6 Oct 7-44
Leipzig, Ger.
10 – 500 [lbs. bombs]
Hit by fighters got one
9 hrs 10 min.

The mission report stated that, "The E/A [engaging aircraft] attacks were very aggressive but pilots seemed inexperienced."[9] Ray agreed with this assessment when relating his personal confrontation with a German Messerschmitt ME 109, "I don't think he was a real experienced pilot."[10] At this point in his story, Ray demonstrated with his hands a pursuit curve used by German fighter pilots so that they came at the B-17 at an angle which made it harder to be hit. As he motioned he explained, "instead of flying straight at the tail, you're supposed to make what they call a pursuit curve, and you slide across, behind that B17. And you get a few shots right over here and a few shots right there and a few shots here, but this boy . . . he flew straight into me! I mean two .50 caliber machine guns firing at you."[11] Amelia, Ray's wife, added that towards the end of the war, Germany ran out of good pilots, many of whom had been either shot down or killed, and the lack of experienced fliers probably explained the enemy actions that day.[12] Author Edward Jablonski reiterated this summation in his book, *America In the Air War*, when he stated, "[Doolittle] knew that the Luftwaffe, although evidently still receiving an adequate supply of planes despite repeated bombings of the aircraft factories, was losing its irreplaceable veteran pilots."[13] German Gen. Adolf Galland, in his biography *The First and the Last*, stated that toward the end of 1944: "the decline of our fighting strength was not merely a question of material but also of personnel. The more the standard of the new pilots sank, the more important it became for our units to be led by able and experienced officers. But naturally there was a greater shortage of these than ever."[14]

Continuing with his story, Ray related that the German fighter headed straight for the tail of his B-17. He restated that his guns were air cooled, so they were to be fired in short burst, but with the ME 109 breathing down on him, getting so close he could clearly make out the pilot in the cockpit, he said he just held the trigger down, closed his eyes, and prepared for impact!

The impact did not happen. When he realized he still lived, he opened his eyes and the fighter was gone. Later, other crews from neighboring B-17s told Ray that he had hit the German fighter, and that the plane went right under the tail of *Heavy Date*, trailing heavy smoke, flying into a dive. When asked if he was scared, he grinned his lopsided grin and said he was too busy to be scared. He reflected for a moment and said maybe later when he was back in his bunk he felt scared, but at the time, he did not remember feeling fear.[15]

This sketch was one Ray clipped out from a newspaper and was in his scrapbook. Although it is not certain that this was drawn during the sixth mission, it demonstrates what Ray would have seen that fateful day.

MISSION 6: THE DEADLY MISSION

The same could not be said for all the crew. Charles "Chuck" Buda, the waist gunner, also had his hands full. German fighters rained down on them, and while they watched helpless, the two bombers on either wing were shot down. A total of three American bombers were shot down during this engagement. The mission report stated, "A/C [aircraft] 7050 at 1210 was set afire by bullets from E/A and there was a fire raging inside the fuselage towards the tail at 1211 this A/C jettisoned its bombs and went into an uncontrolled dive. Its tail came off and three chutes were seen."[16] The report further read, "A/C 7264 went down at 1211 hours with #3 [engine] afire and smoking badly. Four chutes were seen. A/C 482 went down; same attack; no chutes."[17] Neighboring B-17s reported seeing the chutes. As Ray recalled, when a plane went into a spin after being damaged, "we'd watch them go down and we'd sit there and count the boys that got out."[18]

With enemy aircraft attacking, and neighboring planes being shot out of the sky, the crew of the *Heavy Date* kept busy protecting their own. Two German fighter planes were shot down by American bombers that day. Ray took down one, the inexperienced pilot that flew straight at their tail, and assisted on the other. He recalled, "one was just to my left, which he'd be coming in on the right-hand side of the tail of the airplane . . . this airplane was coming in kind of to my left, and I was shooting at him and I'm sure that [Chuck] was shooting at him also. Course, he had one single .50 caliber that he was using . . . his intercom mike [sic] was right here top on the right-hand side of that gun . . . [Ray noted that the] airplane passed us on fire . . . I imagine me and Chuck both put bullets in him."[19] But the small victory came at a heavy cost, as Ray remembered, "I'm pretty sure that's the airplane that got [Chuck]."[20] After five fairly easy missions, the crew experienced their first fatality of the war. "[Chuck's] thumb was shot off. That bullet that

Charles "Chuck" Buda, 1943
Senior Year, High School Yearbook photo.

got him, hit in the chest, tipped that thumb, so I'm sure he was shooting at [the German fighter] also."[21] Chuck was killed instantly, Ray explained, "It just blowed him to pieces right in here (pointing to his chest). Twenty millimeter see, it explodes when it hits, and he went down, and he still had his oxygen mask on laying there in the waist. Course, we didn't do anything with him. We were airborne."[22] The shot that took off Chuck's thumb, also shot out all communications in the plane. The crew had been heavily attacked and they knew their waist gunner had been shot, but they could not communicate to check on Ray. He remembered, "the pilot sent the radio operator back there to see if they got me. They couldn't talk to me. And he climbed, crawled, right there beside the side of that tail wheel, and he never did get back all the way where I was at, but he told Barney he saw me sitting up and he saw me move a little. So, he went back and told the pilot, 'I guess he's alright. I think he's still alive.'"[23] There was not much time to do more than a quick check. Although the attack they just experienced only lasted fifteen minutes, another ambush may come at any time. In fact, the mission report stated that about twenty-four minutes later, two ME 163s, Germany's rocket fighter planes, also attacked the group.[24]

Bert Railton

MISSION 6: THE DEADLY MISSION

Shot up and heavy hearted, the crew made it back their base at Horham, England. Ray remembered what happened when they landed, "[the] medics come in to get [Chuck's] body, they took his oxygen mask off and it was full of vomit, bloody vomit. He died immediately."[25] After taking a moment to assess themselves, making sure they were all in one piece, the crew began to check on each other. The ball turret gunner, Bert Railton, had the hardest time. The death and destruction he witnessed, although it only lasted fifteen minutes, had a traumatic effect on him. Ray recounted:

> Bert Railton . . . never did like [the ball turret gunner position]. Barney assigned us to our gun positions, and he never did like it. He was scared most of the time. But . . . after this sixth mission where we got shot up so bad and killed Chuck Buda, Sandy and I had to help Bert Railton out of that ball turret. He was just so mortified and he couldn't get out. We helped him get out of there and kind of get his head screwed back on . . . he had urinated all over himself . . . and it was pretty traumatic because . . . that many fighters jumping on [us] and airplanes going down all around you . . . we were the only ones left of that three . . . old Bert saw all of that and he just locked down. And you know the [armament] people told us that he hadn't fired any bullets.[26]

Later, the ground crew counted 174 holes in the fuselage and wings of the *Heavy Date*.[27]

Picture of the Heavy Date *after a German attack.*

After Ray's fire fight with the German pilot, the state of his weapons was a sight to behold. Ray explained, "those armament people took my guns out of the airplane and they looked down the barrels and one of those old boys told me, he said, 'When them last bullets come out of there they was going end over end.' . . . I burnt them guns plumb up."[28] Ray again expounded that his guns were air cooled, so the gunner was supposed to shoot in short bursts to give the barrels time to cool between firing. Ray laughingly defended himself, "Well, a couple of German fighters coming in on you, you can see the firing on his wings, the flash on his wings, you can't get off the trigger. I didn't care whether I burnt them guns up or not. If they'd keep shooting that's all I wanted."[29]

Although the *Heavy Date* safely landed after their fatal mission, the incident was not yet over. The mission went terribly wrong, and the commanding general of the Eighth Air Force, with which the Ninety-Fifth Bomb Group was a part of, immediately descended onto the base to investigate. Lt. Gen. James E. Doolittle, who garnered fame for his bombing of Japan as retribution for the Pearl Harbor attack, arrived in an extreme state of agitation. He had many questions for those that participated in the mission, including Ray's pilot, Barney. Ray remembered, "that day that we got shot up so bad, and Chuck got killed, the next day Jimmy Doolittle come to our base, and interviewed Barney . . . we lost too many airplanes that day. And he wanted to know why. If he'd a been there he would've known why! (laughs) I don't know who told me . . . they claimed that we had a security leak. See we was supposed to pick up a group of P-51 fighters at a certain point. Well, the Germans knew about that for some reason or 'nother. And they sent up a group of fighters and picked a fight with our escort, led 'em off over yonder maybe 50 miles or so . . . and they sent up another group to jump us." Amelia added that the book *Contrails* showed a picture of Barney standing with Doolittle and Ray positioned right behind him.[30] She said, judging by the picture, Doolittle was "hot under the collar." Ray elaborated that in the picture, "the fire was just flying out of his eyes when he was talking to Barney."[31]

German Gen. Adolf Galland described the German surprise attack in his memoirs: "on October 7, 41 bombers were shot down. In those days the reports of the missions created great anxiety at Allied headquarters."[32] The mission report involving the *Heavy Date* only detailed the operation of the 95A and 95B Bomb Groups; General Galland's determination of forty-one bombers reflected the total number of bombers from all bomb groups lost that fateful day.

MISSION 6: THE DEADLY MISSION

Barney Glovick

After being debriefed at length over the mission, Barney and the crew still had to deal with the death of their friend. The very next day, Ray attended church services at a local Episcopalian Church.[33] The service, different from the Methodist services he attended back home, helped Ray process his feelings after that mission: "When you get in stiff combat, you get to thinking about the Good Lord and hope he's thinking about you."[34]

Not only was October 7, 1944, the day Chuck was killed, but it was also his nineteenth birthday. The men had planned to celebrate with him after they returned that day.[35] Instead of leading a birthday celebration and chaperoning his young crew, Barney wrote a letter to Chuck's parents, explaining to them how their son gave the ultimate sacrifice. Ray said Barney struggled with this letter, and Ray kept a copy of a rough draft that Barney worked on before sending the final copy. The mark outs, additions, and notes clearly showed a man struggling to write such a hard letter.[36]

Dear Mr. & Mrs. Buda:

It grieves me deeply to correspond with you about so tragic an incident as was the unfortunate fate of your fine son, Charles. This and the fear of re-opening a healing wound are the only reasons that I can offer for my negligence. I sincerely hope this inflicts no further injury to the great bereavement which I know must be yours from the loss of so fine a son. There is so little that I can say or do at a time like this that would be of any help. However, I am eager to do the proper thing and to the greatest extent possible, and I feel there are details that you would like to know.

We were on a deep penetration into Germany on our sixth raid — to a treacherous target — when without warning eighty F.W. 190s hit our formation in a mass attack. The two planes beside us [went] down in flames and at the same instant, our plane was (so) badly damaged and crippled that it was necessary to immediately ~~jettison~~ drop our bombs to maintain our altitude and speed. It was at this instant that ~~a round cannon shell hit~~ Charles was hit. ~~Chest, penetrating both sides of his flak suit and knocking him away from his gun~~. He passed away very quickly in the arms of his buddy — ball turret gunner, Bert A. Railton, and I'm certain he knew of no pain. Charles was a very fine gunner and ~~was returning the fire at one of the~~ not caught off guard. He ~~kept firing at the~~ exchanged shots with the fighter until the very last instant and inflicted considerable damage on one — perhaps destroyed it, because as they passed by, two went down badly smoking.

We ~~had to leave formation,~~ dropped out of our formation, straggled back to the base. ~~The~~ Our plane was badly shot up and had more holes than we could count, but fortunately there were no other casualties.

It might ease the pain somewhat to know that Charles was the best liked person on the crew. ~~Chu~~ Charles was always very cheerful and performed his work with pride and was an admirable inspiration to us all. Before we started combat, I had an extra crew member. I offered to obtain a good non-combat ground duty for Charles, but he pleaded to remain with us. He stated that he wanted to fly and fight in spite of all the dangers that I pointed out to him. I was proud to have him . . . [illegible].

~~So~~ Please consider that a fine compliment because I am very fortunate in having a crew that is far superior to the average ~~one~~ crew, every man is completely ~~competent~~ capable of efficiently knowing his specific duties. It was ~~Chu~~ Charles 19th birthday and [planned] a big party for him that night.

The entire crew ~~crew~~ paid tribute and last respects at an American Cemetery, where a ~~funeral~~ beautiful services were performed with full military honors. ~~The service was very beautiful.~~ We contacted (   ) [this was left blank] but ~~she was unfortunately~~ she was unable to be present at that time.

I am enclosing some pictures of Charles that are the only ones I have of him. They were taken during our training in the States. I hope they pass ~~the~~ censorship.

> If there is any ~~other~~ way in which I can be of further assistance, please do not hesitate to grant me the privilege and pleasure.
>
> I shall take advantage of the earliest opportunity to ~~visit you in the States~~ do so. I am anxious to meet you ~~folks.~~ My home is in Grand Rapids, Mich. and that detour should not present much of a problem after our return.
>
> The crew also desires to meet you ~~and~~ some live close enough to make it possible.
>
> ~~In closing~~ My entire crew joins me in extending our sympathy. ~~We~~ Wish you all the best for future happiness — with sincere hopes that the unique tragedies of war never again strikes so close.
>
> Sincerely —[37]

Between Barney's letter, the "official" mission report, and Ray's interviews, some inconsistencies emerged. In every interview, Ray stated the crew heard around eighty German fighters attacked them that day. The mission report stated thirty to forty FW 190s and ME 109s participated in the assault. Inconsistencies between official documents and personal remembrances prove common. Sometimes official documents do not accurately record facts, either because of misinformation, or a need to relate the narrative differently. Ray addressed one discrepancy himself. When Barney said the *Heavy Date* was attacked by FW 190s, Ray clarified: "In this letter here, [Barney] calls them FW 190s, but all Barney saw was when they went past us. He just looked at the tail of that airplane, but the ME 109 . . . had inline engine . . . and the FW 190 had a radial engine. But I was looking right straight at them, you know."[38] Another discrepancy between Ray's account and Barney's letter was the part where Chuck died in the arms of his buddy Bert, the ball turret gunner. Ray did not mention this point in his interviews, nor does he allude to it when he explained how he and Sandy helped Bert out of his position. Perhaps Barney wanted to give as much comfort as he could to Chuck's parents, and so he added this bit to ease their pain.

Ray's letters home neglected mentioning this air battle until four months later, whether from a confidentiality agreement with the military, or simply because Ray refrained from sharing bad news with his family. Ray sent twenty-nine letters home after that mission, but not until one dated February 15, 1945, did Ray relate that the crew just returned from the "rest home." This was a time to relax after a series of several missions, or a particularly rough one. He told about the sixth mission about half way through his letter:

> You asked if we really needed a rest. I guess we did or they would not have sent us. We were hit by about eighty enemy fighters and two of them picked on our plane. One of them came in on the tail and I got him. He went down in flames and then exploded. Chuck was the youngest one on our crew. His name is Charles Buda and he was from Ohio. You met him the night at the service club after the donkey ball game [in Dyersburg, Tennessee]. He was with Bert the one from Calif. He had dark straight hair. We were allowed to go to his funeral. He had a very nice military funeral. He is buried in Cambridge . . .
>
> Love, Ray[39]

Imagine Ray's mother reading this letter. At first, it was not clear what Ray was trying to convey until he wrote the phrase "allowed to go to his funeral." One can feel the sick feeling start in the pit of her stomach, working its way to her rapidly closing throat, and finally feeling tears pricking her eyes. Not only was she thinking of this young man that was killed, and the danger that held for her own son, but knowing that Ray was a part of this horrific incident and she could not shield him from it. Then the sympathy for the family that lost their son, that must come close on the heels of her concern for her own. The next mention of the incident came roughly three weeks later on March 3, 1945:

> We got a letter from Mrs. Buda (Chucks mother) today. She wrote a very nice letter. She has got the Purple Heart and is going to be presented the Air Medal. Her address is: Mrs. W.H. Buda, Bryan, Ohio, Route 3 . . .
>
> Love, Ray[40]

Ray wanted to give his mother a chance to write to Chuck's mother, but it is unknown if such a letter was ever sent.

With one less crew member, changes came. Bert moved to the position of waist gunner and a substitute was found for the ball turret position. The sixth mission rattled them all, some more than others, but the war still raged on, and duty called.

CHAPTER 9
FINISHING OUT 1944: AIDING THE VICTORY IN EUROPE

*"**Cpl. Davis Missing in Action** – Cpl. Thomas R. Davis, 18, has been missing in action over Germany since October 6, the War Department notified his parents Mr. and Mrs. Tom O. Davis, Haskell, on Monday. Cpl. Davis was on his second or third mission as a gunner on a B-17 at the time, his parents think. He had arrived in England about the middle of July . . . Thomas is the only son of Mr. and Mrs. Davis."*

—Haskell (TX) Free Press, October 27, 1944[1]

Thomas Davis, known affectionately as Tommie by those who knew him, was actually a tail gunner on a B-17, just like his buddy Ray. Ray's parents had no electricity, let alone a radio, on their homestead, so their main source of information and news came from the local newspaper, the *Haskell Free Press*. To see a front page article about one of their son's friends must have been hard on the Perrys. Tommie was known to them, same age as their son, and flying in the same position on the same type of airplane as their son. Ray previously mentioned Tommie in a few letters home. Both were stationed at Sheppard Field in Wichita Falls in the beginning of their training. On February 9, 1944, Ray wrote home, "I got the letter today with Tommie's address in it, and Bill & I went over to see him at dinner. He washed out [of pilot training]."[2] Then again while stationed at Kingman Army Air Field in Kingman, Arizona, Ray wrote home on March 11, 1944, "There was another bunch of boys from Sheppard Field come in here this evening and Tommy [sic] Davis was with them . . . he was really glad to see me."[3] The danger that came with each mission was very real. Ray's thirty-fifth mission still seemed far away.

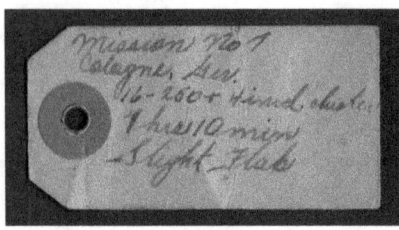

Mission No 7
Cologne, Ger.
16 – 250 [lbs. bombs] & 4 incd [incendiary] cluster
7 hrs 10 min
Slight Flak[4]

The "16–250" represents sixteen 250 lbs. bombs. The bomb tags revealed that the type of bombs dropped on the mission were incendiary cluster bombs (Inced or Incd). "They were just fire bombs. They're small, a hundred pounds . . . [Their job was just to] start fires," explained Ray.[5]

Dear Folks,   England, Oct. 17, 1944

I got a letter and paper [Haskell Free Press] from you today and was very glad to get them. You asked how long it takes for the paper to get here. The one I got today was mailed Sept. 30. That isn't so bad. I am always glad to get it even if it is a little late.

I guess all the cows are looking good now. The grass is probably good since the rain. How is my horses. I bet Stormy is really pretty. I would really like to ride her. I guess she is as mean as ever.

I will be glad when I get a package from home. Some good eats from [home] is going to taste good . . . I may go to London sometime next month. Some of the boys spent two days down there and spent $40. I think I can get by on less than that. I must close. I am out of anything to say.

Love, Ray[6]

FINISHING OUT 1944: AIDING THE VICTORY IN EUROPE

Ray with his horse Stormy

Stormy, Ray's horse that he asked about in his letter, was given to him by his grandmother. This horse was very special to Ray, not just for the monetary value, but for the sentimental value, as Ray was very close to his grandmother.[7]

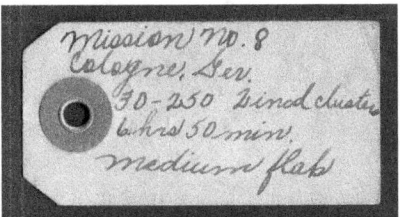

Mission No. 8
Cologne, Ger.
30 – 250 [lbs. bombs] 2 incd [incendiary] clusters
6 hrs 50 min.
Medium flak[8]

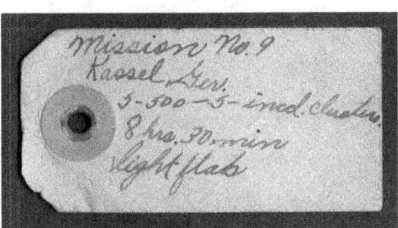

Mission No. 9
Kassel, Ger.
5 – 500 [lbs. bombs] 5 – incd. [incendiary] clusters
8 hrs. 30 min
light flak[9]

Dear Folks, England, Oct. 21, 1944

The packages have started coming in so I should start getting some before long. I will be glad when I start getting some of mine. We have just got back from the show. It was a western. There is a show here every night. It don't cost anything to go and we don't have to dress up that is what I like about it. There is a USO show here every once in a while. We have quite a bit of intertainment [sic] around here.

In your last letter you had Tommie's address in it. He is not at this base, but I don't think he is very far from here. I am going to try to see him before long. I will write him in a few days and try to find out where he is.

Well, I must close and get to bed. I may have to get up early in the morning.

Love, Ray[10]

[Note: this letter was written before Ray knew Tommie was missing in action.]

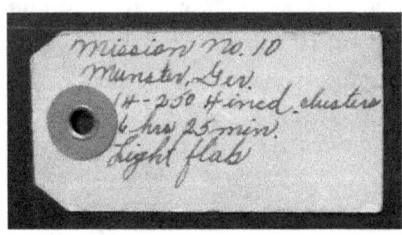

Mission No. 10
Munster, Ger.
14 – 250 [lbs. bombs] 4 incd [incendiary] clusters
6 hrs 25 min.
Light flak[11]

Dear Folks, England, Oct. 24, 1944

I got three letters today. One from you, one from Pearleta and one from Aunt Thelma. I was really glad to get them. It really helps a guy along when he gets a few letters from home. Some of the boys are getting packages, but it takes about two months. I should start getting some of mine before long. I sure hope I get one before long.

It will be nice to say I have been to London, but I am not going back, it cost too much money. I spent about $40 down there and don't know where it went to. I don't like the place it is so old. There is no modern things here in England at all. The people over here are about a hundred years behind.

FINISHING OUT 1944: AIDING THE VICTORY IN EUROPE

Dad, you had better take care of yourself. Don't do something that you can't work. I will be home before long and we will get together and see what we can do.

We haven't been flying lately and we are pretty well rested up now. I guess I had better close and write Pearleta.

Love, Ray[12]

When asked what the most impressive thing he saw in London, Ray replied, "Gosh, I don't know. I wasn't too fond of London. I went to a . . . I don't know what you call it, a theater, I guess. It was a show. 'Course I's an ol' country boy." Amelia chimed in that he probably attended the opera and did not know it! A little indignant, Ray continued, "No!" Then he blurted out, "Well . . . all the women in there were naked! (laughs) They done everything without any clothes on!" When asked if he was shocked, he said, "Oh yeah! I'd never seen anything like that! (laughs)" In a bit of teasing, Ray was asked what his Mama would think, and he laughed and said he never told her.[13] They definitely did not have burlesque shows in Paint Creek, Texas!

Barney Glovick in a bomb shelter in London.

Besides the sight of a theater troupe full of naked ladies, London in 1944 could be as dangerous as any combat zone, due to the bombardment of buzz bombs. While in London, Ray recalled the damage caused by the bombs and the air raids. In fact, Ray and his buddies stopped to pose in front of a bomb shelter in London. These appeared to be scattered throughout the city in alleys. As they stayed overnight in a hotel room, the men experienced the terror that the people of London endured since the war began, "We were all in a hotel room down in London, it was on that 48 hour pass. 'Course those buzz bombs, they was falling around London, and that V2, it was a rocket that shoot straight up and run out of fuel and they just fall. We's there in that hotel room one night, and there's one, I don't know how close it was, but it . . . man, it jarred the building. It would get you awake!"[14]

Dear Folks,   *England, Oct. 26, 1944*

I hit the jack-pot today. I got three letters and a package. It was the package with the peanuts and the hard candy. That is the kind of candy I like. I was really glad to get the package. Sandy got one today also. His was about the same kind of package as mine. It seems that is the kind of packages the boys want, I know it is the kind I like. The package was in very good shape. It wasn't crushed at all and all the peanuts and candy were all in good shape.

You asked me to tell you how many missions I have in. Some of the boys have been telling how many they have so I don't see why I can't. When we first got here I heard we couldn't tell. I have ten in now which ~~is 1/3~~ 1/3 means I am one third finished.

They issued us two pair of thick wool socks, but I will be glad to get the ones you are sending. It will save washing. I got a letter from Pearleta today and she said Truett and Allen had joined the Navy. I think they are going to have a pretty tough time of it. The navy is going to play an important [part] in the S.P. [South Pacific]

. . . every letter I get from you, you say something about daddy being sick. What is wrong with him. Say, Pa, you had better try to take care of yourself . . .

Love, Ray[15]

FINISHING OUT 1944: AIDING THE VICTORY IN EUROPE 111

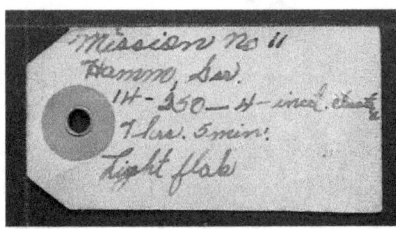

Mission No 11
Hamm, Ger.
14 – 250 [lbs. bombs] 4 incd
[incendiary] clusters
7 hrs. 5 min.
Light flak[16]

Dear Folks,   England, Oct. 30, 1944

    I got two packages from home today one from you and one from Aunt Ruth. I got a letter from Frances too. I was very glad to get the packages. I had about finished the first one, or that is the crew had. I haven't started on Aunt Ruth's cake yet, but I opened it and it was in good shape. I think I will wait until everybody is gone except our crew. That would be mean wouldn't it. Sandy got a cake in one of his packages and it was molded. I am going to write Aunt Ruth tonight and thank her for the cake.

    I was going to write you last night, but we had to do some night landings and I couldn't write.

    We haven't been flying lately. We have been doing some training for lead crew. When we start leading we won't fly as often and won't finish as quick, but we will be flying a much safer position . . . I have been over Germany a few times by now. I can't tell you how many or where we went. It isn't so bad, but I will be glad when we get in all of them.

    I told you Gene would be stepping out before long. He will probably be stepping out regular before long if you don't watch him. I guess I had better close and get to bed. I am pretty tired tonight.

                                                                                   Love, Ray[17]

Dear Folks,   England, Nov. 1, 1944

    I haven't heard from you since I got the last two packages. The mail just comes in bunches over here. We won't get any for a few days and then we will get a lot. Sandy and I finished Aunt Ruth's cake today. It was really good. I think I will write and ask for another one pretty soon. I will be glad when we get your cakes.

Nov. 2

I started this letter last night and ran out of anything to say so I will try it again . . . If we don't do any more flying than we have been doing lately we will be here for the duration, plus trying to get our missions. We have flew one mission in the last week. Lead crews don't fly as often as the other crews.

Sandy and Pop made Tech sergeant today. That is as high as they will go and the ~~others~~ rest of us have Staff Sergeant. All of us are as high as we will go. Staff is pretty good for me to make in ten months.

I had better close and get to writing my girl. I got a letter from her today and it was awful sweet.

Love, Ray[18]

Dear Folks, England, Nov. 7, 1944

I got a letter from Pearleta and she said Tommie was missing. I found out where he was and was going to go see him as soon as I got a pass. I wrote him a few nights ago. He is probably alright. Most of the time when they are reported missing they are usually P.W. [prisoner of war] I don't know if I told you or not, but I got to see him for about thirty minutes before we took off from Kearney, Neb. I was looking for him and found him in the P.X. We talked for about half hour and I had to leave.

Tommie Davis

> *I got a letter from LaVern and Underhill today. Underhill has 29 missions now. If I had that many I would have one to go. He said there was a lot of boys down there that we knew back in training. Sturdivant is alright and he has in twenty-six missions.*
>
> *We haven't flew in almost two weeks now. I don't know why we are not flying. I guess when we start again it will be just like starting over. I guess I had better close as I have several letters to write.*
>
> Love, Ray[19]

Ray always liked the English people, and commented on how welcoming they were to Americans. With a lot of time on their hands, he and his buddies frequented a pub called the Green Dragon. In typical West Texas jargon, he explained that it, "was down the road a ways." Trying to relate the experience, Ray described their time in the pub, "you go to these places and sit around, and the old English people would come by, you know, and we'd visit and throw darts and drink a little of their mild or bitter beer. No ice at all on it."[20] Neither Paint Creek nor Haskell had any "pubs" to speak of, but the camaraderie the men sought could be found in places like the Green Dragon.

Back Row: (l to r) Pop Bowman, new ball turret gunner (unnamed), and Bert Railton; Front row: (l to r) Sandy Herron and Ray Perry.

Dear Folks, *England, Nov. 14, 1944*

I haven't had a letter in little over a week. I got a package from you today. It was the one with the bill fold in it. I really am proud of the bill fold for my old one is worn out. I have another billfold it is a big one, this English money won't fit in ours. There is no use to send me anymore chewing gum, I get a package a week and a package every time we go on a mission. I got a package from Pearleta and it had a little gum in it. She sent some candy and a cake. I don't know if she cooked it or not, but if she did she is going to be alright, if you get what I mean. Pop told me to tell her he passes his approval on it. The candy in your package is really good. I am really proud of the socks and handkerchiefs, I was needing some. The Christmas card in the package was really nice too. I was really glad to get it.

I am sending you a picture we made, it isn't very good, but I thought you might like it. I must close and write Pearleta.

Love, Ray[21]

Dear Folks, *England, Nov. 23, 1944*

Well, today is Thanksgiving. We had a real good dinner. We had turkey and all the fixings. We had pumpkin pie and ice cream, it was really good. I didn't get to go to church this morning, we were going, but were busy. We had to clean our guns and that takes quite a while. Today, I have been in the army eleven months. That don't sound long but it seems like a long time. I sure hope I can be home by next Thanksgiving.

I guess we will have a big dinner Christmas. It isn't going to seem right to not be home for Christmas. I guess all the people at home will have a big time. Are you having a tree up at Grandads? I guess he will have his little tree out in the front of the house all lit up. What is Frances going to get Curtis for Christmas, and what is he going to get her? You probably know, every body except Frances usually knows.

How is the cigarette situation at home, we have been hearing that there is hardly none . . .

Love, Ray[22]

FINISHING OUT 1944: AIDING THE VICTORY IN EUROPE

The Army Air Force tried to simulate a traditional Thanksgiving for the men, probably to ease their homesickness. Ray actually celebrated two Thanksgivings that year, one in a homier setting. The elderly couple that befriended Ray and his pilot Barney invited them to their home for a "Thanksgiving" meal. Ray remembered, "She baked a goose, just like you would cook a turkey. And she had all the trimmings and everything for it."[23] For Ray, a rural boy from Texas with a close family and a community of friends, this meal probably reminded him of home more than the traditional food served at the mess hall.

> *Dear Folks,* *England, Nov. 26, 1944*
>
> *I got a letter from you today and was very glad to get it. It was the first letter I have had in several days. It was dated Oct. 31 almost a month old. I was glad to get it though.*
>
> *It will be a month in three days since we flew. I guess we will start flying in a few days. The crew that was flying our position finished a few days ago.*
>
> *I have not run on to anybody close to home, but have seen some of the guys I went through gunnery school with.*
>
> *Underhill said a lot of the boys we knew were in Italy with them. If we ever go on a shuttle raid to Russia and Italy I am going to try to see them.*
>
> *We saw a lot more sights this last time in London than we did the other time.*
>
> *[Is] Aunt Thelma still home? I have been waiting to get her address to write her, but I guess I will just write her at grandad's . . .*
>
> *Love, Ray*[24]

"English plane lands on U.S. base . . . breaks apart . . ."

Dear Folks, England, Nov. 27, 1944

I got two nice long letters from [you] today and was very glad to get them. I also got a letter from Miss Warden and have already answered it. I got a package from Aunt Ruby and one from LaVern. I don't see why Aunt Ruby didn't write me, but she did send me several nice things. Besides eats she sent me two pair of sox. LaVern sent me a lot of eats and a tooth brush and some tooth paste.

I didn't need the brush and paste for before we left the states I bought three extra brushes and a lot of paste and a lot of other stuff. I have got seven packages now and I know of several more on the way.

They pulled several rough missions along the first of the month, but we were not on any of them. The boys from our outfit had good luck, we didn't loose [sic] a plane. We haven't lost a plane in quite a while. We all hope our luck just holds out.

I am glad you are about finished pulling cotton. You never did tell me how much you made. Did you make a lot this year?

Our cigarettes have been cut again we only get three packs a week now. That is really hard on some of these guys around here. I guess I had better close now and write Pearleta.

Love, Ray[25]

Crash Landing on Base

FINISHING OUT 1944: AIDING THE VICTORY IN EUROPE

The scrapbook that Amelia lovingly made for Ray to showcase the pictures he brought home with him from the war showcased four pictures showing damaged airplanes, all bombers. One photograph was captioned, "English plane lands on U.S. base . . . breaks apart." The photo was of a Lancaster bomber that cracked in half at the waist of the plane with the tail twisted to a vertical stance. In the background was a crane used to lift the plane so it could be transported away from the runway. The next photo in this group featured parts of airplanes after crash landings. Busted wings, mangled fuselages, and panels from all parts of the planes were twisted beyond recognition. The collection of wreckage was simply captioned, "Crash Landings on Base." The photo accompanying the "Crash Landings on Base" photo reminded Ray and his crew that at least the crashes occurred back "home" where Allied personnel, doctors, firemen, and first responders could readily aid the crew. But what about the planes that were forced to crash land in enemy territory? One photo displayed a fuselage where the nose had completely torn away, wings ripped from the body, and the tail shredded to merely wires and bits of metal panels. If you look closely, the nose art of a scantily clad young brunette still decorated the side of the plane, along with stenciled bombs showing the crew's completed missions. With twenty-eight bombs painted on the side, the picture represented the plane of an experienced crew. The only part of the plane not completely destroyed was the cockpit. The caption eerily stated, "At least they came down on friendly soil." The last photo in the collection showed the tail of a B-17 bomber intact, except for the large hole in the tail, just a few feet above the tail gunner position. The dangers of being assigned to a bomber crew were evident all around Ray.[26]

"At Least they Came Down on Friendly Soil"

"This One Came Home with Damage"

Dear Folks, England, Dec. 1, 1944

    I am sorry I haven't written you in several days, but there is just nothing to write about. The lights were out last night and I couldn't write.

    It just don't look like we will ever get to fly again. We flew our last mission 28th of October. Just setting around is getting on our nerves. We have missed some good missions and we have missed some rough ones, but if we don't fly we will never finish.

    I got a phone call from a friend of Aunt Thelma the other night. Her name is Ruth Pound or I think she said Pound these phones over here aren't much good. I don't think I know her, but I remember Aunt Thelma talking about Ruby. We had a nice little talk and I might get to see her sometime.

    I guess I had better close as I am out of paper I can't even write Pearleta.

Love, Ray[27]

FINISHING OUT 1944: AIDING THE VICTORY IN EUROPE

Dear Folks,   *England, Dec. 6, 1944*

I just got back from London last night and had seven letters. I was really glad to get all that many. I got one from Bill Shaver and he is at Lincoln, Neb. He is just a Pfc. He said he was going to be put on the B-29. If he is he won't come over here. He said he got my address from one of my old school teachers, I don't know who it was.

Yes, I had thought about Pearleta having a birthday this month, but there isn't nothing I can do about it. I am glad you are buying her something. Let me know what it is. I was very sorry to hear U.S. was missing. Maybe he will show up before long.

I got a letter from Mr. & Mrs. Montgomery, she really did write a nice letter and I got a Christmas card from Mr. & Mrs. Frank Underwood.

We just stayed in London one day. We went to another base to see one of Sandy's buddies. I am going to send some money home as soon as we get our flying pay. I must close and write Pearleta.

                                                                         Love, Ray[28]

Servicemen received forty-eight-hour passes periodically, and they would pool their money to go to London and stay in a hotel, just to ease the boredom. Ray described their base at Horham as, "about a hundred miles northeast of London . . . occasionally we'd get a 48-hour pass and we'd catch the train at Diss and ride to London. I only went to London a couple of times. Course, you know, back in those days those were little old narrow gauge tracks, that train was . . . they [had] that walk across that you would walk upstairs and walk across. I guess you couldn't get in those trains except on one side. The truck let us off on one side of those tracks. Course, it was a little old building there, and they had an overpass over that you'd walk across and get on the other side of that track, and that's where you got into the train."[29]

Dear Folks,   *Dec. 13, 1944*

I still haven't got a letter from you. There is no one getting mail around here. Are you getting my mail?

I am going to write just a short letter, there is nothing to write. We won't be doing nothing tomorrow so I will try to write you again. I am sending a money order for fifty dollars. You can just put it in the bank with the rest of my money. Be sure and let me know when you get my first allotment for $95. You are suppose to get one for November.

We will probably get another pass before we fly again. If we do it will make four passes since we flew. Sandy and I are not going on this one, we are going to stay on the base. I am not going to London anymore. I don't like that place. These English people almost starve us to death. Whenever we go to London and come back this G.I. chow really looks good. I must close for now.

Love, Ray[30]

At the end of October, Ray made arrangements to have his $60 allotment increased to $95.[31] Although still very young in the eyes of the world, war and living through the Depression matured him beyond his years. Ray sent money home to help him get a decent start when the war ended and returned to civilian life. He always felt that he would return home, but his sixth mission proved to him that nothing was certain. Ray also realized that should he perish overseas, his parents could use the money. Growing up, money was too hard to come by, and through his letters one gets a sense of Ray's frugalness. Ray's wartime experience with managing money helped him become a successful farmer and rancher later in life.

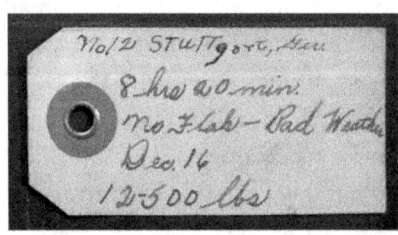

No 12 Stuttgart, Ger
8 hrs 20 min.
No Flak – Bad Weather
Dec. 16
12 – 500 lbs[32]

Dear Folks, Dec. 17, 1944

I haven't had a letter from you in almost three weeks. I don't know what is wrong. Are you getting my mail? It sure is hard to come in from a mission and not have any mail especially when I haven't had any in so long.

We went on a mission yesterday. It was a pretty good one. I would like to have several more just like that one. We flew a practice mission today and I am pretty tired so I will close and write again tomorrow.

Love, Ray[33]

Somewhere in Italy December 17, 1944
Dear Folks,

I received your package a few days ago and want to thank you for it. It's appreciated very much.

Well, Christmas is just around the corner again, one week from tomorrow. I can well remember what Ray and I did last Christmas Day, K.P. at Ft. Sill. I wish we were there to do it again this Christmas though.

The last time that I heard from him he had eleven missions. Hope he has a lot more by now. I have flown very little since the last time I wrote you. Only about thirty-eight missions now. Do you remember Ray ever mentioning a boy named Sturdivant? He has forty-six missions now. We three all came into the Army together and stayed together until we left Kearney.

How are all of you now? I guess the boys are going to school and will be glad when it turns out for the Christmas holidays. That was always the case with me.

Mail has been rather slow in coming through. I suppose its due to the rush on packages. Some days there is no mail at all for the entire squadron. Most of it gets here sooner or later though usually later.

I have just gotten back from church. We always try to go on Sunday nights. During the week we go to two or three shows. Even that gets pretty monotonous here at times.

Guess I'll close now and get some sleep. Take it easy and answer soon.

Preston Underhill[34]

Dear Folks, Dec. 18, 1944

I got a letter from you today and I was really glad to get it. Today is the first time I have had a letter since I got back from pass. I also got a letter from Pearleta and she said Tommie was [a] prisoner. I was really glad to hear that. I was almost sure he would be taken prisoner. When I got the paper with his *picture it said what date he went down and we were on the same one. I might have even seen his plane. I will tell where we went that day. I can't tell you anything like that in a letter.*

I don't guess we will finish as soon as I had thought. We have a much better position now, but we only fly every other mission.

Pearleta also told me something that really surprised me. She said Lou and Buzz was married. I didn't know that was about to happen. I guess John and Bell are pretty lonesome now unless J.B and Elva Mae are living with them. Frances when are you and Curtis going to get hitched, you are about the only one left now. What is wrong can't Curtis get up nerve enough to ask?

Has J.B. and Elva had their new edtion [sic] yet. I know when I was home they were expecting one. What is J.B. doing now? Is he fixing to go into the army? Or is he going to volunteer for something?

I had better close now and write Pearleta. I got a nice letter from her today.

Love, Ray[35]

When reading this letter, Ray's relief upon hearing of Tommie's prisoner status was evident. The paper he referenced was the *Haskell Free Press* dated October 27, 1944.[36] The next mention of Tommie Davis in the *Haskell Free Press* was November 17, 1944: "**Davis Is Prisoner of Germans** – Cpl. Thomas R. Davis, who was reported missing in action over Germany on October 6, is now a prisoner of the Germans, according to a telegram received Wednesday morning in Haskell by his parents, Mr. and Mrs. Tom Davis. The telegram was from the Red Cross and contained no information other than he was a prisoner of war. Presumably he was uninjured. Cpl. Davis was a gunner on a B-17 and had been overseas since July."[37]

This article reiterated what Pearleta wrote to Ray about Tommie's capture. Ray often said that although being a prisoner of war was not fun, the Germans did follow the Geneva Convention on how to treat Allied personnel.[38] The Red Cross actively monitored the prisoners and their treatment.

Dear Folks,   *Dec. 21, 1944*

I got five letters from you yesterday and was going to write you last night, but I went to a dance at the NCO Club. We had a good dance and believe it or not I got out and cut a rug. We haven't been able to get Sandy to dance yet. He says all he does is intermission. These girls aren't so good looking, but they get prettier the longer we stay here. They can dance pretty good.

    I sure hope you do make a good grain crop this year. I guess you have most of it in wheat don't you. How many bales of cotton did you make this year? I sure hope you made a good crop.

    I haven't got a letter from you telling me if daddy killed a deer or not. I got a letter saying you had venison to eat.

    I got a letter from Pearleta yesterday and she really acted like she was really proud to get the compact. It seems to me like Irvin is getting a long fourlough [sic]. Where is he stationed now? Is he fixing to go overseas or something? I sure do hope Kermit will come over to see me. I sure would like to see him. Is he a pilot on a fighter or not.

    I got a nice long letter from Aunt Ruth yesterday too. She really wrote a nice letter. I guess I had better close and write Pearleta.

Love, Ray[39]

Western Union Telegram to Mr. & Mrs. Hoyt Perry   December 23, 1944

Thinking of you and wishing I could be with you. Ray Perry[40]

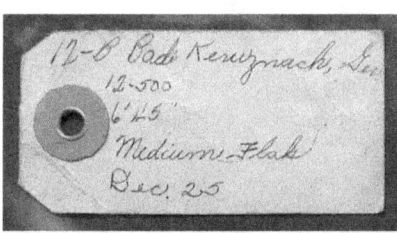

12-B Bad Kerwznach, Ger.
12 – 500 [lbs. bombs]
6' 45"
Medium Flak
Dec. 25[41]

    Although not stated on the bomb tag, Ray remembered dropping fragmentation bombs on his thirteenth mission: "We did have . . . fragmentation bombs. They'd just bust and make little pieces of shrapnel . . . They were used on personnel . . . We used them at the Battle of the Bulge . . . on German troops."[42] The Battle of the Bulge was a last-ditch effort for a German offensive. It was launched on December 16, 1944, and lasted until January 25, 1945. Ray clarified their part in this battle, "The only day I remember using them [fragmentation bombs] was Christmas Day of '44. We had been snowed in for two or three days and couldn't get off to go help those boys over there at the Battle of the Bulge, and they finally packed the snow on the runway with GI trucks. They didn't have any snowplows or anything like that, and they packed that snow . . . so we could get off. And we got off on Christmas Day and went over there, and we carried I don't know how many, but hundred-pound fragmentation bombs . . . Anyway, it's the only low-level mission I ever flew. Below five thousand [feet] . . . There wasn't a lot of heavy antiaircraft fire there, because the Germans were advancing and we went after the front line, maybe after equipment, troops, whatever. You know, their supply line, trying to stop them. Course, they were headed to Antwerp . . . I got the Battle of the Bulge ribbon."[43]

The vast amount of snow that fell in England proved a real treat for Ray. West Texas was lucky to see snowfall every three years, and when it did come, it only fell one to six inches. Ray's scrapbook contained several pictures of snow covering the countryside, snow blanketing a house at least several feet deep, and a very majestic photo of a B-17 doing a run up on the runaway made of packed snow. The captions read, "Christmas in England, 1944."[44] Ray truly experienced a white Christmas, and what a memory to share with loved ones on those chilly West Texas nights in December.

Flying on Christmas Day 1944

White Christmas in England 1944

Dear Folks,   Dec. 27, 1944

    I am sorry I haven't written you in the last several days, but I have been pretty busy and tired. We flew a mission Christmas Day, but it was not very rough. They really had a good meal waiting for us when we got down. We had turkey and everything to go with it. This really didn't seem like Christmas to us, but maybe we can all be home for next Christmas day, I guess you had a good dinner I hope you got my telegram pretty close to Christmas. Sandy and I sent two each. I think we sent them the twenty first, I am not sure.

    Our crew is on pass now, but Sandy and I are not going anywhere. Some of the officers went to London. We might go over to another bomb group and see some boys we know. It isn't but about ten miles though. The pictures our pilot made turned out pretty good and I am going to send you some of them. Our pilot made the pictures, printed and developed them hisself [sic]. He is really good.

    I am sure glad dad got a deer. I wish I could have been there to go with him. When the war is over I am going deer hunting with him.

    I got some pictures from Pearleta a few days ago and I was really glad to get them. They are pretty good. She is going to send me some more. I wish you would send me some.

    I must close now and write Pearleta.

                                                                            Love, Ray[45]

Dear Folks, *Dec. 30, 1944*

I haven't heard from you in several days. It seems like our mail just comes in bunches. We get a lot one day and then we don't get any for about two weeks. I had rather get one or two every other day. I wish you would write two or three Vmail letters with your air mail each week. The Vmail seems to come a lot faster now. The only trouble with Vmail is you can't write much on it and it don't seem like you are getting a letter. I am going to start writing a few Vmail.

I got a cluster to my air Medal a few days ago. They just give you a cluster instead of another Medal.

I wish you would send me a lot of canned stuff. Just anything that I can open and eat. In one of your packages (I think it was yours) I got some cheese and it was really good. Only send a few crackers. Just send anything that you think I might like. Some of the boys are getting sardines, but I don't want any of them. I think our packages will come a lot faster now.

I must close now, we are making some coffee and I want some of it.

Love, Ray[46]

With the end of 1944, and their flying time very erratic, Ray and his crew were anxious to get their missions completed. According to records, during the second half of 1944 "nearly half a million tons of bombs were dropped by American heavy bombers on targets in Germany."[47] In his letters, Ray seemed optimistic about the war ending in favor of the Allies. With the dawn of 1945, the foremost goal for these aviators was ending the war and returning home.

CHAPTER 10
A NEW YEAR: 1945

"LET'S DO OUR SHARE – *Another year of war has drawn to a close. Volumes will be written about the awful destruction of the past twelve months. Puny efforts will be made to describe the suffering of the men of the armed forces, who face death day after day, year after year, far from home and loved ones. Actually, there are no words that can adequately sum up 1944, the most critical year in American history. The astounding thing about the home front is the fact that except for the families of service men, it lives normally and has no conception of the horrors of war. As we enter a new year . . . faced daily by our fighting men, [we] owe our men and women in service a full measure of support in every phase of war activity. No sacrifice can be made on the home front that is worthy of comparison with the grim task faced daily by our fighting men."*

—Haskell (TX) Free Press, January 5, 1945[1]

Dear Folks,   Jan. 1, 1945

I got two more packages from you yesterday and a letter saying you had sent them. The package came as fast as the letters. One of the packages was from Frances with the nuts. The other had the stationery [sic] in it, but it was damp and most of the envelopes were ruined but that is alright I needed the paper most.

I got paid yesterday and I got a little better than 12 dollars with the $95 allotment coming out it don't leave me much, but I will get my flying pay the tenth of the month. I will draw almost $60 dollars then.

Yes, I am a little heavier than I was when I was home. I guess I will weigh that much I haven't weighed since I have been over. All my clothes still fit though. I got a letter from Miss Warden yesterday too. She seems to like her school. I sent the pictures yesterday I think you will be surprised when you get them, I think they are pretty good especially for our pilot making them he is pretty good. I must close for now.

Love, Ray[2]

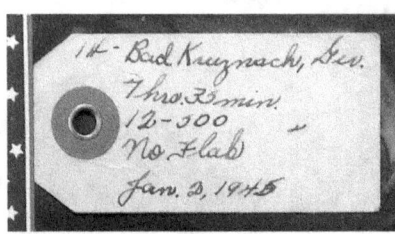

14 – Bad Kreuznach, Ger.
7 hrs. 35 min.
12 – 500 [lbs. bombs]
No Flak
Jan. 2, 1945[3]

Dear Folks,   Jan. 4, 1945

I haven't heard from you in several days. I got a letter from Pearleta today. We have been flying for the last few days until today. None of the missions lately have been very bad. We really had a good one yesterday, but it

Ray Perry c. 1945

was pretty long. We flew eight hours and twenty minutes. We got up at three and got back at three thirty that afternoon.

I have had a slight cold, but it is gone now. The doctors gave me something good. The Sucrets came in handy. In Pearleta's letter today she asked me what I wanted for my birthday. I don't want you to send me anything. I might be home by then, but if I am not it won't be long after that. We expected to finish a lot quicker than we are, but we have had a little hard luck and got delayed in our missions a little. I can't tell you anything now but I will when I get home. I must close for now.

Love, Ray[4]

Dear Folks,   Jan. 6, 1945

I got two letters from you today and I was really glad to get them. It had been several days since I had had a letter from you. I got the paper today too. Not much news though, but I enjoyed it.

I stay plenty warm at night, we have as good a barracks to stay in as we did back in the states. We are supposed to have only four blankets, but I have seven. Sandy and I both have that many. We have decided it isn't what you

Flying through the flak.

know in the army, it is who you know. We have to take some kind of pills every day to prevent us from getting a cold.

I have got a few pictures our pilot took and I am going to send a few home at a time in a letter. I have got some good combat pictures. I will send you a few flak and formation pictures. I have some good battle damage pictures but I can't send them home.

I got another package from Pearleta yesterday. She sent me a cigarette case and five packs of cigarettes. She sent some nice soap and few other things. I got a letter from her today and she said John M. was going to get discharged. How come he is getting a discharge? Is there anything wrong with him, he didn't get wounded did he?

We have in fifteen missions now and will probably fly tomorrow. As soon as we get in three or four more missions we will get to go to the rest home. We call it the Flak Shack. There is one crew in our barracks at it now. I must close for now.

Love, Ray[5]

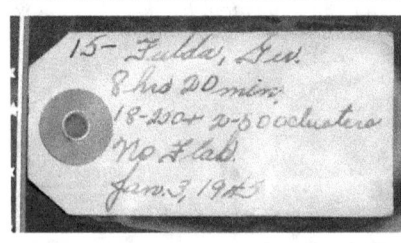

15 – Fulda, Ger.
8 hrs 20 min.
18 – 250 [lbs. bombs] & 2 – 500 clusters
No Flak
Jan. 3, 1945[6]

Dear Folks,   Jan. 9, 1945

I didn't get a letter from you today, but got some yesterday and day before. Have you had any snow at home this year? We had a little snow last night and have been having some fun today. Sandy and I and some other guys had a little snow ball fight.

We haven't flew lately, but we were supposed to fly today. We will probably fly tomorrow. We still have in fifteen I don't remember if I have told you lately or not.

We got paid our flying pay today, but I don't think I will send any of it home. I may need a little money before we get paid again. I know I will when we go to the rest home and we will probably go before next pay day. I guess we

A NEW YEAR: 1945

will get another pass before long, but I don't think we will go.

I am anxious to know if you got my telegram and when you got it.

I must close and write Pearleta.

Love, Ray[7]

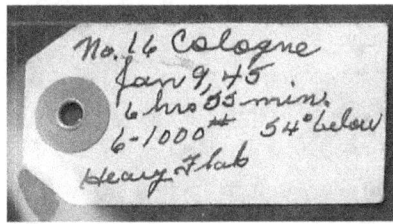

No. 16 Cologne
Jan 9, 45
6 hrs 55 mins
6 – 1000# [lbs. bombs] 54° below
Heavy Flak[8]

Ray's sixteenth mission was so cold, fifty-six degrees below zero, that Ray recalled his ears stuck to his headset—literally froze to the leather.[9] This was the coldest weather that Ray had ever experienced. Back home in Texas, temperatures in winter rarely dropped below freezing. Once in a while, a winter may have a really cold snap, but even then, temperatures rarely dropped

Ready, Aim, Fire

below zero degrees. Ray shared this memory with his family members once he returned home.

Once in a while, engine trouble forced a bomber back to base, causing the crew to abandon the mission. Enemy fighters, antiaircraft fire, and freezing temperatures were all dangers experienced by the crew. Ray described this situation, "We got hit with fighters more than that one time, but they never did really get in there and do a whole lot of damage like they did [on the sixth mission]. And there was times that antiaircraft fire was terrific. You know, there'd be times that we'd just get that old airplane plumb full of holes . . . from shrapnel from those 88-milimeter shells that they shot up at us. And there was times . . . that we'd lose engines, you know. That old airplane would fly pretty good on two engines. You couldn't stay in formation, you'd have to drop out . . . [so] if a German fighter happened to come along, you was pretty vulnerable because you was out there by yourself."[10] If the bombs that the crew carried had not been released, then the crew dropped them before returning to base. Ray stated, "There was a location out there in the North Sea that we'd have to go over and get rid of those bombs." Laughing to himself, Ray mused, "I've often wondered how they managed to drill for oil out there!"[11] Crews jettisoned thousands of bombs in this location through the years.

[from Preston Underhill to Mr. and Mrs. Perry]

Somewhere in Italy   *January 15, 1945*
Dear Folks,

I received a letter from Mrs. Perry and one from Ray the same day. Really was glad to hear from both of you. It took about two weeks less time for yours to get here than [it] did Ray's letter.

He and I are in the same book on this flying deal. I'm not flying very often, either. Only once since Christmas. Have forty-three missions now. Ray is probably gaining on me, since he stated in his letter that they would start flying again soon. I sure wish that it were possible for us to be home at the same time. Coincidence like that don't happen very often, though. Sturdivant is still here. I think that maybe he and I will get to go back together. Sure hope so, anyway.

I have gotten quite a lot of mail the last two days. Most of it was written about six weeks ago. It must have come by water. Your letter got here in twelve days though.

I hope that Frances has gotten, or does get to go see Dorothy. They could probably find a lot to talk about. I seriously doubt if they could find much to do in Rotan though.

Christmas was as good as could be expected here. I flew a mission that day but we had a hot turkey supper when we got back.

I never have seen such a rainy country as this. It rains practically all the time. This black mud gets mighty gummy and slick, too. Has it been dry enough there for Mr. Perry to start farming again?

I'll have to close now. Take it easy and answer soon.

Love, Preston I[12]

Preston's sister Dorothy was about Frances' age. Frances was Ray's younger sister. Dorothy spent time with Ray's family during the summer of 1944. Families of service boys were drawn together in a way they had never been before. Although Rotan and Paint Creek were not very far from each other by today's standards, it was quite a distance in 1945, especially when gas and rubber (tire) rationing were considered. Some families rarely traveled farther than the nearest town once a week for supplies.

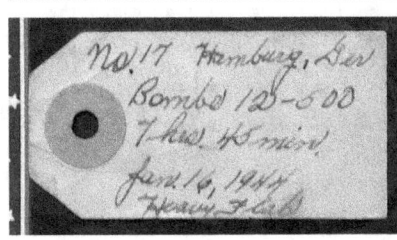

No. 17 Hamburg, Ger
Bombs 12 – 500 [lbs.]
7 hrs. 45 min.
Jan. 16, 1944 [1945]
Heavy Flak[13]

Dear Folks,   Jan 19, 1945

I really hit the jackpot today. I got fifteen letters. Some of them was old, but most of them was new ones. I got several written in December and one or two written in January. I am sorry I haven't written you in the last three or four days, but we have been pretty busy. I was really glad to hear you got my cablegram. Pearleta got hers on Christmas day. I was going to send it a day earlier, but never got around to it.

I guess I have got all my packages. I have got seventeen so far.

I haven't heard from Underhill in a long time now. I wished I was back at Ft. Sill on K.P. as I was over Germany.

I got six letters from you today and I still can't think of a thing to write. When I get back to the states I don't think I will write a letter.

I got a letter from Irvin a few days ago and he didn't seem to think he would be coming over here. He might though you can never tell. I got a letter from Bill Shaver today and he is at Pyote, Texas taking his O.T.W. I guess he will be going overseas before long, but I think he will be going the other way too.

I must close for now.

Love, Ray[14]

V-Mail   Jan. 23, 1945
Dear Folks,

I got a letter from you yesterday and one today. I was very glad to get them. I still haven't had a letter from you since Christmas. I am anxious to know if you got my telegram and when you got it. I might have waited a little late to send it, but I guess you will be glad to get it. I didn't even know I had a calf big enough to sell. I guess I will have more money when I get home than I thought. I don't know how much I have and I haven't been keeping track of it. I would send some more this month, but I may need it when we go to the rest home. I sure wish I could have a thousand dollars in the bank when I get home and get back. I got back from pass alright, but we didn't look up [illegible]. I didn't know how to look her up. All I know is her phone and I just didn't get around to phoning her. I guess I had better close and write Pearleta.

Love, Ray[15]

Dear Folks,   Jan. 24, 1945

I haven't had a letter from anyone since I got that fifteen a few days ago. I had rather have one or two every day instead of a lot in one group.

Well, things are really looking good over here now. We haven't flew a mission in several days now. We may fly tomorrow. I sure hope so. I would like to have twenty or twenty five missions when the war is over. Sandy and I made a bet on the war about two months ago. We bet eight dollars. He bet that it would be over by the end of this month. I think I will collect. He had about $25 bet in all.

A NEW YEAR: 1945

Has Curtis and J.B. every joined anything yet. I think J.B. waited a little late, but I guess that is what he wanted to do. I bet Mrs. Cox really don't want Curtis to get in anything. I thought they would try to keep him out.

I got to write Underhill tonight. I haven't heard from him in several days or I should say weeks. I should write his mother. I have to write Pearleta too.

Love Ray[16]

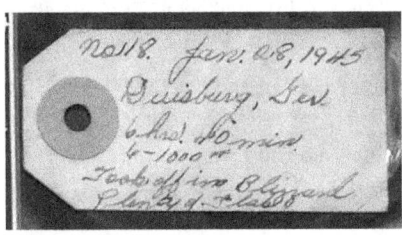

No 18. Jan. 28, 1945
Duisburg [sic], Ger.
6 hrs. 40 min. / 6 – 1000# [lbs. bombs]
Took off in Blizzard
Plenty of Flak[17]

Vmail
Dear Folks,   Jan. 30, 1945

I still haven't had any mail. There is no mail coming through except Vmail I sure hope you are writing two or three Vmail letters each week. I haven't been doing much lately. We have flew a couple of missions in the last few days. We have had a snow here and have really been having some fun. Every time we go to chow we have a big snow fight. J.B. really picked a good time to go into the army. I would kinda like to see his baby. What does he think about it? I guess he is really proud of it. I wonder if he wanted a girl or had rather have a boy?

Pop is fixing to go to the Red Cross Club and get a bowl of soup and sandwich so I am going too. I will write again tomorrow as I am now flying.

Love, Ray[18]

Dear Folks,   Feb. 5, 1945

I will write you a few lines tonight. I guess I can't write you for a day or two. We are going to the rest home tomorrow or the next day. We are supposed to go tomorrow, but may have to wait until the next day. I haven't had a letter from you in several days and I guess I won't get any until we get back. We will get to stay at the rest home seven days with two days travel time.

I will try to write you a few times while we are there. While we are there we get to wear civilian clothes and get breakfast in bed.

We opened a can of your sausage a few nights ago and it was really good. There was just a few of us in the barracks so we had about two pieces each. The boys really like it. We are going to take the other can to the rest home with us. Maybe we can get them fried with our eggs at breakfast. You said Olie said she bets my glasses were new. No, they are not new they were issued to me just before we come over. They are just like the ones I priced when I was home for $18.95. I sure am glad I didn't buy a pair. I got another letter from Olie. I am going to write her tonight. I got two letters from Pearleta a few days ago, but none from you. I got a letter from Underhill, too. I think he has forty two missions now. He said Sturdivant had in forty eight, he just liked two. I sure would like to be home the same time they are, but I know it won't be.

I guess I had better close for now and write another letter or two.

Love, Ray[19]

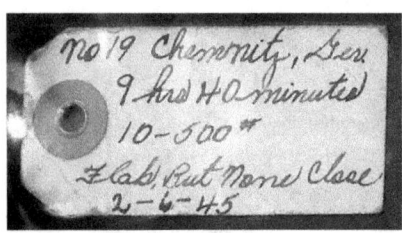

No 19 Chemnitz, Ger.
9 hrs 40 minutes
10 – 500# [lbs. bombs]
Flak, But None Close
2-6-45[20]

Dear Folks, Feb. 15, 1945

We just got back from the rest home yesterday. We really had a nice time there. I am sorry I didn't write you while we were there, but we just found too much to do. We didn't write a letter while we were there. When we got back we really had a lot of mail. I had twenty four letters and three papers. I have just finished reading them all. They are the first I had had in about a month except for a few of those V things. You asked if we really needed a rest. I guess we did or they would not have sent us.

We were hit by about eighty enemy fighters and two of them picked on our plane. One of them came in on the tail and I got him. He went down in flames and then exploded. Chuck was the youngest one on our crew. His name is Charles Buda and he was from Ohio. You met him the night at the

A NEW YEAR: 1945

service club after the donkey ball game. He was with Bert the one from Calif. He had dark straight hair. We were allowed to go to his funeral. He had a very nice military funeral. He is buried in Cambridge.

I tell you a way you can tell him. In the picture of us made by the plane he is the one on the right end. I will send you his folks address as soon as I get it. Our pilot has it, he wrote them a little while back.

You asked who that little fellow in the middle is, he is the one that took Chuck's place. He is really a good guy, he had one more mission to go. We will probably fly it tomorrow. I guess I had better close now and write Pearleta.

Love, Ray[21]

Although Chuck was killed at the beginning of October, Ray refrained from telling his family until February 15. He may not have been able to tell them because of a military gag order, or Ray simply did not want to worry his family, and so kept it to himself. In either case, keeping the information from his family must have weighed heavily on him.

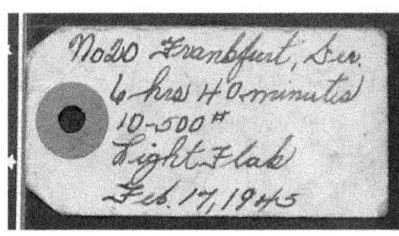

No 20 Frankfurt, Ger.
6 hrs 40 minutes
10 – 500# [lbs. bombs]
Light Flak
Feb. 17, 1945[22]

Dear Folks, *Feb. 19, 1945*

In one of your letters you asked me if Kermit Howard was close to me. He is on the same base as I am, even in the same squadron. I was going to ask you if you knew him, but had just forgot about it. I don't remember him. One morning we started on a mission and our plane was out of order so we had to fly another one. We flew his, he is a crew chief. We were in the tent and I noticed he kept looking at me and finally he found out I was from Texas and Haskell. He said he thought he recognized me. We have flew his plane several times.

We have flew one mission since we got back from the rest home. We have to go to school for three days now. I sure wish we could fly now the weather is really good here. If we could get a good stretch of weather we could finish in less than two months. I think we will fly pretty regular when we finish this school I sure hope so, I really want to finish and get home by late spring.

I guess I had better close and write Pearleta.

Love, Ray[23]

Dear Folks,   Feb. 28, 1945

I am sorry I haven't written you in the last few days, but we have been on pass and I just haven't felt like writing. We haven't flew in several days, but I think we will start now and fly pretty regular until we finish. There is a crew here in our barracks that came here after we did and they are almost finished.

I would really like to see all those old men skating. While we were at the rest home I went ice skating. We really had a good time.

Our pilot and I have been going out to a farm here and hunting. The other day they invited us out to supper and they had goose and everything you can imagine to eat. They are really nice people. We use to go out there and hunt quail and they would give us eggs and take it all to our barracks and have a feed.

I sure hope Frances is still working in the Drug Store when I get home. If she is I am going after her every night and eat ice cream until I can't eat any more. That is something we don't get over here.

I must close and write Pearleta.

Love, Ray[24]

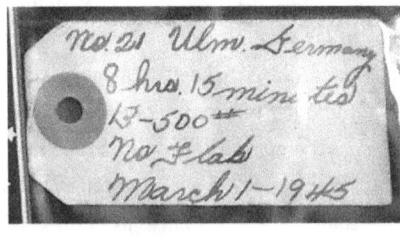

No. 21 Ulm, Germany
8 hrs. 15 minutes
13 – 500# [lbs. bombs]
No Flak
March 1 – 1945[25]

Dear Folks,   March 3, 1945

I have been getting a few Vmail from you lately, but haven't been getting any regular mail from you. I got two from Pearleta today. We have been having some pretty weather the last few days, but we haven't been doing much flying.

We got a letter from Mrs. Buda (Chuck's mother) today. She wrote a very nice letter. She has got the Purple Heart and is going to be presented the Air Medal. Her address is:

Mrs. W.H. Buda, Bryan, Ohio, Route 3.

I guess you will be planting feed and stuff pretty soon won't you. I would really like to be home helping out this year. These English really have a poor excuse for farming. It is so wet over here they have to plow in mud almost.

Well, we are not flying tomorrow. I guess we won't be home until the war is over. I wish we could get started and finished before the war is over.

I must close for now.

Love, Ray[26]

I have been getting a Vmail from you almost every day now. I am glad you write a few of them, but don't stop writing air mail. I got both of the packages today and Sandy got two also. I got one from Mrs. Heron a few days ago. I am going to write to her in a few days.

We started on a mission today and was almost ready to leave England and one engine went out. I was really mad for it was a easy mission too.

I really would like to be home now and see all the pretty green fields. I guess the place is pretty now. How is my horses? I bet Stormy is really big now, have you been riding her any?

You asked why I didn't ask for anymore packages. I have been thinking the war would be over or we would be finished soon. I am not going to ask for anything else.

I guess we will be going on pass in a few days, but I don't think I will go.

I must close for now.

Love, Ray[27]

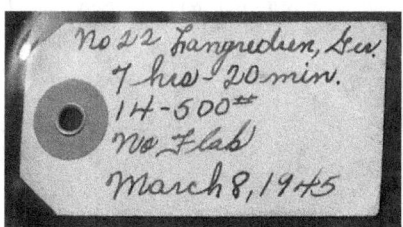

No 22 Langredren [sic], Ger.
7 hrs – 20 min.
14 – 500# [lbs. bombs]
No Flak
March 8, 1945[28]

Dear Folks, March 11, 1945

I am sorry I haven't been writing much lately, but I just haven't felt like writing. I haven't been writing anybody, but will try to write more often from now on. I have been getting Vmails from you pretty regular, that is all that is coming across now. I got three from you today.

When you get Curtis address send it to me and I will write him. I think he got in a pretty good thing. I think they make pretty good money and it isn't so dangerous now.

Yes, I got the card from the Sunday School and was very glad to get it. It was a very nice card.

If I was Ray Jr. I wouldn't be so anxious to get across. I don't think he will have to worry about not getting in on any of the war. He probably won't get over here, but I think he will see plenty on the other side.

I guess I will be home before school is out if it isn't out before July. I guess I will get home and you will put me to work.

I must close for now.

Love, Ray[29]

Dear Folks, March 15, 1945

I got a Vmail from you today and was very glad to get it. The mail is not coming through . . . for some reason.

We are going on a three day pass tomorrow. Sandy and I are going to another base to see a guy we know. I don't think Pop is going anywhere, he doesn't go on pass much. He does a lot of worrying, his wife is to have a baby about the last of this month. That makes three for him and he said he hoped it was twins.

We went out to a farm today and got a dozen eggs and had hard boiled eggs. We do that a lot, we get eggs and fry them sometimes.

Have you started work on the house yet? I hope you have that bath tub in when I get home. If it is I am going to get in it and soak about an hour. I haven't had a good bath since I left the states. The water is always too hot or too cold.

I must close and write Pearleta,

Love, Ray[30]

Dear Folks, March 18, 1945

Well, today is Sunday and of course I didn't get up in time to go to church. I took a shower and dressed up and went to the show this afternoon.

There is a lot of guys finishing now that we come over. The reason we haven't finished is because we layed [sic] around about two months when we got shot up by fighters. We should be finished by the last of April. I sure hope so anyway. We can wear khaki when we get home then.

I haven't had a letter from you in several days. I got one of those Vthings from Pearleta today.

Sandy and I finally just fooled around and never did go on pass. I am kinda glad we didn't, we are all rested up and ready to fly tomorrow. Pop has been flying the last two days, he was six behind us. He broke his arm on one of our missions and was grounded for awhile.

I guess I had better close and write Pearleta.

Love, Ray[32]

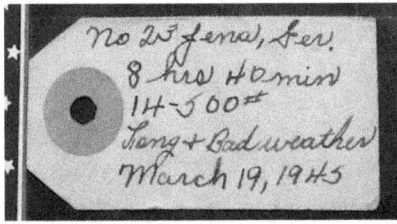

No 23 Jena, Ger.
8 hrs 40 min
14 – 500# [lbs. bombs]
Long & Bad weather
March 19, 1945[31]

Ray's normally cheerful persona was taking a hit. Every time *Heavy Date* flew through heavy flak or experienced mechanical trouble, it was grounded for repairs. A grounded plane meant no flying—and no completed missions. The crew sometimes used another plane, but not too frequently. Lack of mail, boredom from not flying, and homesickness took its toll. The adventure turned monotonous, and Ray dreamed of returning home.

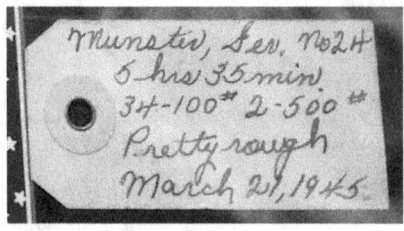

Munster, Ger. No 24
5 hrs 35 min.
34 – 100# [lbs.] 2 – 500# [lbs. bombs]
Pretty rough
March 21, 1945[33]

Dear Folks,   March 21, 1945

    I am just going to write you a short note to let you know I am alright. We flew a mission today and are going to fly again tomorrow. That is the reason I am not going to write much, I am pretty tired tonight.

    I am beginning to get pretty mad about this mail situation. I haven't had a letter in every bit of three weeks. I know it isn't your fault. I think they must be sinking the mail boats for they sure are not getting here.

    I think we are going to fly regular until we finish now. When a crew gets almost finished they usually fly them and finish up pretty quick. We had a pretty rough mission today. I think it was the roughest we have had for some time, but we always seem to make it alright.

    I will close for now and get to bed. I should write Pearleta, but I am pretty tired and need to get to bed.

Love, Ray[34]

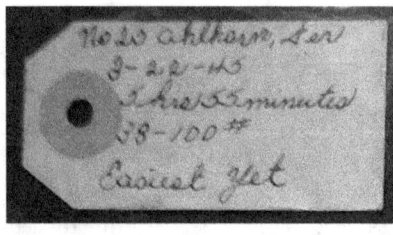

No 25 Ahlhorn, Ger
3-22-45
5 hrs 55 minutes
38 – 100# [lbs. bombs]
Easiest Yet[35]

Dear Folks,   March 23, 1945

    I got a little mail today for a change. I only got four, but that is better than I have had since we got back from the rest home. I got one from you, two from Pearleta and one from Frances.

A NEW YEAR: 1945

I am going to send you a telegram when we finish. Sandy and I have been intending to do that. We have been flying pretty regular lately. We have in twenty five now. We're getting pretty close to the end now. We will probably be home sometime in May.

We are going to fly tomorrow so I had better hurry this up and get to bed. I have to write Pearleta yet too.

So Pa is getting pretty good at skating is he. I guess I will have to go skating when I get home. I haven't been roller skating since I have been here, but I went ice skating when we were at the rest home.

I guess I had better close and write Pearleta.

Love, Ray[36]

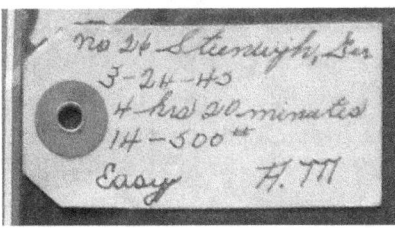

No 26 Steenwijk, Ger [Netherlands]
3-24-45
4 hrs 20 minutes
14 – 500# [lbs. bombs]
Easy A.M.[37]

Ray recalled that the Tuskegee airmen, the African-American military pilot group, escorted their bomber on at least one occasion. When asked how he knew, Ray replied, "by the red tails! You see they went by Red Tails, and they had the rudder and all, back there on the tail was painted red and the spinner on the prop painted red. And we could identify them a good ways off."[38] Although Ray's recollection of the mission date proved imperfect, research on the movements of the Tuskegee airmen, especially the fighter escorts over Germany, put the group as escorts on Ray's twenty-sixth and twenty-seventh missions on March 24, 1945.[39] The aviators made such an impression on Ray, who passed that respect and admiration for this group of men to his son, Rick. When Rick was governor of Texas, he invited all the Tuskegee airman to the Texas Capitol in Austin. Ray and Amelia attended as well, and Ray enjoyed visiting with these men that played such a crucial role, not just in World War II, but on the missions of B-17s crews as well.[40]

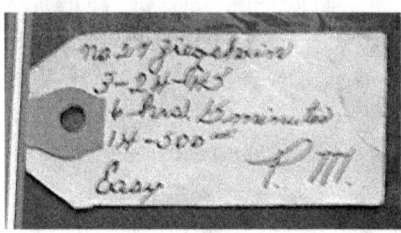

No 27 Ziegenhain [Germany]
3-24-45
6 hrs. 15 minutes
14 – 500# [lbs. bombs]
Easy P.M.[41]

The war changed Ray's way of thinking. Texas, especially the rural areas, held deep prejudices against northerners (Yankees) and minorities. These were not traits developed through association, but because of prejudices passed down through families. Isolation in rural areas continued to encourage these prejudices, but the war put Ray in direct contact with these groups of people. The war removed him from his isolated environment and forced him to make his own judgement of people. Almost every member of his crew was from the North, and early in his service, he discussed how different he found "Yankees." Ray's experiences with the Tuskegee airmen had the same effect, and he came to have great respect for the airmen's capabilities. These types of experiences were not unique for Texas boys; barriers put up through prejudice began to crack and crumble all through the United States due to wartime experiences.

Dear Folks,   *March 25, 1945*

I was going to write you last night, but we got in a little more than ten hours flying time yesterday, so you can guess I was pretty tired. We got all day off today. We have been flying pretty regular for the last few days. I think they are going to finish us up pretty fast now, we have been overseas longer than any other crew in our group. I will really be glad when we finish and get home, I am getting tired of this place.

I am going to have my allotment stopped for April. You won't get any check after the one for March. I guess I will have a lot of money the last of this month. I have fifty six dollars loaned out this month and I will draw about that much. I hope I can get home with enough money so I won't have to use any I have sent home. I haven't kept track of my money, but I should have quite a bit.

I must close and write Pearleta.

Love, Ray[42]

A NEW YEAR: 1945

Dear Folks,   *March 27, 1945*

I got two letters and a paper from you today. I was very glad to get them. I have been getting the papers pretty regular here lately. Your letters were only thirteen days old, that is the best I have had in a long time.

Have you heard from Underhill? He must be home by now the last letter I got from him he only had two to go. I would really like to see him and Sturdivant and some of the other guys. I thought Frances was staying at Ivy's. Why did she change, had she rather stay at a rooming house? I guess she is staying at the place where LaVern was staying when I was home. I remember Bill and I took LaVern home the last night I was home and then we went on to Abilene. I guess he will be the only one at home when I get there.

I guess I had better close and get to bed as we are flying tomorrow.

                                                                                Love, Ray

[P.S.] *I had my allotment stopped but you will get a check for April. I was already too late to have it stopped for then. I will have plenty of money to get home on anyway. What is Frances address now, I might decide to write her ever now and then.*[44]

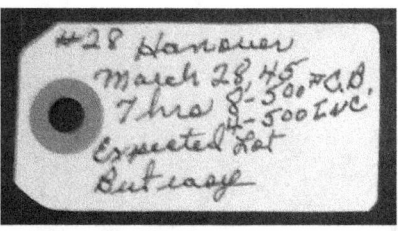

#28 Hanover [Germany]
March 28, 45
7 hrs 8 – 500# C.B.
4 – 500 Inc [incendiary bombs]
Expected Lot
But easy[43]

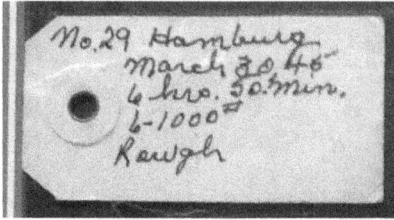

No. 29 Hamburg [Germany]
March 30, 45
6 hrs. 50 min.
6 – 1000# [lbs. bombs]
Rough[45]

The war was not just for the average young man, but celebrities wanted to do their part as well. Hollywood leading man Jimmy Stewart flew B-17s, and in early 1945, he transferred to Buckenham Base, located close to Horham where Ray was stationed. Just like Ray, Stewart considered his service in a bomber during World War II as, "one of the greatest experiences of his life." Author Richard Hayes wrote about Stewart's feelings on fear, "The war eventually got to everyone, even calm, mild mannered Jimmy Stewart. 'Fear is an insidious thing,' he [Stewart] said. 'It can warp judgement, freeze reflexes, breed mistakes. And worse, it's contagious. I felt my own fear and knew that if it wasn't checked, it could infect my crew members.'"[46] During one of Ray's missions, Stewart flew the lead plane. Like most of the other aviators, Ray was a little awed by Jimmy Stewart, but he also respected and admired the man more because of Stewart's active participation.[47]

Fear was truly crippling to some of the young men that experienced traumatic ordeals. During the 2016 interview, Ray described the photos in his scrapbook. When he came across one picture of a small bomb shelter in London where two of his buddies posed for a picture, Ray said, "This guy [that] was sitting there with Charlie Clark, his name was Miller." He explained that Miller and his crew were part of the Caterpillar Club, a club whose membership requisite was bailing out of your damaged plane and living to tell the tale.

Capt. C. R. Miller

"[Miller] was from Fort Worth and they got shot down . . . his tail gunner [was] from down here at Dublin, Texas, his last name was Brown . . . he got direct hit antiaircraft fire in the tail of that airplane and shot him, guns, and ammunition, everything, out of that tail. The rudder was still standing and they flew that airplane back over American lines, bailed his crew out. They were over Belgium, France or somewhere . . . but anyways, the Americans had done taken that area. And he bailed the whole crew out there, nobody was hurt or anything, but that radio operator (he shakes his head sadly) . . . they all got picked up and brought back to England. And after several days they brought them up to fly a mission and this radio operator, he . . . went beserk." Ray explained that the man could not get back in the plane and fly, "They grounded him and busted him, back to a buck private, and he never [flew again] . . . last time I saw him, he was out there in the yard, picking up cigarette butts."[48] When asked about his own bouts of fear, Ray replied, "I never was rattled. . . . I could never remember really being scared. I know I was. Had to be. But I had control of it."[49]

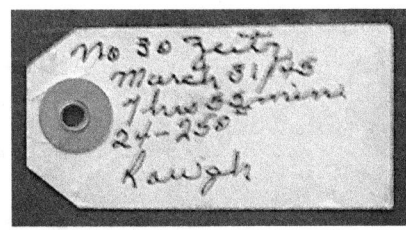

No 30 Zeitz [Germany]
March 31/45
7 hrs 55 min.
24 – 250 [lbs. bombs]
Rough[50]

Capt. C. R. Miller's Plane. Tail Gunner W. W. Brown from Dublin, Texas, was killed in action on September 28, 1944, while flying in his first mission.

Dear Folks,   March 31, 1945

   We have been flying a lot lately and are flying again tomorrow. We flew ten missions this month, more than we have flew before. If we keep on going like that we will be home before long.
   I got two letters from you yesterday, but I didn't get any today. We come in pretty tired tonight and I sure would like to have had a letter. Our last two missions have been pretty tough, but we made it.
   I am going to make this short as I am tired and want to get to bed. We will probably get up pretty early in the morning. I don't guess I will have time to write Pearleta tonight. I guess Sandy is all in tonight he is already in bed and it is only eight thirty. They got us up at twelve thirty last night. We didn't get but about two hours sleep so we aren't going to let that happen again.

                                                            Love, Ray[51]

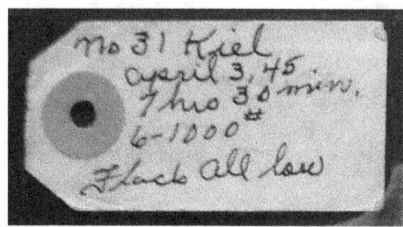

No 31 Kiel [Germany]
April 3, 45
7 hrs 30 min.
6 – 1000# [lbs. bombs]
Flak all low[52]

Dear Folks,   April 4, 1945

   I got several letters from home today and was really glad to get them. I am sorry I haven't written you in the last few days, but they have just been flying the hell out of us. We are not flying tomorrow and I am a little glad of it. I am really tired tonight. I got two letters from Frances, I guess I will just write her to home address. I am going to do a lot of letter writing tomorrow.

                                                            April 5

   I was just so tired last night I quit and went to bed. One of the letters I got from you yesterday was written March 24 and that is really good. That is better than any I have got in a long time.
   Yes I am going to have to get me a new pair of shoes when I get home. I am just wondering if we [will] get home for sun tan time. If they are wearing

khaki then I am going to buy me a nice pair. I guess I will spend a lot of money when I get home.

I must close and write Pearleta.

Love, Ray[53]

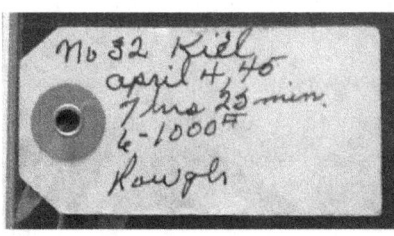

No 32 Kiel [Germany]
April 4, 45
7 hrs 25 min.
6 – 1000# [lbs. bombs]
Rough[54]

Bert Railton, the crew member that moved to waist gunner after the death of Chuck Buda, was wounded in the second-to-last mission. Bert, who was so paralyzed with fear after Chuck's death that Sandy and Ray had to pry him out of the ball turret, had his worst fear realized. Ray explained what happened, "We were on our way home, on the way back. We'd done finished the bomb run and started back, and really we'd started letting down before we got to the English Channel and flew over a few antiaircraft guns for some reason or another. I think everybody ought to knew they were there, because we'd run into them before. But anyway, they shot antiaircraft fire at us, and he took a chunk of shrapnel in his right chest. Course we hauled him back . . . he went down in the waist [of the airplane] there, and Sandy and I was right there and I was just right behind him, and we give him morphine on the way back."[55] Wounded by flak, or anti-aircraft fire, Bert took shrapnel in several places. One piece lodged in his right chest, another piece went through to his lungs, a third piece cut him on his forehead, and the last piece stuck in his arm. Ray recalled visiting him in the hospital, "They loaded him up and took him to a big . . . military hospital. And we went over there to see him. Cause we knew we was fixin' to ship out. And I walked up beside his bed, and what it reminded me of was a dead cow. I could smell him. He wasn't very well taken care of. Well, the military just had too durn many wounded. And they were trying to take [care] of them all. Anyway, he survived. Pop . . . the flight engineer . . . saw him after the war . . . and said Bert loss the use of his right arm. Paralyzed it. And I'll never will forget the way he smelled [in that hospital]."[56]

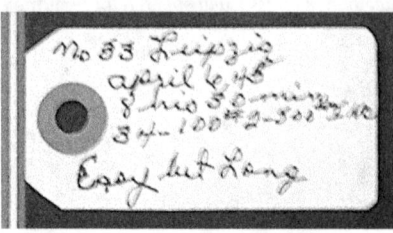

No 33 Leipzig [Germany]
April 6, 45
8 hrs 30 min
34 – 100# [lbs.] 2 – 500# Inc [incendiary bombs]
Easy but long[57]

Ray further described Bert as always "on the edge of the group."[58] Belonging to their crew, but not really a part of it. He recalled that after the war, Ray stayed in touch with all the other guys, but he never heard from Bert. Only through Pop's encounter after the war did the crew receive any news concerning him. Today, Bert may have been diagnosed with post-traumatic stress disorder (PTSD), but at the time, doctors and fellow soldiers did not know how to treat trauma, and the stigma of those who reacted to trauma in certain ways prevented many men from discussing their problems. Bert probably dealt with his problems as best he could, but it makes one wonder how many other young men also suffered silently.

No 34 Newmunster
[Kaltenkirchen, Germany]
April 7, 45
7 hrs 30 min
6 – 1000# [lbs. bombs] Fighters
Bert wounded[59]

Following the completion of his missions, Joseph Ray Perry, of the Ninety-Fifth Bombardment Group (B), received the Oak Leaf Cluster to wear with the Air Medal previously awarded. The citation accompanying the award stated, "For meritorious achievement while participating in heavy bombardment missions in their offensive against the enemy over Continental Europe. The courage, coolness, and skill displayed by these Officers and Enlisted Men upon these occasions reflect great credit upon themselves and the Armed Forces of the United States."[60] Ray made it! Not only did he complete his missions without a scratch, he was rewarded for his bravery and diligence to his duty. Recalling the end of this missions, Ray recounted that he was, "in the tail of that airplane with the same pilot, every mission, and never got a scratch."[61]

A NEW YEAR: 1945

This was quite a feat, not only surviving without any injuries, but flying with the same pilot every time. In fact, four of the original nine crew members completed the thirty-five missions together.[62]

No 35 Egar, Czech
April 8, 45
4 – 1000# [lbs.] 4 – 500# [lbs. bombs]
8 hrs 30 min
The End[63]

Roughly a week later, Ray transferred to a processing center to await his orders home.[64] True to his word, the first chance he got, Ray sent a telegram home telling his parents that he had safely completed all his missions.

Western Union Telegram   24 April 1945

DEAR FOLKS COMPLETED MISSIONS FEELING FINE HOPING TO YOU SOON STOP WRITING LOVE= RAY PERRY[65]

CHAPTER 11
GOING HOME

"HOME ON FURLOUGH AFTER 35 MISSIONS OVER GERMANY —
Staff Sergeant J.R. Perry, veteran of 10 months service with the U.S. 8th Air Force in Europe arrived home Sunday on a 30 day furlough to visit his parents, Mr. and Mrs. Hoyt Perry of Paint Creek and other relatives and friends. S-Sgt. Perry was a tail gunner on a B-17 bomber and completed 35 missions over Germany during the ten months he was overseas. He has been awarded the Air Medal with five Clusters. A graduate of Paint Creek high school, he enlisted in the Army Air Force in December 1943. At the end of his furlough, S-Sgt. Perry will report at Santa Anna, Calif., for reassignment."

—Haskell (TX) Free Press, June 1, 1945[1]

Ray recalled his activities after completing his tour, "I finished my missions on the 8th day of April, '45 . . . I was just laying around there in the bunk and waiting for my orders to go wherever they was going to send me to catch a boat to come home. On the 12th day of April I was laying there in my bunk and the loudspeaker . . . announced that the president had died. I'll never forget that. I caught a boat in South Hampton, England . . . it was an old converted refrigerated boat, they put bunks in there and made it a transport boat . . . nothing fancy at all . . . they had bunks down in that thing five high, and for some reason or another I drew that top bunk, and I'd have to tie myself in it with a GI belt, you know, if we got into rough seas, and we did."[2] According to his service record, Ray left England on April 30, 1945.[3] "We joined a convoy out there, off of England, I don't know how far out there we got with that convoy, but then we started across the Atlantic. It took me 13 days to get across the Atlantic. But anyway, about the second day, after we joined that convoy, a German . . . submarine . . . fired a couple of torpedoes through that formation. It didn't hit nobody . . . 'course we had our escorts . . . two or three or four destroyers . . . dropped . . . depth charges . . . I don't know whether they hit anything or not."[4]

While in route to the states, news came that Germany surrendered on May 8, 1945. Ray remembered, "everybody celebrated. Course, all you can do is whoop and holler . . . no cognac (laughs), and you couldn't go anywhere (laughs)."[5] Although this news was greatly praised and brought relief to many, America still found itself embroiled in a conflict in the Pacific theater with Japan. Many of these bomber crews worried that they would return home, only to be sent to the Pacific. Ray continued with his narrative of his trip, "[We] paddled right by the Statue of Liberty, and went over there and docked on the New Jersey side. And they put us on a barge or something, paddled us across there to Camp Shanks, New York."[6] Ray's ship docked on American soil on May 12, 1945. His first thoughts were of his family, and as soon as he could, he sent a telegram home.[7]

Western Union Telegram   May 13, 1945

ARRIVED SAFELY EXPECT TO SEE YOU SOON DON'T ATTEMPT TO CONTACT OR WRITE ME HERE LOVE RAY PERRY.[8]

The military proved expeditious at getting their servicemen home for their furloughs, but soon was not soon enough for Ray, "See after we came back to the United States . . . we weren't there [Camp Shanks, New York] but just a day or two . . . they put us on troop trains. We went from New York to Chicago and Chicago down to St. Louis and St. Louis to the Fort Worth-Dallas area and then to San Antonio . . . They gave me a 30-day furlough, so, I caught a bus in San Antonio, and I stood up all the way, there weren't no place to sit . . . the bus was full. And [the driver] said, Yeah, you can ride, if you want to . . . [I stood up but eventually] sat down there in the door steps. 'Course I had a B-4 bag and a duffel bag, full of all my junk. We got to Stamford . . . I told him where I was going, there was a county road off of 277 that turns east,

Ray home on leave.

and I said if you'll let me out there . . . 'course I had a ticket to go to Haskell [another nine miles north], if you will let me out on the county road . . . he agreed . . . and he let me out there. There I was with those two big ol' bags, I started walking down that ol' county road and a feller . . . come along and saw me, picked me up . . . [and dropped me off at my Grandad's]. Grandad loaded me up and carried me [to my house]."[9] Ray explained that his parents had no telephone, so it was a surprise when he showed up on that Sunday morning. Ray's service record recorded that he was on furlough from May 19 until June 22, 1945.[10]

Dear Folks,   May 28, 1945

Received your letter today and was glad to hear from you. I was doubting if you would have time to answer while you were home. Guess you are having a swell time.

So you got thirty days. You lucky lug. Glad to hear that combat men are getting more than the plain 15th air force. By the way, how was the Hollywood outfit? You boys must have had it soft. Did they have any of that stuff they call "flak" over there? No, I'm kiddin'.

> *Now to be serious. Ever since I left the states, I had been wondering where Melvin Thomason went to. So when I got down here, I wrote his mother. Received the answer today. He has been M.I.A. since April 10th, was on his 32nd mission when he went down. Only two men were seen to come out, so I doubt if he had a chance. He was flying waist that day, though. He was stationed around Foggia somewhere, probably not far from me, but I didn't know it.*
>
> *Old Burwick is here. He is in his last week now. We have pulled one good drunk already. Rogers (from Colorado City) is also here. Troy is in my barracks. You will run into everybody you ever knew if you come down here.*
>
> *Now, as far this place, it's hell. I'm in my second week now and damn it the work they are giving us. Speeches and more speeches.*
>
> *Yep, we came down here from Santa Ana on a troop train. Some enlisted man that is coming down here for C.I.S. will be in charge though. You are less on your own.*
>
> *Rex Fleming was just in to see me. Remember him at Dyersburg. His twin was on my crew. He still can't believe that Max is dead. Sure feel sorry for him.*
>
> *Guess I'd better stop for now. Don't tear up anything in Haskell, and be damn sure to go see my folks. Answer when you can.*
>
> *As Ever, Preston*[11]

Ray's orders stated that after his furlough, he was to report to Santa Ana Army Air Base in California. Ray figured that the military would put him on B-29s and send them to the Pacific theater, "That was the plans, but before they got that done, they'd done figured out they was going to drop those old big bombs."[12] All indications showed that Japan could not win the war, but fighting in the Pacific proved still heavy. Between mid-April and mid-July 1945, the Allied casualties added up to one-half of the previous three full years of combat in the Pacific.[13] At the end of July 1945, Truman called for Japan's surrender or he would be forced to launch "prompt and utter destruction."[14] Japan rejected the peace offering, and, consequently, sealed their fate. The first atomic bomb, "Little Boy," was loaded on to the *Enola Gay* bomber, piloted by Col. Paul Tibbets, and was dropped on Hiroshima, Japan, on August 6, 1945. This one bomb devastated 90 percent of the city and killed 80,000 people instantly. Japan still would not surrender. On August 9, 1945, "Fat Man" was loaded on to the *Bockscar* bomber, and Maj. Charles Sweeney dropped it on the city of Nagasaki, Japan. Japan formally surrendered on August 15, 1945.[15] So, in June 1945, while Truman and his advisors hashed out what to do in the Pacific, Ray took advantage of sunny California.

Dear Folks,   *[Santa Ana, California] June 23, 1945*

I made it fine. I got here about five Friday afternoon (yesterday). I have already found Sandy and some of the other boys. I don't have much time so I will close and write more later.

Love, Ray[16]

Dear Folks,   *[Santa Ana, California] June 25, 1945*

I am sorry I haven't written you more, but we have really been busy. Our first five days are busy ones. They check our records and give us a physical. I have to go to a lecture in a few minutes.

I don't know if you got my card from El Paso or not, I couldn't find any stamps so I just sent it free. We had a three hour lay over there. I got a seat in Sweetwater, so I didn't have to stand up very long.

I told you I had found Sandy. I don't guess I had been here two hours when I found him. I went to the mess hall and there he was. He fooled me, he is still single. Sandy hasn't heard from any of the crew yet either. Just as soon as I got to Los Angeles I phoned Bert's mother and she said as far as she knew Bert is still in England. Sandy and I are going to see her the first chance we get. I don't guess we will get to go until this weekend.

This is really a nice base. I would like to stay here. The food is really good.

I went to see about getting out of the army and they told me they were not giving out any agricultural discharges now that the point system is in use. I may get out on that before long if they lower them any. We have got two more battle stars now so that makes us ten more points. Sandy only likes three points having enough. I guess I will like seven. So it may not be so long at that. I have heard they are going to lower them the first of July.

I don't think I am going be an instructor I don't much want it. I can get a lot of other jobs. They want a lot of M.P.s down at San Antonio so I think I will try to get that. I don't much like being an M.P., but that is just about as close to home as I think I can get. I am going to try to stay here for quiet [sic] a while and maybe I can get out. If I stay here it won't take so long to get out if they lower the points.

Love, Ray[17]

Dear Folks, [Santa Ana, California] June 28, 1945

I am finished here now, but guess I will stay around a few days before I ship. I am hoping I will be sent to San Antonio, they told me I probably would. I guess I am going to be an M.P. I signed up for it. They didn't want to let me in because I have too much rank, but they finally did. Another boy that is in my barracks in England signed up for it, too. I sure hope we both get sent to the same place and I guess we will.

We have found several of the boys that was in England with us. Monk, our bombardier, is here. One of the guys came in my barracks today while I was asleep. He said he found out some way I was here and had been looking for me for a couple days.

I hear they are going to lower the points to seventy eight and they do that is going to make me mad for I have seventy six. It looks to me like they would lower them to seventy five anyway. That is going to be awful just liking two points.

We have been going to some of the places out here you hear so much about. We went to Los Angeles and Hollywood. Last night we went to Long Beach and no telling where to tonight. We decided we had better see a few of them while we are here or we probably won't be out here again. When we were at Long Beach we could see Catalina island way off on the ocean. While we were in Hollywood we went to the Hollywood canteen and saw Kay Kieser and his band and a couple of movie stars. The Canteen is a pretty place.

I am sending you a money order for $100.00 I will try to send some more as soon as I get my pay for June. I think we get that Saturday. I got a little over fifty dollars for the travel pay. I made a little in the deal.

I haven't got any mail yet. I thought I would get some today for Sandy got a letter yesterday and he got here a day before I did.

I guess I better close for now.

Love, Ray[18]

Dear Folks,   [Santa Ana, California] *June 30, 1945*

I will write you a few lines this afternoon. I don't have time to write much 'cause Sandy and I are going to Long Beach in a few minutes. Sandy is shipping out Monday, he is going somewhere in Kansas. I guess I will get sent somewhere in Texas. Sandy asked for Nebraska and got sent about three hundred miles from home.

I am sending another money order, this one is for $80.00. I didn't get any flying pay for this month. I am supposed to get it. I guess I will get it a little later on.

I still haven't got any mail. I wish I could get some. Sandy has got a couple of letters, he got one from Frances. I thought for sure I would get some today.

I must close as Sandy is about ready.

Love, Ray[19]

Dear Folks,   [Santa Ana, California] *July 4, 1945*

I got your letter and was very glad to get it. I had begun to think I wasn't going to get a letter from you while I was here. I won't be here much longer now. I am shipping out Friday. I am going to San Antonio. There is no use to write me anymore until you hear from me again. I am glad to leave this place. This is no place for a soldier, everything is too expensive.

This has really been a quiet fourth for me. I really would like to be home now and take in the rodeo. Have you gone to it any?

I got a letter from Frances too and should write her, but I am just going to wait until I get to San Antonio.

There is a boy going to San Antonio with me that come back on the boat with me. I guess I am pretty lucky staying with some of the guys I know.

I hope you got my two money orders O.K. Be sure and let me know if you did.

I hear they are going to lower the point to 74 sometime this month. I sure hope they do. I have 76. I sure would like to get out and land me a good job before all the other guys get out.

Did the pictures Frances and I had made come out any good? I will really be glad to see them. You can send one to me as soon as I get stationed again.

I bet the house really does look good. I sure would like to get home and see it. I don't think it will be very long before I get another furlough. And not <u>too</u> long before I get out.

I must close for now.

Love, Ray[20]

The rodeo that Ray referred to was the annual TCR, Texas Cowboy Reunion, held in Stamford, Texas. It began in 1930 and continues today. The rodeo lasts four days and always falls on the fourth of July. Besides the traditional rodeo events, the TCR included wild cow milking, wild mare race, fiddlers contest, cowboy poetry, chuckwagon cookoff, and many more events celebrating the cowboy way of life. As its name portrays, this event was a time for cowboys to get together and reminisce about the past. Ray loved this time of the year, and besides during the war years, he rarely missed a performance throughout his life.[21]

Dear Folks,   [San Antonio, Texas] *July 11, 1945*

I got here a couple of days ago and was going to write you but we had to move so I decided I would send you my permanent address.

I am out here at Kelly field and guess I will be here for quiet [sic] a while. This is really a nice place and I think I am going to like it here. There isn't many men here now, but they are getting them in all the time.

I don't know when I will get my furlough. I guess it will be quiet [sic] a while yet for there isn't many men here and they can't let very many go at once.

It is really hot here now, I guess it is at home too. It was pretty cool in California. I thought it would be warm there but a lot of the guys were wearing their wool clothes. I had a lot of fun out there, but everything is pretty expensive. That is no country for a soldier.

I did get me some more sun tan clothes. When we were at Santa Ana they gave us two more suits and when I got here I went to the P.X. and bought me two pair of pants. They cost $2.85 a pair, that is pretty cheap isn't it?

If I get a weekend off I may try to sneak off up home if I can. If I go I will hitch-hike for it takes too long going by bus. I have a long lay over in Abilene. I think I can make it a lot faster by thumbing it.

> *One of the boys I went into the army with is here. I saw him in Santa Ana, but didn't know he was here. There is several guys here I know.*
>
> *I guess I had better close for now.*
>
> Love, Ray[22]

Western Union Telegram   *July 18, 1945*

> DEAR FOLKS I WONT BE HOME ON MY FURLOUGH AS SOON AS I THOUGHT I GUESS IT WILL BE ABOUT THE FIRST OF AUGUST I AM SORRY I HAVEN'T WRITTEN SOONER BUT I WILL EXPLAIN A LITTLE LATER ON WE MADE IT BACK JUST FINE LOVE RAY.[23]

Ray's military records showed he went on furlough not long after his telegram, from July 27, 1945, to August 12, 1945.[24]

Three days after arriving back at his post at Lackland Air Force Base, adjacent to Kelly Field, in San Antonio, news came that Japan had formally surrendered. The war was officially over! Ray recalled, "The day the war ended, we were in a picture show there in . . . downtown San Antonio theater . . . and they went to blowing those sirens . . . we thought [the war] was fixing to end . . . you talk about a celebration! They fenced off a big area downtown . . . a lot of blocks . . . I never saw so many people. Well, they was just crazy, you know. Everybody was drunk. We were trying to get back on the base the next morning, you know, after daylight (laughs)."[25] Although the treaty ending the war in the Pacific would not take place until September 2, 1945, to these civilians and soldiers the war was over and done!

While in San Antonio, Ray met up with lots of his buddies. Of course, it was never hard for Ray to make friends. Ray recalled one friend in particular: "Raymond Reddell was an old friend of mine; we went into service together and we trained together, and he went with one bomb group and I went with the 95th. And we never did see one another anymore after we were training, but when we come home we both got together. We run into one another, and we were both down there. He was from Abilene."[26] With money he had saved from his pay, Ray bought his first car, "I'd come home nearly every weekend, and he'd ride with me to Abilene and I'd drop him off and I'd come on up here [to Paint Creek]."[27]

GOING HOME

At Lackland, Ray was assigned to oversee the shooting range, "That was my duty, which didn't amount to a durn thing, because there wasn't anybody hardly wanting to use the shooting range anymore. But that was my duty, and I just hung around there until I accumulated enough points to be discharged, which was in October 1945."[28] Ray's official discharge date was October 18, 1945, and according to Ray, he "got in the car and come home."[29]

CHAPTER 12
LIFE GOES ON

"*Married in Double Ring Ceremony* – *The First Methodist Church of Haskell was the scene recently of a double ring ceremony uniting in marriage Amelia June Holt, daughter of Mr. and Mrs. J.C. Holt, and Joseph Ray Perry, son of Mr. and Mrs. Hoyt Perry of Haskell.*"

—*Abilene (TX) Reporter News*, July 9, 1947[1]

Ray came home to Paint Creek in October 1945. He felt a little unsettled, not really sure what he wanted to do. He explained the feeling, "When I got discharged out of the Air Force . . . me and another old boy here we got in the car and we went down to College Station. I was going to go to school, go to college down at A&M. Well at that time, you were required to be in the Corps, and I said thunderation, I don't want to *play* soldier, you know, I just got through being a soldier."[2] At first Ray was not sure farming was where his future lay, "When we were discharged, the government or the Department of Defense, I guess . . . paid us a hundred dollars a month, you know, for a few months. Well, a hundred dollars back in 1945 was a lot of money."[3] He helped his dad out on the farm, kicking around, spending time with friends. Not much had changed back home. Ray recalled, "My daddy did not have electricity when I come home in 1945. Didn't have it when we married in '47. It was so far down there REA [Rural Electrification Administration] never had got down there."[4]

When asked about his feelings toward the German people after the war, Ray had an interesting insight, "Oh, I like the German people . . . course,

I wasn't in . . . personal contact [with the German people]. I don't think I was bitter at the German people themselves. Now I was the Japanese . . . the Japanese were vicious people. They treated our prisoners terrible. And the Germans—course, I talked to several airmen who were shot down over Germany and were held prisoners, and . . . one guy over here at Stamford, he got shot down on his second mission, and he said, 'They like to starved us to death.' You know, [the Germans] didn't have much food . . . he said he ate potatoes . . . and they marched them all over Germany, but they didn't just shoot him just because he couldn't stay up, you know. But the Japanese did . . . on that Bataan Death March."[5]

Ray paused to collect his thoughts and continued, "We had a boy from here . . . from Haskell that was shot down pretty early. He was in the [training] classes just behind me. I was just ahead of him . . . and I had got word from my mother where he was, what air base he was [at] in England, and I was fixing to go see him, and he got shot down. Got shot down out in the edge of the North Sea and they ditched. They ditched that old airplane out there in the sea and they managed to get in lifeboats. And the air-sea rescue from England was on their way out there to pick them up and the Germans got out there before they did . . . and carried them back and held them prisoners. They were treated decent, I guess you would say. Course, they didn't like what they was having to put up with, but at least they didn't mistreat them. [The Germans] went by the Geneva Convention. They pretty well abided by that . . . [the Japanese] were terrible."[6] The young man Ray spoke about was Tommie Davis. Tommie was released in May 1945. The *Haskell Free Press* printed the following article in the June 8, 1945, edition:

> Sgt. Tommie Davis, son of Mr. and Mrs. Tom Davis of this city, came home Sunday, one month and four days from the date he was liberated from a German prison camp at Moosburg, after being held seven months as a prisoner. Sgt. Davis, tail gunner on a B-17 was on his second mission, over Berlin, when his ship was badly damaged over the target and later landing in the North Sea. All the ship's crew were unhurt, and after being dropped a small boat by the English Air Service Rescue they drifted 24 hours before being spotted by the Nazis. The young airman was first held at Stalag Luft 4, was moved in January to Nuremburg, and eight weeks later to Moosburg.[7]

After Tommie returned home, he eventually became the postmaster for Haskell.[8]

Ray was a little lost at first after being discharged, "I would just go to town on Saturday night . . . just pretty well behaving myself, you know, for a 20-year old . . . [My friends and I] tried to rodeo a little bit, you know, rodeo cowboy. I had a horse and a saddle, and we'd try to rope at the rodeos and things like that. They were good friends of mine."[9]

Then in 1946, Ray found the love of his life, "Amelia . . . was working over at Stamford at the old hospital. She got her a job over there, and there was one of [my] friends that was going with a girl that was working with Amelia."[10] Although Amelia and Ray grew up relatively close to one another, they had not met before Ray left for the war. Amelia June Holt was the third of nine children born to J. C. and Clara Holt, who farmed between Rule and Haskell.[11] As Ray told it, "[I] had some old buddies I was runnin' [with] . . . [one] Saturday morning a friend of mine said, 'Would you like to have a date tonight?' I wasn't too durn interested. He said, 'There's a girl over there at the hospital that you ought to meet — you ought to go with.' And I said, 'Well, what are we going to do?' He said, 'We're going to go out to Tuxedo to a softball game.' And [I said] I guess so, I'll go. Well, we went over there, and of course, here come these two girls and I knew immediately when I saw her that she's the one I wanted (laughs). That's right. Wasn't any question about it. And we went on to the ballgame and I asked her for a date the next Saturday to go to the picture show. But anyway, I went to get her there at the hospital the next Saturday and she wasn't there. Dadgum!" He laughed and continued, "She stood me up. I began to question around about where she was at, and all this and that, and she and

Ray on Stormy

two or three other girls had gone to that picture show that I was going to take her to. Well . . . you take a 20-year-old boy that's pretty proud of himself, you know, that didn't suit him at all (laughs). So, I found out where she was and I just pulled my car right up in front of that picture show and sat there until she come out. So, she come out and said, 'Oh, my goodness.' She claimed she forgot it, but I tell you what, that's just as bad as standing me up. But anyway, we got past that and, you know . . . I went to dating her pretty regular . . . and we hit it off pretty good . . . she finally took me up there to show me to her folks. And shortly after that, well—I knew we was getting kind of serious about this situation and I decided I needed to take her down to see my folks."[12]

Ray recalled that first meeting with a smile, "Her folks was up there where they had electricity and running water." Ray's parents did not have these amenities out in the country. Ray was a little concerned about how Amelia would react to their simple home. "But anyway, I had bought a '41 model Buick. It was a fine automobile. It was a straight-8. Had two carburetors setting up on top of it (laughs) . . . I loaded Amelia in that car and we started down to where my folks lived. See, it was 22 miles from Stamford down there and it was all dirt roads. Wasn't no highways down in there at that time. And Amelia thought I was carrying her to the boonies . . . she had never been down in that country . . . but anyway, after that, you know, we went to making plans. We married in June of '47."[13] Ray and Amelia married in the Haskell Methodist Church on June 29, 1947.[14] According to an article that ran in the *Abilene Reporter News*, the wedding was beautiful. Phrases such as, "an altar decorated with greenery and baskets of white gladioluses and tall lighted white tapers," "a medley of love songs were played . . . the bride wore a period gown of traditional white satin, fashioned with long shirred sleeves, fitted bodice . . . full shirred skirt just touching the floor. A full length veil [and] . . . bridesmaids . . . wore identical floor length dresses of eyelet embroidery in pastel shades." Amelia had chosen her sister, Tommie Holt, as maid-of-honor, and another sister, Mrs. Edwin T. Jeter as matron-of-honor. She also had Mrs. Roy Pitman and Ray's sister, Frances Perry, as bridesmaids. Ray chose his brother Gene Perry as his best man, and Amelia's brother, J. C. Holt, Jr., and his other brother, Don Perry, as groomsmen. The couple took a honeymoon trip to Nebraska, Wyoming, Colorado, and New Mexico.[15]

After returning home, Ray tried his hand at a few jobs, a laundry, farming, and then a drought hit the Paint Creek area. So, Ray took a job in Wink, Texas, for Shell Pipeline. At the time, Amelia was very pregnant with their first child, so she could not go with him. On June 27, 1948, Amelia gave birth

Amelia and Ray

to a baby girl that they named Milla. When the baby was six weeks old, they joined Ray in Wink. Amelia remembered that Ray was a wonderful dad and he loved his little girl. After about a year, Amelia said Ray came home from work one day and said, "I'm going home. You wanna go with me?" She said that Ray was always a farmer at heart, and she did not have to think twice, "Give me a minute to pack my things." And with that they moved back to Haskell County where they have been ever since.[16]

Milla was always very bright in school and was a talented basketball player. Amelia remembered, "Ray and I were always at their school events, no matter how much farming needed to be done, Ray put his kids first." Milla grew up calling her dad "Honey." Amelia explained, "I called Ray 'honey' all the time, so Milla thought that was his name. She called him that until she went to school and the kids made fun of her."[17] Milla would go on to be extremely successful, graduating from Texas Tech in less than three years, working as a dietician for Hendrick Medical Center, then taking a job with Baylor Medical in Dallas. She changed positions at Baylor from dietician to fundraiser for the hospital before retiring. She came out of retirement to work for United Surgical Partners International (USPI) until she retired a second time at the end of 2017. Ray was extremely proud of her accomplishments.[18]

Ray's son, James Richard "Rick" Perry was born on March 4, 1950. Ray recalled Rick's achievements after graduating high school from Paint Creek, "[Rick] went down to A&M and he wanted to be a veterinarian, or that was his ambition, but then he got involved in the Corps, the military, and he loved the military. And he called us one day and said, 'Mother, I think I'm going to drop out of school.' That kind of excited Amelia. And he said, 'No, I don't mean quit school, I mean when I graduate, well, I'm going to go into the Air Force.' Course, I was glad he did that. He wanted to be a pilot, and he was. He managed to do what I had ambitions of doing at one time."[19] Rick went on to fly C-130s and was stationed a large part of the time at Dyess Air Force Base in Abilene, Texas, not far from home. Ray explained, "He was stationed there, but Rick was single and he was on rotation an awful lot. He was all over Europe, well, Turkey and Saudi Arabia and Iraq."[20]

Ray proved to be a successful farmer over the years. As he explained, "There were some years in there in the sixties and seventies that we made some good cotton crops, and of course I've always had some cattle."[21] Ray began to acquire land around the area. He explained that fence improvements had to be made immediately to keep the cattle in, "Rick come home in '77 out of the Air Force, and one of his A&M classmates had gone to work for me. [Rick]

The Perry Family: Rick, Ray, Amelia, and Milla

wanted to cowboy . . . Well, I put Rick and [Kenny Stephens] down there one summer . . . building fence. And I think that's what made a politician out of Rick. [Because] I kept him and old Kenny down there all summer long building fence, and that's pretty tough!"²² Eventually the Perrys ended up ranching more than farming, "Course, we always had a lot of farmland, but we pretty well quit cotton and went to wheat and cattle. This all happened about the time Rick come home . . . He didn't like to drive tractors. He was a good cowboy. Old Rick, he'd get on a horse to work cattle, gather cattle, whatever he was doing, and Rick was a lot better on horseback than I was."²³ Rick ended up with a successful career in politics, serving three terms in the Texas House of Representatives, then as Agriculture Commissioner until he was elected Lieutenant Governor of Texas, then became Governor of Texas from 2000 until 2015. Rick ran for President of the United States twice without success, but afterwards served under President Donald Trump as Secretary of Energy.²⁴

Ray was also a leader in the community and local politics. In 1968, Ray ran for county commissioner and won, "I was elected county commissioner. I took office [the] first of January 1969."²⁵ Ray held this office for the next

Four Generations of Perry Men: Hoyt, Ray, Rick, and Griffin

Don Perry

twenty-eight years. He only relinquished this office due to his failing eyesight. Ray also served ten years on the Paint Creek School Board. Not only had Ray attended Paint Creek School, but both his children graduated as Pirates. Other local offices held included six years on the board for the West Central Texas Council of Government, with two years as acting president. Ray was instrumental in organizing the Paint Creek Water Corporation, and served several years on the Board and as president two times.[26]

Ray's family grew with the addition of grandchildren and great-grandchildren. Milla had a daughter, Caitlyn Jones. Rick went on to marry Anita Thigpen from Haskell and they welcomed a son, Griffin, and a daughter, Sydney. Griffin and wife, Meredith, have two daughters, Ella and Piper.[27] These grandchildren and great-grandchildren kept that sparkle alive in Ray's eye. He loved his family and was proud of every one of them.

Ray's younger brother, Don Perry, ended up in Germany during the 1950s. Don recounted how he ended up there, "I graduated from college, WTS [West Texas State]. Went to Fort Sill, Oklahoma. Sent to Germany about ten years after the war, in 1955. Went over on a boat and came back on a boat. I was a forward observer on an artillery battery. Parts of Germany were still torn up."[28] According to Ray, after Don had been over in Germany he told him, "Ya'll just made a mess of that place!"[29]

Keeping up with the crew after the war brought joy to Ray and Amelia throughout their almost seventy years together. Ray loved visiting with these buddies who had become like brothers. Amelia remarked, "We kept in touch with everyone of Ray's crew members, the only one we ever lost touch with was a man . . . Bert Railton. He lived in California and went back there, I suppose. We never did keep up with him. But the other boys we kept in touch with. Christmas cards, visiting in their homes, spend the night with some of them."[30] Amelia explained that they tried to make contact with Bert, but he never replied to their cards or letters. It was not until Pop Bowman happened upon him and shared with the rest of the crew that Bert had lost the use of his arm after he was wounded on their thirty-fourth mission.

Rick was just as proud of his dad's accomplishments as Ray was about Rick's. Amelia said that Rick kept a portrait of his dad in the governor's office during the fifteen years he held that position.[31] During Rick's term as Governor of Texas, he held a Ninety-Fifth Bomb Group celebration in Austin. Ray remembered the event, "He invited the families, not just the members, but the families of the members of the crew down at Austin, and the co-pilot and I were the only two there. The navigator was Norman Sacks. He was so sick he couldn't come."[32] Not only did Ray and Amelia keep up with the old crew members, and after the veterans passed on, they kept in contact with their children. They all had a special bond indeed. By 2017, Ray was the last living member of the crew of the *Heavy Date*. All others had all passed on, but the legacy they left behind lasted through the memories of their families and through their stories that they shared with others.

EPILOGUE

"Returning to Normandy – I am so proud of my dad and the many soldiers like him who fought that devastating war. I have longed for the day I could return with him to the place where he and his fellow soldiers demonstrated their utter devotion to freedom, and their sacrificial love for fellow man."

—Rick Perry, *Austin (TX) American-Statesman*, June 6, 2000[1]

Rick had the opportunity, while he was in the Air Force, to visit Horham Airfield in England, the base Ray had been stationed at while overseas. Amelia showed me a brick and explained, "That is a brick from one of the Quonset huts that Ray lived in . . . Rick went over there . . . and he brought that all wrapped up in newspaper for his dad."[2]

In June 1999, Rick and his parents embarked on a trip to Europe. This would be the first time Ray had returned overseas in fifty-four years. Rick had always wanted to do this for his dad, and he spent a lot of time planning the places they would go. Of course, they revisited the base at Horham, England, walked along the beach of Normandy, and traversed many sites around Europe that had importance in World War II.[3] Ray spoke with pride as he related this trip. He was proud to revisit those sites, especially with his son, who also served in the military.

When they visited Horham, Ray was surprised at what little was left of the base and familiar landmarks from 1945. The Green Dragon Pub that Ray visited as a young GI in England was one of the places Ray wanted to re-visit, "It was still there when Amelia and I . . . [went] over there in 1999, and it's closed, but it was still there."[4] Another stop that Ray wanted to make was at the home of the older couple that was so hospitable to Ray and his pilot, Barney, "I don't know why . . . I didn't write [their names] down. I'd have give anything in the world if we'd a had that when we went back to England and I could have gone over there. I couldn't even find the place anymore . . . but I would love to have gone back and see if any of the family was still there." Ray said the English were always a welcoming people, and his trip back, fifty-four years later was no exception, "They really like us. And they still do. When we went back over there we were well received by the English people. They're good people."[5]

As Ray described his visit to his old base that held the Ninety-Fifth bomb group, he lamented, "There's not much of it. There's just a short piece . . . of the main runway. They're farming it all, and the old hospital building is still there and they're turning it into a museum. There's some of those farmers around there that bought it . . . We went to [the museum], and they've got some stuff that was left there . . . none of the old huts are still there . . . but the old bathhouse [was]."[6] He continued, "There was a big ammunition and bomb storage area . . . in these bunkers, you know these bunkers that were covered in dirt. Besides the bathhouse I was telling you about that was still there in our area, the old bomb shelter was still there. Course, it's all concrete and covered over with dirt and grown up in weeds and trees."[7]

Ray standing in front of the Bomber Glass Monument at Duxford Airbase in Cambridgeshire, England.

EPILOGUE

Ray went on to say, "Some farmer that had acquired [the bathhouse] after the war, he was a hog farmer and he'd turned that old shower into a farrowing house."[8] "Some of those people that acquired [the hospital building] . . . [are] turning it into a museum . . . they're still pretty enthusiastic about the 95th," remarked Ray.[9] In fact, the museum, named The 95th Bomb Group Museum, is the official U.K. museum dedicated to the bomb group that was so instrumental in bringing victory to England and the Allies.[10]

The church that the crew of the *Heavy Date* attended the day after Chuck's death was still there. When the B-17s landed at Horham, they passed over the steeple above that church. If they carried wounded or dead crewman, they dropped a flare to signal that further aid was needed when they landed. Rick was so intrigued by this story and seeing this church, that he had a painting commissioned showing a B-17 flying over the church steeple as it was coming in to land. He presented this to his dad when he hosted the Ninety-Fifth Bomb Group at the Texas Capitol, and it hung in the capitol until Rick left office.[11]

When asked how it felt to revisit these places, Ray replied, "Oh, it brought back a lot of memories." He went further on to say that he had photos he showed Rick of what these areas looked like when he was there.[12] Amelia recalled a special moment for her when they visited the Cambridge Cemetery and stood before the wall that had all the names of the Americans that had lost their lives in England. She said Ray searched for his buddy, Chuck Buda's name, and when he found it, he walked up and placed his hand over the name.[13]

Ray and Dr. Thomas M. Hatfield, who accompanied the Perry family on their trip to Europe, sitting at the train depot at Diss, England.

Dr. Thomas M. Hatfield, from the University of Texas at Austin, accompanied the Perry family on their journey through Europe. As they visited areas that Ray saw during his war years, Dr. Hatfield asked him questions. One question that kept coming up was if Ray was scared, "I told him I could never remember really being scared. I know I was. Had to be. But I had control of it." This sentiment was reminiscent of what Jimmy Stewart said about fear, that you had to master it or it would master you, and affect those around you. Ray's sense of duty was stronger than his sense of fear, "I was ready to go anytime that we were assigned to fly."[14]

While at Horham, England, Ray ran into a man named Allen Johnson. Mr. Johnson had been a child of six or seven during the war, and hung around the base with the soldiers. When Ray reminisced about a buzz bomb that exploded close to the base, and how all the GIs ran for cover in a ditch, he could not quite recall where the bomb landed. Mr. Johnson spoke up and said, "Oh, yeah, I know exactly where that hit." Ray was amazed that Mr. Johnson remembered that particular buzz bomb hitting over there. But what an impression the American soldiers with their huge B-17 bombers must have made on a little boy who grew up during war.[15]

In 2000, Rick wrote an article published in the *Austin American-Statesman* that remembered the young men that sacrificed so much on June

Allen Johnson as a boy on the Base. He is third from the left, right in the middle.

Ella and Ray

6, 1944, D-Day. He titled his article, "Returning to Normandy," and in the article, he related how these men did their duty and in essence preserved the freedom that Americans enjoy. Describing these courageous young men, Rick wrote, "They did not complain, because it was their job. To this day, those who remain keep a humble, quiet aura to themselves. They seek not recognition for what they did, only a simple assurance: that America never let down its guard, that it always strive to keep the peace."[16]

In early 2017, Ray's health failed. He entered the Hendrick Hospice Care Center in Abilene, Texas, shortly before his ninety-second birthday. In fact, he celebrated this birthday, the last he would see, in this facility. Surrounded by family, Ray looked upon the legacy he left behind, so very proud of his family and their accomplishments, but more importantly in the people they had become. During his stay at Hendrick Hospice Care Center, someone snapped a picture of Ray lying in his hospital bed, holding hands with his great-granddaughter, Ella. When looking at this photograph, Rick's words from the end of his article in 2000 come back clearly, "They were so brave that day. They changed the world as we know it. I hope my dad sees that in the eyes of a young French child, in the gleam of a young British lad or in the admiring gaze of his own grateful son."[17] Ray would tell you very quickly that he wasn't a hero, he was just doing his duty. And I like to think, that as he held his great-granddaughter's hand, as he felt her youthful strength, just as his life was ebbing away, that he felt great contentment for a job well done. Because of his service, and many others just like him, his family can live in peace and know freedom.

Ray passed away on April 27, 2017. His funeral program said it best, "Joseph Ray Perry, a lifetime resident of Haskell County, has moved to a new address."[18] He is not really gone, because his service, his dedication, his love for his God, his family, and his country, will be remembered long after his time on this Earth.

ENDNOTES

FOREWORD

1. "Eighth Air Force Combat Losses," online article, *Taphilo.com*, found online at: http://www.taphilo.com/history/8thaf/8aflosses.shtml [accessed February 28, 2018].

2. Since Ray's eightieth birthday, a group of Ray's friends have gotten together at Lynne and Cliff Teinert's Collins Creek Ranch on or about April 23 each year to celebrate his birthday. It will continue on as a celebration of a life well lived.

CHAPTER 1

1. "A Happy New Year," *Haskell (TX) Press*, January 4, 1890, page 2, col. 1–2, HTML edition, archived at: https://swco-ir.tdl.org/swco-ir/bitstream/handle/10605/2367/Haskell_Free_Press__1890-0104.pdf?sequence=1&isAllowed=y [accessed July 11, 2017].

2. 1850 U.S. census, Harrison County, Texas, population schedule, p. 115A (handwritten), dwelling 931, family 936, J. Perry; digital image, Ancestry.com website, citing National Archives microfilm publication M432_911, image 234, found online at: http://www.ancestry.com [accessed July 11, 2017].

3. "John Michael Perry (1856-1934)," Find A Grave database, memorial 40993105, Willow Cemetery, Haskell, Haskell County, Texas, created by Carla Carlton Young, found online at: http://findagrave.com [accessed July 11, 2017].

4. Frederick Law Olmsted, *A Journey Through Texas: Or a Saddle-Trip on the Southwestern Frontier* (Lincoln, NE: University of Nebraska Press, 2004), 67.

5. Ibid.

6   1860 U.S. census, Beat 12, Panola County, Texas, population schedule, Grand Bluff Post Office, p. 58 (handwritten), dwelling 388, family 388, John W. Perry; digital image, Ancestry.com website, citing National Archives microfilm publication M653, roll 1302, found online at: *http://www.ancestry.com* [accessed July 11, 2017].

7   David Park, "Nineteenth Texas Infantry," *Handbook of Texas Online*, Texas State Historical Association, uploaded on April 11, 2011, modified on June 8, 2011, found online at: *http://www.tshaonline.org/handbook/online/articles/qkn20* [accessed July 11, 2017].

8   "J. W. Perry, Pvt., Co. E, 19th Texas Inf.," Confederate Compiled Service Records of Confederate Soldiers Who Served in Organizations from the State of Texas 1861, found online at: *https://www.fold3.com/images/14584590* [accessed August 12, 2017].

9   1870 U.S. census, Panola County, Texas, population schedule, Beat 2, Grand Bluff Post Office, p. 273[A] (stamped), dwelling 742, family 742, John Perry; digital image, Ancestry.com website, citing National Archives microfilm publication M593, roll 1601, found online at: *http://www.ancestry.com* [accessed July 11, 2017].

10   1880 U.S. census, Hill County, Texas, population schedule, Precinct 1, p. 298[A] (stamped), dwelling 250, family 264, J. M. Perry; digital image, Ancestry Library Edition website, from NARA microfilm publication, roll 1311, found online at: *http://ancestrylibrary.proquest.com* [accessed July 11, 2017].

11   "John Michael Perry (1856-1934)," Find A Grave database.

12   "Winneyfred Catherine Berry Perry (1862-1935)," Find A Grave database, memorial 40993109, Willow Cemetery, Haskell, Haskell County, Texas, created by Carla Carlton Young, found online at: *http://findagrave.com* [accessed July 11, 2017].

13   "Wayne Willing Perry (1882-1963)," Find A Grave database, memorial 40993108, Willow Cemetery, Haskell, Haskell County, Texas, created by Carla Carlton Young, found online at: *http://findagrave.com* [accessed July 11, 2017].

14   S. C. Gwynne, "Last Days of the Comanches," *Texas Monthly* (Austin, TX: Genesis Park), para. 38, found online at *https://www.texasmonthly.com/articles/last-days-of-the-comanches/* [accessed December 3, 2018].

15   John Leffler, "Haskell County," *Handbook of Texas Online*, Texas State Historical Association, uploaded on June 15, 2010, modified on February 5, 2016, found online at: *http://www.tshaonline.org/handbook/online/articles/hch10* [accessed July 11, 2017].

16   "John Michael Perry (1856-1934)," Find A Grave database.

ENDNOTES

17   Leffler, "Haskell County," *Handbook of Texas Online*.

18   The 1890 U.S. Federal Census was destroyed in a fire in January 1921, so no census data is available for that year. Loretto Dennis Szucs and Sandra Hargreaves Luebking, eds., "Research in Census Records," *The Source: A Guidebook of American Genealogy*, rev. ed. (Salt Lake City, UT: Ancestry, Inc., 1997).

19   1900 U.S. census, Haskell County, Texas, population schedule, precinct 3, p. 5[B] (handwritten), dwelling 76, family 80, Willing W. Perry; digital image, Ancestry.com website, citing National Archives microfilm publication T623, roll 1643, found online at: http://www.ancestry.com [accessed July 11, 2017].

20   "Hoyt Perry (1903-1992)," Find A Grave database, memorial 40993104, Willow Cemetery, Haskell, Haskell County, Texas, created by Carla Carlton Young, found online at: http://findagrave.com [accessed July 11, 2017].

21   1910 U.S. census, Haskell County, Texas, population schedule, Sagerton, p. 9B, dwelling 152, family 153, Hoyt Perry; digital image, Ancestry.com website, citing National Archives microfilm publication T624, roll 1562, found online at: http://www.ancestry.com [accessed July 11, 2017].

22   1920 U.S. census, Haskell County, Texas, population schedule, Justice precinct 3, p. 10(A), dwelling 154, family 182, Hoyt Perry; digital image, Ancestry.com website, citing National Archives microfilm publication T625, roll 1816, found online at: http://www.ancestry.com [accessed July 11, 2017].

23   Interview with Joseph Ray Perry by Jewellee Jordan Kuenstler, Perry Home, Paint Creek Community, Haskell County, Texas, April 6, 2016, transcript in possession of interviewer. Ray related his family history and his experiences in World War II.

24   Hooper Shelton and Homer Hutto, *The First Hundred Years of Jones County, Texas* (Stamford, TX: Shelton Press, 1978), 55–56.

25   1930 U.S. census, Haskell County, Texas, population schedule, Justice precinct 1, p. 41 (stamped) sheet no. 2(A) (handwritten), dwelling 22, family 22, Hoyt Perry; digital image, Ancestry.com website, citing National Archives microfilm publication T626, roll 2354, found online at: http://www.ancestry.com [accessed July 11, 2017].

26   Interview with Joseph Ray Perry, April 6, 2016.

27   Interview with Joseph Ray Perry by Dan K. Utley, Perry Home, Paint Creek Community, Haskell County, Texas), February 7, 2006, transcript in possession of the Perry Family and the Texas Historical Commission, 5. Ray related his family history and his experiences in World War II.

28. Interview with Joseph Ray Perry, February 7, 2006, 6.
29. Ibid.
30. Ibid., 22.
31. Ibid.
32. Ibid.
33. Interview with Joseph Ray Perry, April 6, 2016.
34. Ibid.
35. Ibid.
36. Ibid.
37. Interview with Joseph Ray Perry, February 7, 2006, 11.
38. Ibid., 5.
39. Ibid., 6.
40. Ibid., 6–7.
41. Ibid., 12.
42. Interview with Joseph Ray Perry, April 6, 2016.
43. Interview with Joseph Ray Perry, February 7, 2006, 13.

CHAPTER 2

1. "A Happy New Year," *Haskell (TX) Free Press*, October 29, 1943, HTML edition, archived online at: *http://collections2.swco.ttu.edu/handle/20.500.12255/39049* [accessed July 11, 2017], page 2, col. 7.
2. Interview with Joseph Ray Perry by Dan K. Utley, Perry Home, Paint Creek Community, Haskell County, Texas, February 7, 2006, transcript in possession of the Perry Family and the Texas Historical Commission, 12.
3. Ibid., 6.
4. Joseph Ray Perry to Hoyt and Thelma Perry, letter, Lawton, Oklahoma, December 22, 1943, in the private collection of the Perry Family.
5. Interview with Joseph Ray Perry, February 7, 2006, 13.
6. Joseph Ray Perry to Hoyt and Thelma Perry, letter, Ft. Sill, Oklahoma, December 24, 1943, in the private collection of the Perry Family.
7. Joseph Ray Perry to Hoyt Thelma Perry, letter, Ft. Sill, Oklahoma, December 26, 1943, in the private collection of the Perry Family.

ENDNOTES

8. Joseph Ray Perry to Hoyt and Thelma Perry, letter, Sheppard Field, Texas, December 29, 1943, in the private collection of the Perry Family.

9. Joseph Ray Perry to Hoyt and Thelma Perry, letter, January 2, 1944, in the private collection of the Perry Family.

10. Joseph Ray Perry to Hoyt and Thelma Perry, letter, January 5, 1944, in the private collection of the Perry Family.

11. Joseph Ray Perry to Hoyt and Thelma Perry, letter, January 10, 1944, in the private collection of the Perry Family.

12. Veteran's Administration to Mrs. Thelma Edna Perry, Haskell, Texas, life insurance policy on Joseph Ray Perry, January 10, 1944, in the private collection of the Perry Family.

13. Joseph Ray Perry to Hoyt and Thelma Perry, letter, Sheppard Field, Texas, January 13, 1944, in the private collection of the Perry Family.

14. Joseph Ray Perry to Hoyt and Thelma Perry, letter, Sheppard Field, Texas, January 17, 1944, in the private collection of the Perry Family.

15. Joseph Ray Perry to Hoyt and Thelma Perry, letter, Sheppard Field, Texas, January 23, 1944, in the private collection of the Perry Family.

16. Joseph Ray Perry to Hoyt and Thelma Perry, letter, Sheppard Field, Texas, January 24, 1944, in the private collection of the Perry Family.

17. Joseph Ray Perry to Hoyt and Thelma Perry, letter, Sheppard Field, Texas, February 1, 1944, in the private collection of the Perry Family.

18. Interview with Joseph Ray Perry, February 7, 2006, 48.

19. Joseph Ray Perry to Hoyt and Thelma Perry, letter, Sheppard Field, Texas, February 9, 1944, in the private collection of the Perry Family.

20. Interview with Joseph Ray Perry, February 7, 2006, 4.

21. Joseph Ray Perry to Hoyt and Thelma Perry, letter, Sheppard Field, Texas, February 14, 1944, in the private collection of the Perry Family.

22. Joseph Ray Perry to Hoyt and Thelma Perry, letter, Sheppard Field, Texas, February 27, 1944, in the private collection of the Perry Family.

23. Interview with Joseph Ray Perry, February 7, 2006, 13.

24. Joseph Ray Perry to Hoyt and Thelma Perry, letter, Sheppard Field, Texas, February 29, 1944, in the private collection of the Perry Family.

25. Joseph Ray Perry to Hoyt and Thelma Perry, letter, Sheppard Field, Texas, March 1, 1944, in the private collection of the Perry Family.

CHAPTER 3

1. "County's Quota in Red Cross War Fund is Oversubscribed," *Haskell (TX) Free Press*, March 24, 1944, HTML edition, archived online at: http://collections2.swco.ttu.edu/handle/20.500.12255/39085 [accessed August 10, 2017], page 1, col. 8.

2. Interview with Joseph Ray Perry by Dan K. Utley, Perry Home, Paint Creek Community, Haskell County, Texas, February 7, 2006, transcript in possession of the Perry Family and the Texas Historical Commission, 14.

3. Joseph Ray Perry to Hoyt and Thelma Perry, letter, Kingman, Arizona, March 4, 1944, in the private collection of the Perry Family.

4. "Kingman AAF Boneyard & Kingman Airport (IGM) in Arizona," online article, *AirplaneBoneyards.com*, found online at: http://www.airplaneboneyards.com/kingman-arizona-airplane-boneyard-storage.htm [accessed August 10, 2017].

5. Ray Perry's Junior year in Paint Creek High School. "Pirates, 1942," Paint Creek School Yearbook, Haskell County, Texas, in the private collection of Jewellee Jordan Kuenstler.

6. Joseph Ray Perry to Hoyt and Thelma Perry, letter, Kingman, Arizona, March 5, 1944, in the private collection of the Perry Family.

7. Joseph Ray Perry to Hoyt and Thelma Perry, letter, Kingman, Arizona, March 7, 1944, in the private collection of the Perry Family.

8. J. B. Kuenstler, sophomore, "Pirates, 1942," Paint Creek School Yearbook, Haskell County, Texas, in the private collection of Jewellee Jordan Kuenstler.

9. *Haskell (TX) Free Press*, 1886-2017, Texas Tech University, Southwest Collection, found online at: http://collections2.swco.ttu.edu/handle/20.500.12255/26380 [accessed August 10, 2017].

10. Joseph Ray Perry to Hoyt and Thelma Perry, letter, Kingman, Arizona, March 8, 1944, in the private collection of the Perry Family.

11. Joseph Ray Perry to Hoyt and Thelma Perry, letter, Kingman, Arizona, March 10, 1944, in the private collection of the Perry Family.

12. Interview with Joseph Ray Perry, February 7, 2006, 16.

13. Ibid.

14. Joseph Ray Perry to Hoyt and Thelma Perry, letter, Kingman, Arizona, March 11, 1944, in the private collection of the Perry Family.

15. Ray alternated the spelling of Tommie's name between Tommy and Tommie. The author of the newspaper article spelled his name "Tommie."

16. "Sgt. Tommie Davis," undated article from *Haskell (TX) Free Press*, in Joseph Ray Perry Scrapbook, in the private collection of the Perry Family.

ENDNOTES

17 Joseph Ray Perry to Hoyt and Thelma Perry, letter, Kingman, Arizona, March 12, 1944, in the private collection of the Perry Family.

18 Joseph Ray Perry to Hoyt and Thelma Perry, letter, Kingman, Arizona, March 13, 1944, in the private collection of the Perry Family.

19 Interview with Joseph Ray Perry, February 7, 2006, 14.

20 Joseph Ray Perry to Hoyt and Thelma Perry, letter, Kingman, Arizona, March 16, 1944, in the private collection of the Perry Family.

21 Joseph Ray Perry to Hoyt and Thelma Perry, letter, Kingman, Arizona, March 19, 1944, in the private collection of the Perry Family.

22 D. W. Gipson, "Pirates, 1942," Paint Creek School Yearbook, Haskell County, Texas, in the private collection of Jewellee Jordan Kuenstler.

23 Truett Kuenstler, sophomore, "Pirates, 1942," Paint Creek School Yearbook, Haskell County, Texas, in the private collection of Jewellee Jordan Kuenstler.

24 Joseph Ray Perry to Hoyt and Thelma Perry, letter, Kingman, Arizona, March 21, 1944, in the private collection of the Perry Family.

25 Interview with Joseph Ray Perry, February 7, 2006, 16-17.

26 Joseph Ray Perry to Hoyt and Thelma Perry, letter, Kingman, Arizona, March 24, 1944, in the private collection of the Perry Family.

27 Joseph Ray Perry to Hoyt and Thelma Perry, letter, Kingman, Arizona, March 26, 1944, in the private collection of the Perry Family.

28 Joseph Ray Perry to Hoyt and Thelma Perry, letter, Kingman, Arizona, March 28, 1944, in the private collection of the Perry Family.

29 Joseph Ray Perry to Hoyt and Thelma Perry, letter, Kingman, Arizona, April 12, 1944, in the private collection of the Perry Family.

30 Interview with Joseph Ray Perry by Jewellee Jordan Kuenstler, Perry Home, Paint Creek Community, Haskell County, Texas, April 6, 2016, transcript in possession of interviewer.

31 Joseph Ray Perry to Hoyt and Thelma Perry, letter, Kingman, Arizona, April 16, 1944, in the private collection of the Perry Family.

32 Joseph Ray Perry to Hoyt and Thelma Perry, letter, Kingman, Arizona, April 19, 1944, in the private collection of the Perry Family.

33 Interview with Joseph Ray Perry, February 7, 2006, 15.

34 "HQ 223rd AAF Base Unit, to All Heavy Bombardment Groups, Crews, and Components Thereof, 30 Apr 1944," original, in the private collection of the Perry Family.

CHAPTER 4

1. "Prayer Session Set For Day Invasion of Europe Begins," *Haskell (TX) Free Press*, May 12, 1944, HTML edition, archived online at: *http://collections2.swco.ttu.edu/handle/20.500.12255/39015* [accessed August 10, 2017], page 1, col. 1.

2. "A Brief History: World War II," The Nebraska Aviation Heritage Museum Project website, found online at: *https://www.lincolnafb.org/history.php* [accessed August 10, 2017].

3. Interview with Joseph Ray Perry by Jewellee Jordan Kuenstler, Perry Home, Paint Creek Community, Haskell County, Texas, April 6, 2016, transcript in possession of interviewer.

4. Joseph Ray Perry to Hoyt and Thelma Perry, letter, Lincoln, Nebraska, May 1, 1944, in the private collection of the Perry Family.

5. "Pearleta Ivy, Richard Carothers, Marry Today in Haskell Home," *Abilene (TX) Reporter News*, July 18, 1948, HTML edition, archived online at: *https://www.newspapers.com/image/45003054/* [accessed July 11, 2017], section 2, page 5, col. 3–4 [digital pages 57–58].

6. "In Loving Memory of Joseph Ray Perry, May 2, 2017," funeral program, printed by Smith Family Funeral Home, Haskell, Texas, in the private collection of the Perry Family.

7. Joseph Ray Perry to Hoyt and Thelma Perry, letter, Lincoln, Nebraska, May 2, 1944, in the private collection of the Perry Family.

8. Joseph Ray Perry to Hoyt and Thelma Perry, letter, Lincoln, Nebraska, May 4, 1944, in the private collection of the Perry Family.

9. Interview with Joseph Ray Perry, April 6, 2016.

10. Interview with Joseph Ray Perry by Dan K. Utley, Perry Home, Paint Creek Community, Haskell County, Texas, February 7, 2006, transcript in possession of the Perry Family and the Texas Historical Commission, 17.

11. Ibid., 17–18.

12. Ibid.

13. Ibid., 18.

14. Ibid., 19.

15. Gerald Astor, *The Mighty Eighth: The Air War In Europe As Told By the Men Who Fought It* (New York: Berkley Caliber, 1997), 9.

16. Joseph Ray Perry to Hoyt and Thelma Perry, letter, Lincoln, Nebraska, May 7, 1944, in the private collection of the Perry Family.

17. Joseph Ray Perry to Hoyt and Thelma Perry, letter, Lincoln, Nebraska, May 8, 1944, in the private collection of the Perry Family.

ENDNOTES

18   Joseph Ray Perry to Hoyt and Thelma Perry, letter, Lincoln, Nebraska, May 14, 1944, in the private collection of the Perry Family.

CHAPTER 5

1   "Promoted to Corporal," *Haskell (TX) Free Press*, July 21, 1944, HTML edition, archived online at: *http://collections2.swco.ttu.edu/handle/20.500.12255/39161* [accessed August 10, 2017], page 6, col. 3.

2   "Dyersburg Army Airfield," database, *Historic Markers Across Tennessee*, found online at: *http://www.lat34north.com/HistoricMarkersTN/MarkerDetail .cfm?KeyID=049-008&MarkerTitle=Dyersburg%20Army%20Airfield* [accessed August 10, 2017].

3   Interview with Joseph Ray Perry by Jewellee Jordan Kuenstler, Perry Home, Paint Creek Community, Haskell County, Texas, April 6, 2016, transcript in possession of interviewer.

4   The letter was damaged, but Ray had hoped for a furlough before being shipped overseas and the increase in pay that came with his new promotion. Joseph Ray Perry to Hoyt and Thelma Perry, letter, Dyersburg, Tennessee, May 14, 1944, in the private collection of the Perry Family.

5   Joseph Ray Perry, Report of Physical Examination and Induction, September 3, 1943, Haskell County Courthouse, Haskell, Texas, Service Records, 1943-1945, National Archives, Washington, D.C., copy in possession of the editor, p 49.

6   Joseph Ray Perry to Hoyt and Thelma Perry, letter, Dyersburg, Tennessee, May 18, 1944, in the private collection of the Perry Family.

7   Joseph Ray Perry to Hoyt and Thelma Perry, letter, Dyersburg, Tennessee, May 20, 1944, in the private collection of the Perry Family.

8   Joseph Ray Perry to Hoyt and Thelma Perry, letter, Dyersburg, Tennessee, May 23, 1944, in the private collection of the Perry Family.

9   Joseph Ray Perry to Hoyt and Thelma Perry, letter, Dyersburg, Tennessee, May 26, 1944, in the private collection of the Perry Family.

10   Perkins & Timberlake Co. Advertisement, *Haskell (TX) Free Press*, October 6, 1944, HTML edition, archived online at: *http://collections2.swco.ttu.edu /handle/20.500.12255/39021* [accessed September 20, 2017], page 8, col. 1.

11   Joseph Ray Perry to Hoyt and Thelma Perry, letter, Dyersburg, Tennessee, June 1, 1944, in the private collection of the Perry Family.

12   Interview with Amelia Holt Perry by Jewellee Jordan Kuenstler, Perry Home, Paint Creek Community, Haskell County, Texas, June 6, 2017, transcript in

possession of interviewer. Amelia clarified questions concerning Ray's letters and interviews.

13. Joseph Ray Perry to Hoyt and Thelma Perry, letter, Dyersburg, Tennessee, June 2, 1944, in the private collection of the Perry Family.

14. Joseph Ray Perry to Hoyt and Thelma Perry, letter, Dyersburg, Tennessee, June 5, 1944, in the private collection of the Perry Family.

15. Interview with Joseph Ray Perry by Dan K. Utley, Perry Home, Paint Creek Community, Haskell County, Texas, February 7, 2006, transcript in possession of the Perry Family and the Texas Historical Commission, 17.

16. Joseph Ray Perry to Hoyt and Thelma Perry, letter, Dyersburg, Tennessee, June 7, 1944, in the private collection of the Perry Family.

17. Joseph Ray Perry to Hoyt and Thelma Perry, letter, Dyersburg, Tennessee, June 10, 1944, in the private collection of the Perry Family.

18. Joseph Ray Perry, Authorization For Allotment of Pay, July 11, 1944, AA Fld Dyersburg, Tennessee, Service Records, 1943-1945, National Archives, Washington, D.C., copy in possession of the editor, p 33.

19. Joseph Ray Perry, Authorization For Allotment of Pay, December 23, 1943, Fort Sill, Oklahoma, Service Records, 1943-1945, National Archives, Washington, D.C., copy in possession of the editor, p 34.

20. Joseph Ray Perry, Class E Allotments, March 29, 1945, Service Records, 1943-1945, National Archives, Washington, D.C., copy in possession of the editor, p 17.

21. Joseph Ray Perry to Hoyt and Thelma Perry, letter, Dyersburg, Tennessee, June 13, 1944, in the private collection of the Perry Family.

22. Joseph Ray Perry to Hoyt and Thelma Perry, letter, Dyersburg, Tennessee, June 16, 1944, in the private collection of the Perry Family.

23. Joseph Ray Perry to Hoyt and Thelma Perry, letter, Dyersburg, Tennessee, June 18, 1944, in the private collection of the Perry Family.

24. Joseph Ray Perry to Hoyt and Thelma Perry, letter, Dyersburg, Tennessee, June 21, 1944, in the private collection of the Perry Family.

25. Joseph Ray Perry to Hoyt and Thelma Perry, letter, Dyersburg, Tennessee, June 22, 1944, in the private collection of the Perry Family.

26. Joseph Ray Perry to Hoyt and Thelma Perry, letter, Dyersburg, Tennessee, June 24, 1944, in the private collection of the Perry Family.

27. Joseph Ray Perry to Hoyt and Thelma Perry, letter, Dyersburg, Tennessee, June 25, 1944, in the private collection of the Perry Family.

28. Interview with Joseph Ray Perry, February 7, 2006, 20.

ENDNOTES

29 "Not-So-Secret Weapon: The Norden Bombsight," *Historynet.com* website, available online at *http://www.historynet.com/not-so-secret-weapon-the-norden-bombsight.htm* [accessed September 20, 2017], reprint of a March 2014 *Aviation History* article.

30 Joseph Ray Perry to Hoyt and Thelma Perry, letter, Dyersburg, Tennessee, June 29, 1944, in the private collection of the Perry Family.

31 Joseph Ray Perry to Hoyt and Thelma Perry, letter, Dyersburg, Tennessee, July 2, 1944, in the private collection of the Perry Family.

32 Interview with Joseph Ray Perry, February 7, 2006, 20.

33 Phone interview with Don Perry by Jewellee Jordan Kuenstler, September 21, 2017, transcript in possession of interviewer. Don related his memories of Ray and his family during World War II and his experiences in in the military, specifically Germany, after World War II.

34 Joseph Ray Perry, Remarks Administrative, July 11, 1944, Dyersburg, Tennessee, Service Records, 1943-1945, National Archives, Washington, D.C., copy in possession of the editor, "offered opportunity to make will and power of attorney," p 39.

35 Joseph Ray Perry, Remarks Administrative, July 15, 1944, Dyersburg, Tennessee, Service Records, 1943-1945, National Archives, Washington, D.C., copy in possession of the editor, "Soldier is favorably recommended for good conduct medal," p 39.

36 Joseph Ray Perry, Furloughs, July 21, 1944, Dyersburg, Tennessee, Service Records, 1943-1945, National Archives, Washington, D.C., copy in possession of the editor, p 15.

37 Joseph Ray Perry, Remarks Administrative, August 15, 1944, Dyersburg, Tennessee, Service Records, 1943-1945, National Archives, Washington, D.C., copy in possession of the editor, "ETO Indoctrination Course Completed," p 39.

CHAPTER 6

1 "Is Gunner," *Haskell (TX) Free Press*, September 15, 1944, HTML edition, archived online at: *http://collections2.swco.ttu.edu/handle/20.500.12255/39022* [accessed September 20, 2017], page 1, col. 4.

2 Interview with Joseph Ray Perry by Dan K. Utley, Perry Home, Paint Creek Community, Haskell County, Texas, February 7, 2006, transcript in possession of the Perry Family and the Texas Historical Commission, 20.

3 "Historic Kearney," online article, University of Nebraska at Kearney, available online at: historickearney.unk.edu [accessed September 20, 2017].

4   Ray Perry, Furloughs, July 21, 1944, Dyersburg, Tennessee, Service Records, 1943-1945, National Archives, Washington, D.C., copy in possession of the editor, p 15.

5   Joseph Ray Perry to Hoyt and Thelma Perry, letter, Kearney, Nebraska, July 30, 1944, in the private collection of the Perry Family.

6   Joseph Ray Perry, To: CO, 271st AAF Base Unit, DAAF, Kearney, Nebraska, July 20, 1944, Dyersburg, Tennessee, Service Records, 1943-1945, National Archives, Washington, D.C., copy in possession of the editor, rating his character and efficiency as excellent, p 24.

7   Joseph Ray Perry to Hoyt and Thelma Perry, letter, Kearney, Nebraska, August 2, 1944, in the private collection of the Perry Family.

8   Interview with Joseph Ray Perry, February 7, 2006, 22–23.

9   Ibid., 23–24.

10 Ibid., 24.

11 Ibid., 22.

12 Joseph Ray Perry to Hoyt and Thelma Perry, letter, Kearney, Nebraska, August 3, 1944, in the private collection of the Perry Family.

13 Interview with Joseph Ray Perry, February 7, 2006, 23.

14 Janice Brown, "A Window into World War II: Grenier Field aka Manchester (NH) Airport," New Hampshire's History Blog, *Cow Hampshire*, September 17, 2013, found online at: *http://www.cowhampshireblog.com/2013/09/17/a-window-into-world-war-ii-grenier-field-aka-manchester-nh-airport/* [accessed September 20, 2017].

15 Tom Hildreth, "The World War Two Years," Manchester, New Hampshire Airport (Grenier Army Air Field) in WWII, *Tom's Picture Pages*, found online at: *http://users.vermontel.net/~tomh/AIRCRAFT/AIRPORTS/MHT/MHTWWII.html* [accessed September 20, 2017].

16 Joseph Ray Perry, Foreign Service, August 8, 1944, Grenier Fld., New Hampshire, Service Records, 1943-1945, National Archives, Washington, D.C., copy in possession of the editor, p 15.

17 Interview with Joseph Ray Perry, February 7, 2006, 21.

18 Dimmitt Hughes to Hoyt Perry, letter, Georgetown, Texas, August 14, 1944, in the private collection of the Perry Family.

19 Joseph Ray Perry to Hoyt and Thelma Perry, letter, Horham, England, August 27, 1944, in the private collection of the Perry Family.

ENDNOTES

20 Interview with Joseph Ray Perry, February 7, 2006, 30.

21 "Horham," *American Air Museum in Britain*, found online at: http://www.americanairmuseum.com/place/180 [accessed September 20, 2017].

22 Interview with Joseph Ray Perry, February 7, 2006, 21-22.

23 Ibid., 30.

24 Ibid., 21.

25 Ibid., 32.

26 Eighth Air Force Memorial Association, *Contrails II: Pictorial History, 95th Bomb Group (H), 8th U.S. Army Air Force, Horham, England, 1943-1945* (Marceline, MO: Walsworth Publishing Co., 2003).

27 Interview with Joseph Ray Perry, February 7, 2006, 31.

28 Joseph Ray Perry to Hoyt and Thelma Perry, letter, Horham, England, September 1, 1944, in the private collection of the Perry Family.

29 Joseph Ray Perry to Hoyt and Thelma Perry, letter, Horham, England, September 16, 1944, in the private collection of the Perry Family.

30 Interview with Joseph Ray Perry, February 7, 2006, 34.

31 Joseph Ray Perry to Hoyt and Thelma Perry, letter, Horham, England, September 21, 1944, in the private collection of the Perry Family.

32 "Navigator," *B17 Flying Fortress: Queen of the Skies*, found online at: http://www.b17queenofthesky.com/navigator.htm [accessed September 20, 2017].

33 Gerald Astor, *The Mighty Eighth: The Air War In Europe As Told By the Men Who Fought It* (New York: Berkley Caliber, 1997), 244-45.

34 Joseph Ray Perry to LaVern Livengood, letter, Horham, England, September 23, 1944, in the private collection of the Perry Family.

35 "The Fieseler Fi 103 (V1) German 'Buzz Bomb,'" exhibit description, *The Museum of Flight*, found online at: http://www.museumofflight.org/Exhibits/fieseler-fi-103-v1 [accessed September 25, 2017].

36 Interview with Joseph Ray Perry, February 7, 2006, 33.

CHAPTER 7

1 "In Just 10 Minutes They'll Need Your Help," National War Fund Ad, *Haskell (TX) Free Press*, October 6, 1944, HTML edition, archived online at: http://collections2.swco.ttu.edu/handle/20.500.12255/39021 [accessed September 25, 2017], page 6, col. 5-8.

2. "World War II Operations Mission Briefing Hut," image downloaded from Hill Air Force Base website on September 25, 2017, copy in possession of the editor.

3. Interview with Joseph Ray Perry by Jewellee Jordan Kuenstler, Perry Home, Paint Creek Community, Haskell County, Texas, April 6, 2016, transcript in possession of interviewer.

4. "Mission No. 1, Breman, Germany," Bomb Tag, September 26, 1944, Joseph Ray Perry Scrapbook, in the private collection of the Perry Family.

5. Interview with Joseph Ray Perry by Dan K. Utley, Perry Home, Paint Creek Community, Haskell County, Texas, February 7, 2006, transcript in possession of the Perry Family and the Texas Historical Commission, 25.

6. Ibid., 26.

7. Ibid., 27.

8. Adolf Galland, *The First and the Last* (Popular Classics Publishing, 2014), 106.

9. Ibid., 94.

10. Ibid., 94.

11. "Mission No. 2, Merseburg, Germany," Bomb Tag, September 28, 1944, Joseph Ray Perry Scrapbook, in the private collection of the Perry Family.

12. Interview with Joseph Ray Perry, February 7, 2006, 24.

13. Ibid., 42.

14. Ibid., 44.

15. Ibid., 20.

16. Edward Jablonski, *America In the Air War*, Epic of Flight Series (New York: Time Life Books, 1982), 112.

17. Interview with Joseph Ray Perry, February 7, 2006, 28.

18. "Mission No. 3, Bielefeld, Germany," Bomb Tag, September 30, 1944, Joseph Ray Perry Scrapbook, in the private collection of the Perry Family.

19. Gerald Astor, *The Mighty Eighth: The Air War In Europe As Told By the Men Who Fought It* (New York: Berkley Caliber, 1997), 381.

20. Personal Photos, Joseph Ray Perry Scrapbook, in the private collection of the Perry Family.

21. Interview with Joseph Ray Perry, February 7, 2006, 40.

22. Ibid.

23. "P-51 Mustang Performance," WWIIaircraftperformance.org website, found online at: *http://www.wwiiaircraftperformance.org/mustang/mustangtest.html*

[accessed September 25, 2017].

24 Interview with Joseph Ray Perry, February 7, 2006, 39.

25 Ibid. 44.

26 Preston Underhill to Hoyt and Thelma Perry, letter, Italy, October 21, 1944, in the private collection of the Perry Family.

27 "Rotan Gunner Missed Raid in Which His Crew Went Down," undated newspaper clipping, Joseph Ray Perry Scrapbook, in the private collection of the Perry Family.

28 Interview with Joseph Ray Perry, April 6, 2016.

29 Joseph Ray Perry to Hoyt and Thelma Perry, letter, Horham, England, October 3, 1944, in the private collection of the Perry Family.

30 "Mission No. 4, Nurnburg [sic], Germany," Bomb Tag, October 3, 1944, Joseph Ray Perry Scrapbook, in the private collection of the Perry Family.

31 Interview with Joseph Ray Perry, February 7, 2006, 40.

32 Ibid., 40-41.

33 Various newspaper and magazine articles were found in Ray's scrapbook. See "Nearly 2,000 U.S. Planes Raid Reich War Plants," *Stars and Stripes* Magazine, October 4, 1944, and "Heavies Strike Nazi Ordinance," *Stars and Stripes* Magazine, Joseph Ray Perry Scrapbook, in the private collection of the Perry Family.

34 Galland, *The First and the Last*, 127.

35 "Mission No. 5, Berlin, Germany," Bomb Tag, October 6, 1944, Joseph Ray Perry Scrapbook, in the private collection of the Perry Family.

36 Interview with Joseph Ray Perry, February 7, 2006, 25.

37 Ibid., 36.

38 Ibid., 43.

39 Interview with Joseph Ray Perry, April 6, 2016.

40 Interview with Joseph Ray Perry, February 7, 2006, 24.

CHAPTER 8

1 "Haskell Gets 3.19 Inches of Rain; Scattered Hail at Rule," *Haskell (TX) Free Press*, October 6, 1944, HTML edition, archived online at: *http://collections2 .swco.ttu.edu/handle/20.500.12255/39021* [accessed September 25, 2017], page 1, col. 8.

2. Interview with Joseph Ray Perry by Jewellee Jordan Kuenstler, Perry Home, Paint Creek Community, Haskell County, Texas, April 6, 2016, transcript in possession of interviewer.

3. The official "Mission Report" concerning Ray Perry's sixth mission where Chuck Buda was killed. "S-2 Report 95A and 95B Groups on October 7, 1944," Office of the Intelligence Officer, undated, copy of declassified report, in the private collection of the Perry Family.

4. Interview with Joseph Ray Perry by Dan K. Utley, Perry Home, Paint Creek Community, Haskell County, Texas, February 7, 2006, transcript in possession of the Perry Family and the Texas Historical Commission, 37.

5. "S-2 Report 95A and 95B Groups on October 7, 1944."

6. Ibid.

7. Interview with Joseph Ray Perry, February 7, 2006, 42.

8. Interview with Joseph Ray Perry, April 6, 2016.

9. "Mission No. 6, Leipzig, Germany," Bomb Tag, October 7, 1944, Joseph Ray Perry Scrapbook, in the private collection of the Perry Family.

10. "S-2 Report 95A and 95B Groups on October 7, 1944."

11. Interview with Joseph Ray Perry, April 6, 2016.

12. Ibid.

13. Ibid.

14. Edward Jablonski, *America In the Air War*, Epic of Flight Series (New York: Time Life Books, 1982), 103.

15. Adolf Galland, *The First and the Last* (Popular Classics Publishing, 2014), 115.

16. Interview with Joseph Ray Perry, April 6, 2016.

17. "S-2 Report 95A and 95B Groups on October 7, 1944."

18. Ibid.

19. Interview with Joseph Ray Perry, February 7, 2006, 24.

20. Ibid., 38.

21. Ibid.

22. Ibid.

23. Ibid., 39.

24. Interview with Joseph Ray Perry, April 6, 2016.

ENDNOTES

25 "S-2 Report 95A and 95B Groups on October 7, 1944."

26 Interview with Joseph Ray Perry, February 7, 2006, 39.

27 Ibid., 35-37.

28 Interview with Joseph Ray Perry, April 6, 2016.

29 Interview with Joseph Ray Perry, February 7, 2006, 37.

30 Ibid.

31 Eighth Air Force Memorial Association, *Contrails II: Pictorial History, 95th Bomb Group (H), 8th U.S. Army Air Force, Horham, England, 1943-1945* (Marceline, MO: Walsworth Publishing Co., 2003).

32 Interview with Joseph Ray Perry, April 6, 2016.

33 Galland, *The First and the Last*, 138.

34 Interview with Joseph Ray Perry, April 6, 2016.

35 Interview with Joseph Ray Perry, February 7, 2006, 49.

36 Interview with Joseph Ray Perry, April 6, 2016.

37 For the benefit of the reader, the letter has been transcribed as it was written, with edits included.

38 Barney Glovick to Mr. and Mrs. Buda, rough draft of letter, Horham, England, 1944, in the private collection of the Perry Family.

39 Interview with Joseph Ray Perry, February 7, 2006, 38.

40 Joseph Ray Perry to Hoyt and Thelma Perry, letter, Horham, England, February 15, 1945, in the private collection of the Perry Family.

41 Joseph Ray Perry to Hoyt and Thelma Perry, letter, Horham, England, March 3, 1945, in the private collection of the Perry Family.

CHAPTER 9

1 "Cpl. Davis Missing In Action," *Haskell (TX) Free Press*, October 27, 1944, HTML edition, archived online at: *http://collections2.swco.ttu.edu/bitstream /handle/20.500.12255/38990/Haskell_Free_Press__1944-10-27.pdf?sequence =2&isAllowed=y* [accessed September 25, 2017], page 1, col. 8.

2 Joseph Ray Perry to Hoyt and Thelma Perry, letter, Horham, England, February 9, 1944, in the private collection of the Perry Family.

3 Joseph Ray Perry to Hoyt and Thelma Perry, letter, Horham, England, March 11, 1944, in the private collection of the Perry Family.

4 "Mission No. 7, Cologne, Germany," Bomb Tag, October 15, 1944, Joseph Ray Perry Scrapbook, in the private collection of the Perry Family.

5 Interview with Joseph Ray Perry by Dan K. Utley, Perry Home, Paint Creek Community, Haskell County, Texas, February 7, 2006, transcript in possession of the Perry Family and the Texas Historical Commission, 26.

6 Joseph Ray Perry to Hoyt and Thelma Perry, letter, Horham, England, October 17, 1944, in the private collection of the Perry Family.

7 Interview with Amelia Holt Perry by Jewellee Jordan Kuenstler, Perry Home, Paint Creek Community, Haskell County, Texas, January 9, 2018, transcript in possession of the interviewer. Amelia clarified questions concerning Ray's letters and interviews.

8 "Mission No. 8, Cologne, Germany," Bomb Tag, October 17, 1944, Joseph Ray Perry Scrapbook, in the private collection of the Perry Family.

9 "Mission No. 9, Kassel, Germany," Bomb Tag, October 18, 1944, Joseph Ray Perry Scrapbook, in the private collection of the Perry Family.

10 Joseph Ray Perry to Hoyt and Thelma Perry, letter, Horham, England, October 21, 1944, in the private collection of the Perry Family.

11 "Mission No. 10, Munster, Germany," Bomb Tag, October 22, 1944, Joseph Ray Perry Scrapbook, in the private collection of the Perry Family.

12 Joseph Ray Perry to Hoyt and Thelma Perry, letter, Horham, England, October 25, 1944, in the private collection of the Perry Family.

13 Interview with Joseph Ray Perry by Jewellee Jordan Kuenstler, Perry Home, Paint Creek Community, Haskell County, Texas, April 6, 2016, transcript in possession of interviewer.

14 Ibid.

15 Joseph Ray Perry to Hoyt and Thelma Perry, letter, Horham, England, October 26, 1944, in the private collection of the Perry Family.

16 "Mission No. 11, Hamm, Germany," Bomb Tag, October 28, 1944, Joseph Ray Perry Scrapbook, in the private collection of the Perry Family.

17 Joseph Ray Perry to Hoyt and Thelma Perry, letter, Horham, England, October 30, 1944, in the private collection of the Perry Family.

18 Joseph Ray Perry to Hoyt and Thelma Perry, letter, Horham, England, November 1, 1944, in the private collection of the Perry Family.

19 Joseph Ray Perry to Hoyt and Thelma Perry, letter, Horham, England, November 7, 1944, in the private collection of the Perry Family.

20 Interview with Joseph Ray Perry, February 7, 2006, 30-31.

ENDNOTES

[21] Joseph Ray Perry to Hoyt and Thelma Perry, letter, Horham, England, November 14, 1944, in the private collection of the Perry Family.

[22] Joseph Ray Perry to Hoyt and Thelma Perry, letter, Horham, England, November 23, 1944, in the private collection of the Perry Family.

[23] Interview with Joseph Ray Perry, February 7, 2006, 31.

[24] Joseph Ray Perry to Hoyt and Thelma Perry, letter, Horham, England, November 25, 1944, in the private collection of the Perry Family.

[25] Joseph Ray Perry to Hoyt and Thelma Perry, letter, Horham, England, November 27, 1944, in the private collection of the Perry Family.

[26] Personal Photos, Joseph Ray Perry Scrapbook, in the private collection of the Perry Family.

[27] Joseph Ray Perry to Hoyt and Thelma Perry, letter, Horham, England, December 1, 1944, in the private collection of the Perry Family.

[28] Joseph Ray Perry to Hoyt and Thelma Perry, letter, Horham, England, December 6, 1944, in the private collection of the Perry Family.

[29] Interview with Joseph Ray Perry, February 7, 2006, 42-43.

[30] Joseph Ray Perry to Hoyt and Thelma Perry, letter, Horham, England, December 13, 1944, in the private collection of the Perry Family.

[31] Joseph Ray Perry, Class E Allotments, August 1, 1944, Service Records, 1943-1945, National Archives, Washington, D.C., copy in possession of the editor, p. 16-17.

[32] "Mission No. 12, Stuttgart, Germany," Bomb Tag, December 16, 1944, Joseph Ray Perry Scrapbook, in the private collection of the Perry Family.

[33] Joseph Ray Perry to Hoyt and Thelma Perry, letter, Horham, England, December 17, 1944, in the private collection of the Perry Family.

[34] Preston Underhill to Hoyt and Thelma Perry, letter, Italy, December 17, 1944, in the private collection of the Perry Family.

[35] Joseph Ray Perry to Hoyt and Thelma Perry, letter, Horham, England, December 18, 1944, in the private collection of the Perry Family.

[36] "Cpl. Davis Missing In Action," page 1, col. 8.

[37] "Davis is Prisoner of Germans," *Haskell (TX) Free Press*, November 17, 1944, HTML edition, archived online at: *http://collections2.swco.ttu.edu/bitstream /handle/20.500.12255/39102/Haskell_Free_Press__1944-11-17.pdf?sequence= 2&isAllowed=y* [accessed September 25, 2017], page 1, col. 3.

[38] Interview with Joseph Ray Perry, February 7, 2006, 50-51.

39 Joseph Ray Perry to Hoyt and Thelma Perry, letter, Horham, England, December 21, 1944, in the private collection of the Perry Family.

40 Joseph Ray Perry to Hoyt and Thelma Perry, telegram, Horham, England, December 25, 1944, in the private collection of the Perry Family.

41 Ray's official Service Record listed his thirteenth mission as Badmunster; note that Ray does not label the bomb tag as "No. 13," but instead as "12-B." "Mission No. 12-B [13], Badmunster [labeled as Bad Kerwznach], Germany," Bomb Tag, December 25, 1944, Joseph Ray Perry Scrapbook, in the private collection of the Perry Family.

42 Interview with Joseph Ray Perry, February 7, 2006, 26, 43.

43 Ibid., 43.

44 Personal Photos, Joseph Ray Perry Scrapbook, in the private collection of the Perry Family.

45 Joseph Ray Perry to Hoyt and Thelma Perry, letter, Horham, England, December 27, 1944, in the private collection of the Perry Family.

46 Joseph Ray Perry to Hoyt and Thelma Perry, letter, Horham, England, December 30, 1944, in the private collection of the Perry Family.

47 Adolf Galland, *The First and the Last* (Popular Classics Publishing, 2014), 111.

CHAPTER 10

1 "Let's Do Our Share," *Haskell (TX) Free Press*, January 5, 1945, HTML edition, archived online at: *http://collections2.swco.ttu.edu/bitstream/handle/20.500.12255 /39100/Haskell_Free_Press__1945-01-05.pdf?sequence=2&isAllowed=y* [accessed September 25, 2017], page 6, col. 2.

2 Joseph Ray Perry to Hoyt and Thelma Perry, letter, Horham, England, January 1, 1945, in the private collection of the Perry Family.

3 "Mission No. 14, Bad Kerwznach [Badmunster], Germany," Bomb Tag, January 2, 1945, Joseph Ray Perry Scrapbook, in the private collection of the Perry Family.

4 Joseph Ray Perry to Hoyt and Thelma Perry, letter, Horham, England, January 4, 1945, in the private collection of the Perry Family.

5 Joseph Ray Perry to Hoyt and Thelma Perry, letter, Horham, England, January 6, 1945, in the private collection of the Perry Family.

6 "Mission No. 15, Fulda, Germany," Bomb Tag, January 2, 1945, Joseph Ray Perry Scrapbook, in the private collection of the Perry Family.

ENDNOTES

7   Joseph Ray Perry to Hoyt and Thelma Perry, letter, Horham, England, January 9, 1945, in the private collection of the Perry Family.

8   Service Record listed Himmelgeist, a suburb of Dusseldorf, a few miles from Cologne. "Mission No. 16, Cologne [Himmelgeist], Germany," Bomb Tag, January 9, 1945, Joseph Ray Perry Scrapbook, in the private collection of the Perry Family.

9   Interview with Joseph Ray Perry by Dan K. Utley, Perry Home, Paint Creek Community, Haskell County, Texas, February 7, 2006, transcript in possession of the Perry Family and the Texas Historical Commission, 23.

10   Interview with Joseph Ray Perry, February 7, 2006, 44-45.

11   Ibid.

12   Preston Underhill to Hoyt and Thelma Perry, letter, Italy, January 15, 1945, in the private collection of the Perry Family.

13   "Mission No. 17, Hamburg, Germany," Bomb Tag, January 16, 1945, Joseph Ray Perry Scrapbook, in the private collection of the Perry Family.

14   Joseph Ray Perry to Hoyt and Thelma Perry, letter, Horham, England, January 19, 1945, in the private collection of the Perry Family.

15   Joseph Ray Perry to Hoyt and Thelma Perry, v-mail letter, Horham, England, January 23, 1945, in the private collection of the Perry Family.

16   Joseph Ray Perry to Hoyt and Thelma Perry, letter, Horham, England, January 24, 1945, in the private collection of the Perry Family.

17   The correct spelling for the town is Diusburg. "Mission No. 18, Duisburg [sic], Germany," Bomb Tag, January 28, 1945, Joseph Ray Perry Scrapbook, in the private collection of the Perry Family.

18   Joseph Ray Perry to Hoyt and Thelma Perry, v-mail letter, Horham, England, January 30, 1945, in the private collection of the Perry Family.

19   Joseph Ray Perry to Hoyt and Thelma Perry, letter, Horham, England, February 5, 1945, in the private collection of the Perry Family.

20   "Mission No. 19, Chemnitz, Germany," Bomb Tag, February 6, 1945, Joseph Ray Perry Scrapbook, in the private collection of the Perry Family.

21   Joseph Ray Perry to Hoyt and Thelma Perry, letter, Horham, England, February 15, 1945, in the private collection of the Perry Family.

22   "Mission No. 20, Frankfurt, Germany," Bomb Tag, February 17, 1945, Joseph Ray Perry Scrapbook, in the private collection of the Perry Family.

23   Joseph Ray Perry to Hoyt and Thelma Perry, letter, Horham, England, February 19, 1945, in the private collection of the Perry Family.

24. Joseph Ray Perry to Hoyt and Thelma Perry, letter, Horham, England, February 28, 1945, in the private collection of the Perry Family.

25. "Mission No. 21, Ulm, Germany," Bomb Tag, March 1, 1945, Joseph Ray Perry Scrapbook, in the private collection of the Perry Family.

26. Joseph Ray Perry to Hoyt and Thelma Perry, letter, Horham, England, March 3, 1945, in the private collection of the Perry Family.

27. Joseph Ray Perry to Hoyt and Thelma Perry, letter, Horham, England, March 7, 1945, in the private collection of the Perry Family.

28. The correct spelling is Langendreer. "Mission No. 22, Langredren [sic], Germany," Bomb Tag, March 1, 1945, Joseph Ray Perry Scrapbook, in the private collection of the Perry Family.

29. Joseph Ray Perry to Hoyt and Thelma Perry, letter, Horham, England, March 11, 1945, in the private collection of the Perry Family.

30. Joseph Ray Perry to Hoyt and Thelma Perry, letter, Horham, England, March 15, 1945, in the private collection of the Perry Family.

31. "Mission No. 23, Jena, Germany," Bomb Tag, March 19, 1945, Joseph Ray Perry Scrapbook, in the private collection of the Perry Family.

32. Joseph Ray Perry to Hoyt and Thelma Perry, letter, Horham, England, March 18, 1945, in the private collection of the Perry Family.

33. "Mission No. 24, Munster, Germany," Bomb Tag, March 21, 1945, Joseph Ray Perry Scrapbook, in the private collection of the Perry Family.

34. Joseph Ray Perry to Hoyt and Thelma Perry, letter, Horham, England, March 21, 1945, in the private collection of the Perry Family.

35. "Mission No. 25, Ahlhorn, Germany," Bomb Tag, March 22, 1945, Joseph Ray Perry Scrapbook, in the private collection of the Perry Family.

36. Joseph Ray Perry to Hoyt and Thelma Perry, letter, Horham, England, March 23, 1945, in the private collection of the Perry Family.

37. "Mission No. 26, Steenwijk, Germany [Netherlands]," Bomb Tag, March 24, 1945, Joseph Ray Perry Scrapbook, in the private collection of the Perry Family.

38. Interview with Joseph Ray Perry, February 7, 2006, 15.

39. Molony, Brig. C. J. C., et al., *The Mediterranean and Middle East: Volume V, The Campaign in Sicily 1943 and The Campaign in Italy, 3rd September 1943 to 31st March 1944*, History of the Second World War: United Kingdom Military Series (Uckfield, UK: Naval an Military Press, 2004), 49; "Tuskegee Airmen," online article, *San Diego Air and Space Museum* website, found online at: *http://sandiegoairandspace.org/hall-of-fame/honoree/tuskegee-airmen* [accessed October 17, 2017].

ENDNOTES

40   Interview with Joseph Ray Perry by Jewellee Jordan Kuenstler, Perry Home, Paint Creek Community, Haskell County, Texas, April 6, 2016, transcript in possession of interviewer.

41   "Mission No. 27, Ziegenhain, Germany," Bomb Tag, March 24, 1945, Joseph Ray Perry Scrapbook, in the private collection of the Perry Family.

42   Joseph Ray Perry to Hoyt and Thelma Perry, letter, Horham, England, March 25, 1945, in the private collection of the Perry Family.

43   "Mission No. 28, Hanover, Germany," Bomb Tag, March 28, 1945, Joseph Ray Perry Scrapbook, in the private collection of the Perry Family.

44   Joseph Ray Perry to Hoyt and Thelma Perry, letter, Horham, England, March 27, 1945, in the private collection of the Perry Family.

45   "Mission No. 29, Hamburg, Germany," Bomb Tag, March 30, 1945, Joseph Ray Perry Scrapbook, in the private collection of the Perry Family.

46   Richard L. Hayes, "Mr. Stewart Goes to War," online article, *History.net* website, found online at: *http://www.historynet.com/mr-stewart-goes-to-war.htm* [accessed October 17, 2017].

47   Interview with Joseph Ray Perry, April 6, 2016.

48   Ibid.; Interview with Joseph Ray Perry, February 7, 2006, 58-60.

49   Interview with Joseph Ray Perry, February 7, 2006, 47.

50   "Mission No. 30, Zeitz, Germany," Bomb Tag, March 31, 1945, Joseph Ray Perry Scrapbook, in the private collection of the Perry Family.

51   Joseph Ray Perry to Hoyt and Thelma Perry, letter, Horham, England, March 31, 1945, in the private collection of the Perry Family.

52   "Mission No. 31, Kiel, Germany," Bomb Tag, April 3, 1945, Joseph Ray Perry Scrapbook, in the private collection of the Perry Family.

53   Joseph Ray Perry to Hoyt and Thelma Perry, letter, Horham, England, April 4, 1945, in the private collection of the Perry Family.

54   "Mission No. 32, Kiel, Germany," Bomb Tag, April 4, 1945, Joseph Ray Perry Scrapbook, in the private collection of the Perry Family.

55   Interview with Joseph Ray Perry, February 7, 2006, 34.

56   Interview with Joseph Ray Perry, April 6, 2016.

57   "Mission No. 33, Leipzig, Germany," Bomb Tag, April 6, 1945, Joseph Ray Perry Scrapbook, in the private collection of the Perry Family.

58   Interview with Joseph Ray Perry, February 7, 2006, 35.

59   "Mission No. 34, Neromunster [Kaltenkirchen], Germany," Bomb Tag, April 7, 1945, Joseph Ray Perry Scrapbook, in the private collection of the Perry Family.

60   List of awards including the awards received by Joseph Ray Perry. Headquarters 3D Air Division: Office of the Commanding General, Awards of the Oak Leaf cluster to the Air Medal, April 12, 1945, original, in the private collection of the Perry Family.

61   Interview with Joseph Ray Perry, April 6, 2016.

62   Interview with Joseph Ray Perry, February 7, 2006, 19.

63   "Mission No. 35, Egar, Germany," Bomb Tag, April 8, 1945, Joseph Ray Perry Scrapbook, in the private collection of the Perry Family.

64   127th Reinforcement Battalion (AAF), Processing Sheet Enlisted Personnel, April 20, 1945, original, in the private collection of the Perry Family.

65   Joseph Ray Perry to Hoyt and Thelma Perry, telegram, Horham, England, April 24, 1945, in the private collection of the Perry Family.

CHAPTER 11

1   "Home on Furlough After 35 Missions Over Germany," *Haskell (TX) Free Press*, June 1, 1945, HTML edition, archived online at: *http://collections2.swco.ttu.edu /handle/20.500.12255/39016* [accessed October 17, 2017], page 1, col. 8.

2   Interview with Joseph Ray Perry by Jewellee Jordan Kuenstler, Perry Home, Paint Creek Community, Haskell County, Texas, April 6, 2016, transcript in possession of interviewer; Interview with Joseph Ray Perry by Dan K. Utley, Perry Home, Paint Creek Community, Haskell County, Texas, February 7, 2006, transcript in possession of the Perry Family and the Texas Historical Commission, 45.

3   Joseph Ray Perry, Enlisted Record and Report of Separation Honorable Discharge, October 31, 1945, Service Records, 1943-1945, National Archives, Washington, D.C., copy in possession of the editor, p 2.

4   Interview with Joseph Ray Perry, April 6, 2016.

5   Interview with Joseph Ray Perry, February 7, 2006, 46.

6   Interview with Joseph Ray Perry, April 6, 2016.

7   Ibid.; Interview with Joseph Ray Perry, February 7, 2006, 46.

8   Joseph Ray Perry to Hoyt and Thelma Perry, telegram, New York, New York, May 13, 1945, in the private collection of the Perry Family.

9   Interview with Joseph Ray Perry, April 6, 2016; Interview with Joseph Ray Perry, February 7, 2006, 62.

ENDNOTES

10. Joseph Ray Perry, Furloughs, May 19, 1945, Service Records, 1943-1945, National Archives, Washington, D.C., copy in possession of the editor, p. 15.

11. Preston Underhill to Joseph Ray, Hoyt, and Thelma Perry, letter, Laredo, Texas, May 28, 1945, in the private collection of the Perry Family.

12. Interview with Joseph Ray Perry, February 7, 2006, 48.

13. History.com Editors, "Bombing of Hiroshima and Nagasaki," online article, History.com website, found online at: *https://www.history.com/topics/world-war-ii/bombing-of-hiroshima-and-nagasaki* [accessed November 17, 2017].

14. Ibid.

15. "Japan Surrenders, Bringing an End to WWII," online article, History.com website, found online at: *http://www.history.com/this-day-in-history/japan-surrenders* [accessed November 17, 2017].

16. Joseph Ray Perry to Hoyt and Thelma Perry, letter, Santa Ana, California, June 23, 1945, in the private collection of the Perry Family.

17. Joseph Ray Perry to Hoyt and Thelma Perry, letter, Santa Ana, California, June 25, 1945, in the private collection of the Perry Family.

18. Joseph Ray Perry to Hoyt and Thelma Perry, letter, Santa Ana, California, June 28, 1945, in the private collection of the Perry Family.

19. Joseph Ray Perry to Hoyt and Thelma Perry, letter, Santa Ana, California, June 30, 1945, in the private collection of the Perry Family.

20. Joseph Ray Perry to Hoyt and Thelma Perry, letter, Santa Ana, California, July 4, 1945, in the private collection of the Perry Family.

21. Interview with Amelia Holt Perry by Jewellee Jordan Kuenstler, Perry Home, Paint Creek Community, Haskell County, Texas, January 9, 2018, transcript in possession of the interviewer. Amelia clarified questions concerning Ray's letters and interviews.

22. Joseph Ray Perry to Hoyt and Thelma Perry, letter, San Antonio, Texas, July 11, 1945, in the private collection of the Perry Family.

23. Joseph Ray Perry to Hoyt and Thelma Perry, telegram, San Antonio, Texas, July 18, 1945, in the private collection of the Perry Family.

24. Joseph Ray Perry, Furloughs, July 27, 1945, Service Records, 1943-1945, National Archives, Washington, D.C., copy in possession of the editor, p. 15.

25. Interview with Joseph Ray Perry, February 7, 2006, 48-49.

26. Ibid., 48.

27. Ibid.

28 Ibid., 49.

29 Joseph Ray Perry, Enlisted Record and Report of Separation Honorable Discharge, October 18, 1945, Service Records, 1943-1945, National Archives, Washington, D.C., copy in possession of the editor, p. 2; Interview with Joseph Ray Perry, February 7, 2006, 49.

CHAPTER 12

1 "Married in Double Ring Ceremony," *Abilene (TX) Reporter News*, July 9, 1947, HTML edition, archived online at: *https://www.newspapers.com/image/44946901/?terms=Amelia+Holt+Perry+1947+texas* [accessed November 17, 2017], page 15, col. 1-2.

2 Interview with Joseph Ray Perry by Dan K. Utley, Perry Home, Paint Creek Community, Haskell County, Texas, February 7, 2006, transcript in possession of the Perry Family and the Texas Historical Commission, 11.

3 Ibid., 53.

4 Ibid., 7.

5 Ibid., 50.

6 Ibid.

7 "Sgt. Tommie Davis, . . ." *Haskell (TX) Free Press*, June 8, 1945, HTML edition, archived online at: *http://collections2.swco.ttu.edu/bitstream/handle/20.500.12255/39135/Haskell_Free_Press__1945-06-08.pdf?sequence=2&isAllowed=y* [accessed November 17, 2017], page 1, col. 3.

8 Interview with Amelia Holt Perry by Jewellee Jordan Kuenstler, Perry Home, Paint Creek Community, Haskell County, Texas, January 9, 2018, transcript in possession of the interviewer.

9 Interview with Joseph Ray Perry, February 7, 2006, 53.

10 Ibid., 53.

11 Interview with Amelia Holt Perry, January 9, 2018.

12 Interview with Joseph Ray Perry, February 7, 2006, 53-54.

13 Ibid.

14 Interview with Amelia Holt Perry, January 9, 2018.

15 "Married in Double Ring Ceremony," page 15, col. 1-2.

16 Interview with Amelia Holt Perry, January 9, 2018.

17 Ibid.

ENDNOTES

18. Ibid.
19. Interview with Joseph Ray Perry, February 7, 2006, 51-52.
20. Ibid.
21. Ibid., 54.
22. Ibid., 55.
23. Ibid.
24. "Rick Perry," online article, *Biography.com* website, found online at: *https://www.biography.com/people/rick-perry-20663471* [accessed November 17, 2017].
25. Interview with Joseph Ray Perry, February 7, 2006, 54.
26. *In Loving Memory of Joseph Ray Perry*, May 2, 2017, funeral program, printed by Smith Family Funeral Home, Haskell, Texas.
27. Interview with Amelia Holt Perry by Jewellee Jordan Kuenstler, Perry Home, Paint Creek Community, Haskell County, Texas, June 12, 2017, transcript in possession of the interviewer.
28. Interview with Don Perry by Jewellee Jordan Kuenstler, phone interview, Haskell County, Texas, September 21, 2017, transcript in possession of the interviewer. Don related his memories of Ray and his family during World War II and his experiences in in the military, specifically Germany, after World War II.
29. Interview with Joseph Ray Perry by Jewellee Jordan Kuenstler, Perry Home, Paint Creek Community, Haskell County, Texas, April 6, 2016, transcript in possession of interviewer.
30. Ibid.
31. Interview with Amelia Holt Perry, June 12, 2017.
32. Interview with Joseph Ray Perry, February 7, 2006, 61.

EPILOGUE

1. Rick Perry, "Returning to Normandy," *Austin (TX) American-Statesman*, June 6, 2000, copy in the private collection of the Perry Family.
2. Interview with Joseph Ray Perry by Jewellee Jordan Kuenstler, Perry Home, Paint Creek Community, Haskell County, Texas, April 6, 2016, transcript in possession of interviewer.
3. Interview with Amelia Holt Perry by Jewellee Jordan Kuenstler, Perry Home, Paint Creek Community, Haskell County, Texas, January 9, 2018, transcript in possession of the interviewer.

4   Interview with Joseph Ray Perry by Dan K. Utley, Perry Home, Paint Creek Community, Haskell County, Texas, February 7, 2006, transcript in possession of the Perry Family and the Texas Historical Commission, 30.

5   Ibid., 31.

6   Ibid., 32.

7   Ibid., 33.

8   Ibid., 70.

9   Ibid.

10 95th B.G. Horham Heritage Association website, found online at: *http://95thbg-horham.com/wordpress/* [accessed November 17, 2017].

11 Interview with Amelia Holt Perry, January 9, 2018.

12 Interview with Joseph Ray Perry, February 7, 2006, 33.

13 Interview with Amelia Holt Perry, January 9, 2018.

14 Interview with Joseph Ray Perry, February 7, 2006, 47.

15 Ibid., 69-70.

16 Rick Perry, "Returning to Normandy."

17 Ibid.

18 *In Loving Memory of Joseph Ray Perry, May 2, 2017*, funeral program, printed by Smith Family Funeral Home, Haskell, Texas.

BIBLIOGRAPHY

Abilene Reporter News. Abilene, Texas. July 9, 1947-July 18, 1948.

"A Brief History: World War II." The Nebraska Aviation Heritage Museum Project website. Found online at: *http://www.lincolnafb.org/history.php.*

Brown, Janice. "A Window Into World War II: Grenier Field aka Manchester (NH) Airport." New Hampshire's History Blog. *Cow Hampshire.* September 17, 2013. Found online at: *http://www.cowhampshireblog.com/2013/09/17/a-window-into-world-ar-ii-grenier-field-aka-manchester-nh-airport/.*

"Dyersburg Army Airfield." Database. Historical Markers Across Tennessee website. Found online at: *http://www.lat34north.com/HistoricalMarkersTN/.*

Eighth Air Force Memorial Association. *Contrails II: Pictorial History, 95th Bomb Group (H), 8th U.S. Army Air Force, Horham, England, 1943-1945.* Marceline, MO: Walsworth Publishing Co., 2003.

"Fieseler Fi 103 (V1) German 'Buzz Bomb.'" Exhibit description. Undated. Museum of Flight website. Found online at: *http://www.museumofflight.org/Exhibits/fieseler-fi-103-v1.*

Find A Grave website. Database with images. Found online at: *http://www.findagrave.com.*

Fold3 by Ancestry. *Compiled Service Records of Confederate Soldiers Who Served in Organizations from the State of Texas 1861.* Database. Found online at: *https://www.fold3.com/images/14584590.*

Harrison County, Texas. 1850 U.S. census. Population schedule. Ancestry.com website. Found online at: *http://www.ancestry.com.*

Haskell County, Texas. 1900, 1910, 1920, 1930 U.S. census. Population schedule. Ancestry.com website. Found online at: *http://www.ancestry.com.*

Haskell Free Press. Haskell, Texas. 1886-2017. Texas Tech University. Southwest Collection. Found online at: *http://collections2.swco.ttu.edu/handle/20.500.12255 .36380*.

Hayes, Richard L. "Jimmy Stewart Goes to War." Online article. History.net website. Found online at: *http://www.historynet.com/mr-stewart-goes-to-war.htm*.

Hildreth, Tom. "The World War Two Years." Manchester, New Hampshire Airport (Grenier Army Air Field) in WWII. *Tom's Picture Pages*. Found online at: *http://www.users.vermontel.net/*.

Hill County, Texas. 1880 U.S. census. Population schedule. Ancestry.com website. Found online at: *http://www.ancestry.com*.

"Historic Kearney." Online article. University of Nebraska at Kearney website. Found online at: *http://www.historickearney.unk.edu*.

"Horham." American Air Museum in Britain website. Found online at: *http://www .americanairmuseum.com/place/180*.

Hoyt and Thelma Perry Letters. In the private collection of the Perry Family.

Interview with Amelia Holt Perry by Jewellee Jordan Kuenstler. Perry Home. Paint Creek Community. Haskell County, Texas. June 6, 2017. Transcript in possession of the interviewer.

Interview with Don Perry by Jewellee Jordan Kuenstler. Phone. September 21, 2017. Transcript in possession of the interviewer.

Interview with Joseph Ray Perry by Dan K. Utley. Perry Home. Paint Creek Community. Haskell County, Texas. February 7, 2006. Transcript in possession of the Perry Family and the Texas Historical Commission.

Interview with Joseph Ray Perry by Jewellee Jordan Kuenstler. Perry Home. Paint Creek Community. Haskell County, Texas. April 6, 2016. Transcript in possession of the interviewer.

"Kingman AAF Boneyard & Kingman Airport (IGM) in Arizona." Online article. AirplaneBoneyards.com website. Found online at: *http://www.airplaneboneyards .com/kingman-arizona-airplane-boneyard-storage.htm*.

"Japan Surrenders, Bringing an End to WWII." Online article. History.com website. Found online at: *https://www.history.com/this-day-in-history/japan-surrenders*.

Joseph Ray Perry Scrapbook. Perry Family Collection.

Leffler, John. "Haskell County," *Handbook of Texas Online*. Texas State Historical Association. Uploaded on June 15, 2010. Modified on February 5, 2016. Found online at: *http://www.tshaonline.org/handbook/online/articles*.

Memorabilia from Joseph Ray Perry's World War II service. Perry Family Collection.

BIBLIOGRAPHY

Molony, Brig. C. J. C., et al. *The Mediterranean and Middle East: Volume V, The Campaign in Sicily 1943 and The Campaign in Italy, 3rd September 1943 to 31st March 1944.* History of the Second World War: United Kingdom Military Series. Uckfield, UK: Naval and Military Press, 2004.

"Navigator." *B-17 Flying Fortress: Queen of the Skies.* Found online at: http://www.b17queenofthesky.com/navigator.htm.

"Not-So-Secret Weapon: The Norden Bombsight." Historynet.com website. Found online at: http://www.historynet.com/not-so-secret-weapon-the-norden-bombsight.htm.

Olmsted, Frederick Law. *A Journey Through Texas: Or a Saddle-Trip on the Southwestern Frontier.* Lincoln: University of Nebraska Press, 2004.

"P-51 Mustang Performance." World War II Aircraft Performance website. Found online at: http://www.wwiiaircraftperformance.org/mustang/mustangtest.html.

Panola County, Texas. 1860, 1870 U.S. census. Population schedule. Ancestry.com website. Found online at: http://www.ancestry.com.

"Pirates, 1942." Paint Creek School Year Book. Haskell County, Texas. In the private collection of Jewellee Jordan Kuenstler. Stamford, Texas.

Park, David. "Nineteenth Texas Infantry." *Handbook of Texas Online.* Texas State Historical Association. Uploaded on April 22, 2011. Modified on June 8, 2011. http://www.tshaonline.org/handbook/online/articles/qkn20.

Perry, Joseph Ray. Personnel File. Army Serial No. 38347857 (discharged 1945). Official Military Personnel Files. World War II: United States Army Air Corps. National Personnel Records Center, St. Louis, Missouri.

"Rick Perry." Online article. Biography.com website. Found online at: http://www.biography.com/people/rick-perry-20663471.

Shelton, Hooper, and Homer Hutto. *The First Hundred Years of Jones County, Texas.* Stamford, Texas: Shelton Press, 1978.

Szucs, Loretto Dennis and Sandra Hargreaves Luedbking, eds. *The Source: A Guidebook of American Genealogy*, rev ed. Salt Lake City, UT: Ancestry, Inc., 1997.

"Tuskegee Airmen." Online article. San Diego Air and Space Museum website. Found online at: http://www.sandiegoairandspace.org/hall-of-fame/honoree/tuskegee-airmen.

"World War II Operations Mission Briefing Hut." Image downloaded from Hill Air Force Base website on September 25, 2017. Copy in possession of the editor.

INDEX

A

Abilene Reporter News (newspaper), 162, 165, 182, 202
Abilene, Texas, 19, 20, 145, 159, 160, 162, 166, 175
Ahlhorn, Germany, 142
Alabama, 2
American Air Museum in Britain, 70
Antwerp, Belgium, 124
Arizona, 21, 24, 25, 38, 41, 43, 87, 105
AT-6, 36
Aurora, Nebraska, 43, 75
Austin, Texas, 143, 170, 171
Austin American-Statesman (newspaper), 174
Aviation History Magazine, 60, 187

B

B-17, xi, 26, 35, 36, 40, 43, 45, 48, 60, 63, 65, 66, 67, 68, 70, 76 80, 81, 84, 87, 91, 96, 97, 105, 117, 122, 124, 143, 145, 152, 163, 173, 174
B-29, 119, 155
Bad Kreuznach, Germany, 123, 128
Bataan Death March, 163
Battle of the Bulge, 123, 124
Belgium, 78, 147. *See also* Antwerp.
Berlin, Germany, 92, 163
Bielefeld, Germany, 84
Blackwell, Texas, 37, 41, 46
Bockscar, 155
Bohlen, Germany, 94
Bomb Groups, Ninety-Fifth, vii, 70, 72, 73, 91, 94, 100, 160, 170, 172, 173; 100th, 91
Bomb Squadrons, 334th, 71; 335th, 71; 336th, 71, 79; 390th, 91
Boulder Dam (Hoover Dam), 26
Bowman, Eugene "Pop," 44, 53, 54, 68, 76, 112,113, 114, 135, 140, 141, 149, 150, 170
Bremen, Germany, 79, 80, 91
Bricker, Bill, 33, 76
Bricker, Thelma Perry, 5, 26, 33, 51, 76, 108, 115, 118
Britain. *See England.*
British. *See England.*
Bryan, Ohio, 104, 139
Buckenham Base, England, 146
Buda, Charles "Chuck," 44, 68, 97, 98, 99, 100, 101, 102, 103, 104, 136, 137, 139, 149, 173
Buda, W. H., 104, 139

INDEX

C
California, 8, 22, 35, 44, 155
California Creek, Texas, 7
Cambridge, England, 104, 137, 173
Camp Shanks, New York, 153
Carothers, Richard, 41
Carter, Merlin I., 47
Catalina Island, California, 157
Caterpillar Club, 146
Chemnitz, Germany, 136
Chicago, Illinois, 153
Civil War, vii, 3, 4; Confederate Nineteenth Texas Infantry (Regimental Texas Volunteers), 3
Clark, C. O. "Charlie," 43, 44, 68, 71, 73, 146
Cologne, Germany, 106, 107, 131
Colorado City, Texas, 155
Comanche, 4
Connecticut, 43
Contrails (book), 100
Contrails II (book), 73

D
Dallas, Texas, 11, 17, 53, 57, 153, 166
Davis, Thomas R. "Tommie," 20, 29, 30, 42, 105, 108, 112, 121, 122, 163
Dixon, F. B., 3
Doolittle, James E. "Jimmy," 70, 96, 100
Dublin, Texas, 147
Duisburg, Germany, 135
Dyersburg, Tennessee, 46, 47, 49, 53, 58, 61, 62, 87, 88, 104, 155
Dyess Air Force Base, Texas, 167

E
Egar, Czechoslavakia, 151
El Paso, Texas, 27, 156
England, vii, 156, 63, 65, 68, 69, 70, 71, 73, 74, 78, 81, 85, 88, 90, 91, 92, 95, 99, 105, 106, 108, 109, 111, 112, 113, 114, 115, 116, 117, 118, 119, 120, 124, 125, 139, 147, 149, 152 153, 156, 157, 163, 171, 172, 173, 174, 175
English. *See England.*
Enola Gay, 155
Europe, 41, 45, 47, 54, 62, 63, 67, 68, 69, 70, 82 105, 150, 152 167, 171 173, 174

F
Fleming, Max, 155
Fleming, Rex, 155
Foggia, Italy, 155
Fort Sill, Oklahoma, 11, 12, 13, 15, 21, 169
Fort Sumter, South Carolina, 3
Fort Worth, Texas, 8, 11, 53, 54, 55, 57, 69, 147, 153
France, 147
Frankfurt, Germany, 137
Free, Jim, 69
Fulda, Germany, 130
FW-190, 95, 103

G
Georgetown, Texas, 36, 68
Germany, 29, 38, 59, 68, 69, 78, 79, 80, 81, 82, 83, 84, 89, 90, 91, 92, 94, 95, 96, 97, 98, 99, 100, 102, 105, 111, 122, 123, 124, 126, 132, 133, 138, 143, 144, 145, 147, 148, 149, 150, 152, 153, 162, 163, 169
Gipson, D. W., 33
Glovick, Barney, 43, 44, 68, 71, 72, 74, 98, 99, 100, 101, 103, 109, 115, 172
Goliad Massacre, 4
Goose Bay, Labrador, 68
Grand Bluff, Texas, 3
Grand Canyon, 26
Grand Rapids, Michigan, 43, 103
Green Dragon Pub, 70, 171
Grenier Field, New Hampshire, 68

G

Gulf of Mexico, 49
Gulfport, Mississippi, 57

H

Hamburg, Germany, 82, 91, 133, 145
Hamm, Germany, 111
Hanover, Germany, 91, 145
Harrison County, Texas, 2, 3
Haskell, Texas, 4, 5, 6, 8, 11, 13, 17, 19, 20, 29, 40, 41, 42, 47, 49, 51, 53, 88, 89, 105, 113, 122, 137, 154, 155, 162, 163 164, 165, 169
Haskell, Charles R., 4
Haskell County, Texas, 4, 5, 8, 14, 24, 69, 94, 166, 176
Haskell Free Press (newspaper), 1, 12, 24, 27, 28, 33, 40, 45, 47, 51, 63, 79, 94, 105, 106, 122, 127, 152, 162, 163
Hatfield, Thomas M., 173, 174
Heavy Date, xi, 76, 81, 91, 96, 97, 99, 100, 103, 141, 170, 173
Herron, W. C. "Sandy," 43, 44, 67, 68, 75, 92, 113
Hill County, Texas, 3
Hillsboro, Texas, 3
Hiroshima, Japan, 155
Hollywood, California, 145, 155, 157
Holmes, Raymond D., 64
Holt, Clara, 164
Holt, J. C., 162, 164
Holt, J. C., Jr., 165
Holt, Tommie, 165
Hoover Dam. *See Boulder Dam*.
Horham, England, 68, 70, 73, 81, 99, 119, 146, 171, 173, 174
Howard, Kermit, 123, 137
Hughes, Dimmitt, 68, 69

I

Ireland, 68
Italy, 67, 75, 88, 89, 115, 121, 132

Ivy, John, F., 41, 145
Ivy, Pearleta, 15, 30, 41, 45, 46, 49, 50, 51, 52, 53, 55, 56, 59, 60, 61, 75, 108, 109, 110, 112, 114, 116, 118, 119, 121, 122, 123, 125, 128, 129, 130, 131, 133, 134, 135, 136, 137, 138, 140, 141, 142, 143, 144, 148, 149

J

Japan, 8, 38, 56, 70, 100, 153, 155, 156, 160, 163
Jena, Germany, 141
Johnson, Allen, 174

K

Kaltenkirchen, Germany, 150
Kansas, 41, 43, 158
Kassel, Germany, 107
Kearney, Nebraska, 63, 66, 68, 76, 112, 121
Kearney Army Air Field. *See Kearney, Nebraska*.
Kiel, Germany, 148, 149
Kingman Army Airfield, Arizona, 21, 22, 24, 25, 26, 37, 41, 42, 43, 46, 87, 105
Kuenstler, J. B., 28
Kuenstler, Truett, 33
Kyser, Kay (spelled Kieser in book), 157

L

Langredren, Germany, 139
Las Vegas, Nevada, 35, 42
Lawton, Oklahoma, 13
Leipzig, Germany, 95, 150
Lincoln, Nebraska, 27, 28, 38, 40, 43, 45, 48, 49, 87, 119
Livengood, LaVern, 53, 77, 78, 113, 116, 145

INDEX 211

London, England, 70, 78, 106, 108, 109, 110, 115, 119, 120, 125, 146
Long Beach, California, 157, 158
Los Angeles, California, 22, 156, 157
Louisiana, 3

M
Mackenzie, Ranald Slidell, 4
Manchester Airport, New Hampshire, 68. *See also Grenier Field, New Hampshire.*
ME-109, 95, 96, 103
ME-163, 98
Memphis, Tennessee, 51, 53, 54, 58, 61
Meridian, Mississippi, 53
Merseburg, Germany, 82
Messerschmitt. *See ME-109.*
Michigan, 43, 44. *See also Grand Rapids, Detroit.*
Miller, Clarence, R., 71, 73, 146, 147
Milliken's Bend, Louisiana, 3
Mississippi, 45, 53
Mohave County, Arizona, 25
Monkevich, William "Monk," 44, 68, 73, 157
Monroe, Louisiana, 3
Moosburg, Germany, 163
Munday, Texas, 19

N
Nagasaki, Japan, 156
Nashville, Tennessee, 53
Navy, 110
Nebraska, 40, 41, 42, 49, 51, 70, 75 158, 167
Needles, California, 35
New Hampshire, 68
New Jersey, 153
New Mexico, 42, 165, 167
New York, 153
New York Daily Times (newspaper), 2

Norden Bombsight, 59, 60, 82, 91
Normandy, 171, 175
North Sea, 132, 163
Nuremburg, Germany, 89, 91, 163

O
Ohio, 44, 104, 136, 139
Oklahoma, 4, 11, 13, 170
Olmsted, Frederick Law, 2, 3

P
P-38, 85, 87
P-47, 81, 92
P-51, 81, 100
Pacific, 66, 67, 70, 111, 153, 155, 156, 160
Paint Creek, Texas, 5, 6, 7, 9, 12, 28, 113, 133, 152, 162, 165, 169
Panola County, Texas, 3
Parker, Quanah, 4
Pearl Harbor, Hawaii, xii, 8, 11, 22, 70, 100
Perkins & Timberlake Co., 51
Perry, Amelia June Holt, x, xi, xii, 1, 10, 41, 52, 80, 95, 100, 109, 117, 143, 162, 164, 165, 166, 167, 170, 171, 173
Perry, Clarie, 57
Perry, Don, 61, 62, 169
Perry, Ella, 169, 175
Perry, Frances, 5, 17, 18, 41, 48, 49, 54, 56, 62, 88, 111, 114, 122, 127, 133, 138, 142, 145, 148, 158, 165
Perry, Frank, 3
Perry, Gene, 5, 62, 111, 165
Perry, Gertrude Hamilton, 5
Perry, Griffin, 168, 169
Perry, Hoyt, 5, 6, 12, 13, 18, 47, 57, 63, 68, 123, 152, 162, 168
Perry, Ida, 3
Perry, J. W., 2, 3
Perry, James, 3,

Perry, James Richard "Rick," viii, xi, xii, 143, 167, 168, 169, 170, 171, 173, 174, 175
Perry, Jane, 2, 3
Perry, Joel, 3
Perry, John C., 3
Perry, John Michael, 3, 4
Perry, Press, 57, 122
Perry, Meredith, 169
Perry, Milla, xii, 166, 167, 169
Perry, Piper, 169
Perry, Sydney, 169
Perry, Thelma Dinsmore, 5, 17, 18, 26, 33, 51, 62
Perry, Wayne, vii, 4, 5, 6, 7
Perry, William, 3
Perry, Winneyfred Catherine Berry, 3, 4
Perry, W. J., 3
Phoenix, Arizona, 38
Pikes Peak, Iowa, 41
Post Community School, Texas, 5
Pound, Ruth, 118
Presque Isle, Maine, 68
Pyote, Texas, 134

R

Railton, Bert, 44, 68, 98, 99, 102, 103, 104, 113, 137, 149, 150, 153, 156, 170
Reddell, Raymond, 20, 27, 160
Rekjavik, Iceland, 68
Rice Springs, Texas, 4
Rotan, Texas, 37, 41, 46, 89, 133
Russia, 115

S

Sacks, Norman, 44, 68, 71, 73, 170
Sagerton, Texas, 3
San Antonio, Texas, ix, 153, 156, 157, 159, 160

Santa Ana, California, 155, 156, 157, 158, 159, 160
Saxton, Missouri, 44, 54
Scott's Crossing, Texas, 7
Seymour, Texas, 19
Shaver, Bill, 119
Sheets, Carrol, 41
Sheets, Will, 41
Sheppard Field, Texas, 12, 13, 14, 15, 16, 18, 21, 23, 24, 26, 29, 37, 41, 42, 46, 48, 50, 105
Sherman, Texas, 57
St. Louis, Missouri, 153
Stamford, Connecticut, 43
Stamford, Texas, 5, 6, 19, 41, 69, 153, 159, 161, 164, 165
Stamford Lake, Texas, 5
Steenwijk, Germany, 143
Stephens, Kenny, 168
Stewart, Jimmy, 146, 174
Stormy, 42, 106, 107, 139, 165
Sturdivant, Clarence "Max," 37, 46, 155
Stuttgart, Germany, 120
Sweeney, Charles, 155
Sweetwater, Texas, 156

T

Tennessee, 46, 48, 49, 53, 61, 62, 67, 87, 104
Texas, viii, ix, xi, 1, 2, 3, 4, 5, 6, 8, 10, 12, 13, 14, 16, 21, 24, 26, 27, 34, 36, 41, 51, 52, 57, 61 68, 75, 87, 89, 90, 109, 113, 115, 124, 131, 134, 137, 143, 144, 147, 158, 159, 165, 166, 167, 168, 169, 170, 173, 174, 175
Texas A&M College, 162, 167
Texas Cowboy Reunion (TCR), 159
Texas Historical Commission, xi
The Stars and Stripes (magazine), 91
Thomason, Melvin, 155
Tibbets, Paul, 155
Truman, Harry S., 156

INDEX

Turkey, 167
Tuskegee Airmen, 143, 144

U
Ulm, Germany, 138
Underhill, Dorothy, 133
Underhill, Preston, 46, 87, 88, 89, 121, 132, 133, 155
Underwood, Frank, 119
Union City, Tennessee, 53, 55
University of Texas, 174
U.S. Army Air Forces, xi, 10, 11, 12, 14, 17, 25, 34, 47 63, 105, 115, 152, 154; Eighth Air Force, viii, 70, 86 100, 152; Fifteenth Air Force, 154
U.S. Navy Air Corps, 50
Utley, Dan K., xi, 12, 24, 44, 65

W
Warden, Miss, 20, 116, 128
Waterhouse, Richard, 3
Weaver, George, 7
Wellington, Texas, 49
Wichita Falls, Texas, 14, 16, 17, 105
Wink, Texas, 165
Wolverton Hotel, Oklahoma, 13
World War I, 9
World War II, viii, ix, x, xi, xii, 9, 45, 47, 70, 81, 90, 143, 146, 171

Y
Yucca, Arizona, 30, 35, 36

Z
Zeitz, Germany, 91, 147
Ziegenhain, Germany, 144

www.ingramcontent.com/pod-product-compliance
Lightning Source LLC
Chambersburg PA
CBHW052054110526
44591CB00013B/2209